'Tim Matthews tells an inspirin[...]
ments, challenges and excitem[...]
God. This is a book I would r[...]
anyone starting out to plant a church.'

Rt Revd Graham Tomlin, Bishop of Kensington

'A gripping story of the highs and lows of church planting. Tim's honesty, courage, faith, humility and wit shine through. Both practical and inspiring, it is a wonderful reminder that there is hope for our nation through communities of people who love God, love people and love life.'

Rebecca Stewart, Goldstar Partners

'This is an incredibly helpful book for anyone thinking about church planting, currently church planting or just interested. The combination of practical wisdom, brutal honesty and storytelling makes it a brilliant read! Tim and Debi have been an incredible source of encouragement and help as we have been church planting just a few miles down the coast in Portsmouth.'

Alex and Liz Wood, Harbour Church Portsmouth

'An extraordinary story of faithfulness, courage and obedience.'

Al Gordon, St John at Hackney

'This is a personal and a corporate story, an inspiring and passionate exhortation for the church to thrive and grow, by God's grace, even when it seems impossible. Tim writes an honest account of how our churches can flourish and our communities can be transformed when weak people rely on God, share a vision and keep praying. What are we waiting for?'

Abby Guinness, Spring Harvest

'This is a brilliantly encouraging book reflecting on Tim's own call to ordained ministry, the planting of St Swithun's, and the potential that the gospel has to bring transformation and hope to a local community and wider society through the local church. I highly recommend it.'

Andrew Emerton, St Mellitus College

'The world we live in often shuns real love. Love for God is seen as outdated, love for each other is simply not cool or too much effort and love for life is looked at cynically. Tim Matthews worldview is based on his faith and swims upstream against popular trends. He has the audacity to believe that love is the answer. I know Tim, and what he believes in, he lives.'

Tom Hewitt MBE, Surfers Not Street Children

'Planting churches is essential to reach new generations with the good news of Jesus Christ. In this engaging book, Tim invites us into his own church planting story in honest, real and exciting ways. There's hard-won treasure here and it's available for the taking.'

Rt Revd Ric Thorpe, Bishop of Islington

'It has long been known that the most effective means of growing the Church is through church planting and Tim's humble and honest account of God's grace and the power of His love makes very moving, very inspiring and encouraging reading. I thoroughly recommend it.'

Rt Revd Sandy Millar,
Honorary Assistant Bishop in the Diocese of London and previous Vicar of Holy Trinity Brompton

'This is a punchy, honest and inspiring read. Tim lays his heart bare and invites us into the adventure and reality of church planting. You feel the joy and pain of the journey. Perhaps more than anything this book awakens a sense of hope that God has an adventure for each and every one of us ... if only we'd take the risk and step out!'

Tim and Rachel Hughes,
Worship Central and St Luke's, Gas Street

'In this his first book Tim produces a vision for church planting and practical insights that are both scripturally inspired and born out of on-the-ground experience. He paints a comprehensive picture of the challenges the church planter will face, while giving clear advice on how to overcome these issues. Tim's testimony will encourage, instruct and inspire the next generation of church planters seeking to fulfil their vision. Tim is not afraid to tackle the key challenges in a reassuringly realistic way. A must-read for those planting churches and for leaders hoping to do so.'

Ken Costa, Leadership College London

'With honesty and humility Tim tells his story of church planting, calling us to love Jesus and follow him more coura-geously. Time and time again, the faithfulness of God in the details of a calling comes through and I am left wanting to give more, serve more and trust more. I commend this book as a story through which God can speak to all of us.'

Dr Amy Orr-Ewing,
The Oxford Centre for Christian Apologetics

'The story of what God has done to renew his church at St Swithun's Bournemouth under the leadership of my friends Tim and Debi Matthews is absolutely inspiring. It is another clear sign of great hope for the future of the church in this country and a reminder that the gospel is as relevant and compelling as ever.'

Pete Greig, 24–7 Prayer and Emmaus Rd, Guildford

'Tim Matthews is a man of great faith, great vision and great perseverance. He is also a great friend. We loved working together with him and Debi at HTB, and over the past four years have watched with huge admiration and excitement what God has been doing through them in Bournemouth. We could not recommend this book too highly – it will enthral and inspire you to press on with God.'

Nicky and Sila Lee, authors of *The Marriage Book*

'This book is a gold mine of wisdom for any aspiring church planter. Through telling his personal story, Tim Matthews reveals why church planting is the most exciting missional activity in the UK today.'

Sarah Jackson, Church Revitalisation Trust

'The story of St Swithun's is a remarkable account of the life of the Kingdom being poured out in and through the local church in order to bless the surrounding city and culture. I would encourage anyone to pick up this book and be inspired about the extraordinary things that God can do through those willing to step out and partner with God on his mission to make all things new.'

Pete Hughes, KXC London

'This is a wonderful story of transformation and hope. In a remarkable way, it bears witness to the grace, goodness and dynamic agency of Jesus Christ, in and through human weakness. I have learned much from the attempt to keep up with all the Holy Spirit is doing in the lives of these two beautiful Christian communities; to me they are the good Lord's 'work in progress'. I commend Tim's honest account to all those who seek the renewal of God's church in holiness, ministry and compassionate mission.'

Rt Revd Dr Jonathan Frost, Bishop of Southampton

LOVE CHURCH

An Adventure in Church Planting

TIM MATTHEWS

HODDER

First published in Great Britain in 2018 by Hodder & Stoughton
An Hachette UK company

This paperback edition first published in 2019

1

A CIP catalogue record for this title is available from the British Library

Paperback ISBN 978 1 473 69041 7
eBook ISBN 978 1 473 69042 4

Typeset in Ehrhardt MT by Palimpsest Book Production Limited,
Falkirk, Stirlingshire

Printed and bound in Great Britain by Clays Ltd, Elcograf S.p.A.

Hodder & Stoughton policy is to use papers that are natural,
renewable and recyclable products and made from wood grown in sustainable
forests. The logging and manufacturing processes are expected to conform
to the environmental regulations of the country of origin.

Hodder & Stoughton Ltd
Carmelite House
50 Victoria Embankment
London EC4Y 0DZ

www.hodderfaith.com

For Debi, Josiah, Caleb, Rebekah and our big family
at St Swithun's and St Clement's.

'Let us go forth, then, let us go forth to offer everyone the life of
Jesus Christ. Here I repeat for the entire Church what I have often
said to the priests and laity of Buenos Aires: I prefer a Church
which is bruised, hurting and dirty because it has been out on the
streets, rather than a Church which is unhealthy from being confined
and from clinging to its own security.'

Pope Francis, *Evangelii Gaudium: The Joy of the Gospel*

'God has brought the growth' 1 Corinthians 3:6

The Church exists for others – to serve and to share the good news with non-members. Over the last few years St Swithun's has done just that. People's lives have been touched and transformed.

This is the story of what God has done in the lives of a community of church planters in Bournemouth. It is an inspiring and challenging read. Young people have been finding the meaning of life, addicts have been set free and many have come to Christ. The power of the Holy Spirit has been seen in countless good news stories.

Tim Matthews has faithfully offered courageous leadership and sought to share his vision and his ministry with others. The result is a team of people who have sacrificially given themselves for others.

I recommend this book to everyone who wants to see how God is bringing this growth to his Church. He uses those who plant and those who water, but he is the one who brings the miracle of growth. St Swithun's has grown from about 20 to 600 in little over four years – God has been at work!

The Bournemouth plant has encouraged us to go on planting new churches in the Diocese of Winchester. As the Diocesan Bishop I pray that God will bring the growth of his Church across this whole region.

Tim Dakin

Bishop of Winchester

Contents

Foreword

At Holy Trinity Brompton we first became aware of church planting in the early 1980s when we heard it described by the American missiologist Peter Wagner as 'the most effective form of evangelism known under heaven'. The question was: could church planting work in the Church of England?

We quickly realised that, in addition to the requirements of a non-denominational church, we would need three key elements: the support of a bishop, a church building and a leader ordained in the Church of England. And so it was that in 1985 we embarked on our first church plant when, at the invitation of the then Bishop of Kensington, Mark Santer, a hundred members of our congregation went with curate John Irvine (later Dean of Coventry) to bring new life to the church of St Barnabas West Kensington. That was followed in 1987 by a plant south of the river to St Mark's Battersea Rise at the invitation of the Bishop of Southwark. And from then, with the help and support of Bishop Richard Chartres, we partnered in a succession of church planting initiatives in the London diocese.

In 2009 we were presented with a wholly new challenge when we were invited to partner with the Diocese of Chichester to help revitalise the iconic St Peter's Brighton, known as the 'Cathedral of Brighton', which had been facing closure. We knew by now that church planting worked in London but this was totally unchartered water: could church planting work at a distance?

Our associate vicar Archie Coates took a small team of around twenty, moved to Brighton and got down to work at St Peter's. They started holding services at one end of the huge building (the bit which wasn't falling down); they started Alpha; they began a project for vulnerable women called Safehaven; they started prayer groups and other initiatives as they felt the Holy Spirit was leading them.

Within a short time it became clear that God was blessing their work – and the church began to grow. Now the church congregation is more than a thousand, they have planted five churches (including Portsmouth and Hastings) and the whole city of Brighton is being affected.

Tim Matthews was coming to the end of his first year as a curate at HTB when Archie and his associates went to Brighton. In this book, Tim tells the amazing story of how God led him, his wife Debi and their dedicated team (by quite a circuitous route at times!) to Bournemouth – and what they have seen the Holy Spirit do there. It is a story of highs and lows, battles and blessings; ultimately, though, it is an inspiring story of a group of Christians trying to go where God is leading them.

Like the mustard seed in Jesus' parable, the Love Church project had small beginnings. But, as Jesus told his listeners, when 'planted … it grows' (Matthew 13:31–2) and now Bournemouth is just one of the thriving newly planted 'Resource Churches' growing in university cities around the country as a result of a partnership between the diocese, church and HTB.

None of what is written in this book would have happened if it was not for the vision and drive of Bishop Tim Dakin of Winchester and Bishop Jonathan Frost of Southampton. We are so grateful to them; it has been a privilege to partner with them in this enterprise.

It is so exciting to look at Bournemouth and other church plants and see the tremendous impact they are having on their localities – 'the birds of the air come and perch in its branches' (verse 32) – with many people coming into God's Kingdom as a result of their presence and ministries. All over the world today we see the impact of church planting. Even the media is beginning to notice. Recently, *The Times* wrote about 'moribund churches' coming to life again through church planting – churches that had been closed now being reopened. It spoke of a 'church that is alive and vibrant and growing'.

If you have any doubts about whether church planting works, read this book.

Tim Matthews is a leader whose faith, tenacity and vision in the power of the Holy Spirit have helped turn an empty building into a vibrant church community transforming the local area. He has a great story to tell and I recommend it highly.

Nicky Gumbel
Vicar of Holy Trinity Brompton

Introduction

570,000 reasons to get out of bed

It was a cold, windy, slab-grey day in London in the early spring of 2013. I sat down on a train leaving London Waterloo for the South Coast, cautiously sipped my coffee and thought, 'Not again, Lord, I just can't take more disappointment.' My wife Debi and I had just come through another bruising and discouraging encounter with a church that we'd tried to plant into. We'd failed. Again. It was the twelfth time we'd tried. It felt as if I was the single common factor in things going wrong. The church I loved and where I served as curate, Holy Trinity Brompton (HTB), were being patient with me; they couldn't have been more supportive, in fact, but I'd been there for five years and felt at times a bit of a spare part. Although I was supposed to be fixing my mind on the future, I was stuck in the past. I was depressed. Maybe I'd got it all wrong. I caught my subdued reflection in the window and wondered if I should give up church leadership and go back to making money in the City. As the train left the platform, though, I knew in my heart that would be a faithless backward step.

The train jolted forward and I turned my attention to my travelling companion, relieved at not having to explain my mood. A seasoned church planter himself, Ric Thorpe knew what I was going through. Contrasting my own demeanour, Ric oozed energy and excitement. He slurped his coffee with eager gulps. His eyes shone. He had a huge, permanent grin and he laughed often and loudly. The natural cynic in me tried hard to find him annoying but failed; he was such a nice guy to spend time with and his optimism was infectious. I was soon laughing as Ric told me lame jokes and mischievous stories. I didn't realise what he was doing at the time, but looking back I realise he spent that entire train journey doing just one thing: encouraging me. Here was a guy who clearly knew the importance of, 'encouraging the disheartened'(1 Thess. 5:14). If it wasn't for that day with Ric, none of what follows would have happened. I owe him so much – he'd agreed to accompany me on that trip to the South Coast to look around some potential sites for a new church plant.

We stepped off the train at Bournemouth into bright sunshine. They say there's a micro-climate here with more sunshine and less rainfall than much of the rest of the UK. I'd done my research. There are 570,000 people who live in the area – that puts it in the UK's top twenty largest urban regions. The average age of the population is falling as more and more young people decide to live here. But only a tiny percentage of them go to church. There's surf, there's sun, and there's a lot of people who don't yet know Jesus. As I blinked in the dazzling sunshine, my heart leapt, my energy rose and a single thought filled my mind: 'I can't think of a better place to start a new church.'

We were met by the archdeacon of Bournemouth, Peter Rouch, who had come to explain the bishop's vision for a new church in the city and to show us some of the possible sites under consideration. Peter explained that alarm bells were ringing at the diocese. Numbers in Bournemouth's churches were in decline and the average age of congregations was rising – that, at a time when the background population was doing the exact opposite: growing and getting younger. Overall, it meant that the Church of England in Bournemouth had only a very limited lifespan. An exciting change programme was just getting started in existing churches to reinvigorate mission and alongside that the diocesan leadership believed it was time for a risky new experiment.

After lunch Ric, Peter and I walked down the beach at Branksome Chine. As Peter spoke I glanced at Ric, who was listening intently and, I knew, silently praying. The Holy Spirit seemed to blow through us and our conversation as we walked. Peter became animated as he laid out a fledgling vision for what he had in mind. He started by talking about the questions that needed answering. Had the younger generations of Bournemouth rejected Jesus, or the church? Were those who were poor, addicted, lonely, homeless or who had lost hope beyond reach? Could many Church of England congregations move into a new phase of life, worship and mission through church planting? Peter restated the bishop's intention to start an experimental new church in Bournemouth to answer these questions: a church that, while being open for all, would focus its energy on reaching unchurched younger generations; a church that would enact mission and ministry so as to be a beacon of hope; a church that, in time, would be able to act as a resource to others, and partner with them to plant or revitalise other church communities throughout the diocese. I was hooked. Peter turned to me and asked what I thought of it all. My reply was simple: 'Where do I sign?'

This book is the story of the church that emerged following that conversation. Through some highs and many lows, I have clung to a conviction that the church really is the only hope for the future of our nation. The UK's society is breaking down as if falling into a chasm between the opposing cliffs of several paradoxes. Thanks to the revolution in communications and social media we have never been more connected and it has never been easier to contact friends and lovers instantly. Yet loneliness and isolation are at record levels. We have never been so wealthy or had so much opportunity to express our true identities. But depression and anxiety-related mental health problems are at record levels. Billy Graham's phenomenal TED talk highlighted how, despite breathtaking technological advances, no solution has been found for the problem of evil in every human heart or the universal experience of suffering. No government institution, health service, business or law enforcement agency is going to fix these societal ills. But if in every community we were to see friendship groups declaring the freedom from guilt and shame uniquely found in experiencing the good news about Jesus, enacting their practical hope through service, compassion and justice, then everyone in this nation would have a better life.

This is the movement that Jesus came to start and what he's still doing every day in the UK, right now. This movement is called church. When church is good, there's nothing like it: a group of friends helping one another and everyone around them to become everything that God has in mind for them, driven by God's own delicious, unquenchable love. Who doesn't want that? That's what we've tried to do in planting St Swithun's Bournemouth and later at St Clement's Boscombe. With so many church plants now being considered all around the UK, this book is my attempt to fuel the fire. It is not offered as a tale of success but simply as an honest account giving you the opportunity to learn from the few things we've got right and the many mistakes we've made. My aim is to encourage you that even with all our fear, frailty and failures, God

4

wants to partner with us on his great adventure to reach everyone everywhere by building his church in every community.

In July 2014 St Swithun's was an idea that existed only on paper. Our team consisted of eleven adults, three children and a baby. The only kit we had was a large box of sunglasses with our website address and twitter handle printed on the arms. We thought it might be a fun way of getting the word out, so we spent the summer giving them away and listening to locals' wisdom. Four years later Debi and I look around with amazement each Sunday as we find ourselves joined by six or seven hundred worshippers at five services across two sites. We've run Alpha throughout, welcoming over eight hundred guests. There are growing children's, youth, student and millennial ministries. There are people leaving highly paid jobs to enter ordained ministry. Together with other churches in the town, we've run a homeless shelter every winter and we've also helped hundreds of people with addictions to seek freedom through our Recovery Community. We've purchased our first site and started up at a second site. We run an exciting intern scheme to disciple young leaders. Sounds good, doesn't it? Am I impressing you? God save me. I'll try and tell the real story.

The reality is that these headlines have come through a great deal of trouble, a lot of confusion, a huge number of mistakes and several outright failures. If you're hoping for a book that tells you how to lead a successful church plant without putting a step wrong, written by a seasoned A-grade leader, I'm so sorry, but this isn't it. Don't waste your money. (Sorry if you did that already.) If you finish this book and don't get anything from it, let me know and I'll make it up to you. If you are a church planter, then please don't read this until you've read *The Purpose Driven Church* by Rick Warren.[1] It's brilliant and I'm still learning from it. The truth is that most of the time I don't have a clue what I'm doing. I've taken a while to think about why things happened and what I've learned from them. Be sure that, as I tell our story, all the mistakes are certainly mine, and all the successes are probably someone else's!

I trained as a curate at HTB, the home of Alpha, for six years, leaving to start St Swithun's four years ago. What I've seen occur at HTB, St Swithun's and many other so-called 'successful' churches has not been a result of strength, skill or expertise. It doesn't make for the kind of great, heroic keynote addresses we might imagine hearing at church conferences, but here in Bournemouth I simply stumbled into a move of God that many other people had been praying to see for years. Each day I feel I'm clambering to keep up with the Holy Spirit as he moves forward. On my rare best days, I feel as if I'm not messing it up too much; on my worst days, I fail it completely. Most of the time I live in a state of mild confusion, if not utter bewilderment – though I'm learning that this ongoing weakness and powerlessness is the reality of the Christian life and certainly the reality of leadership in the church.

I am slowly accepting (if not yet exactly embracing) the paradox that to learn to live in the power of the Holy Spirit I must also learn to live in the weakness of self. In both of his letters to the Corinthian church, St Paul talked about the wonder of weakness. He considered himself a strong leader because he was aware of his weakness. He writes: 'I came to you in weakness with great fear and trembling . . . if I must boast, I will boast of the things that show my weakness' (1 Cor. 2:3; 2 Cor. 11:30). In my own much smaller way, I've also learned that owning your own 'stuff' is fundamental to Christian leadership and I'll endeavour to reflect on that as I tell the story of what I have been a part of here.

The truth is, the whole idea of church has been in my bloodstream since birth even though I spent much of my early life feeling very confused about it. What I first understood about the character of God was learned primarily from my parents. But their warm, enthusiastic and tactile love seemed at odds with the Christian faith that I often saw in church settings. At home there was a loving, fun God who clearly inspired the very best in my mum and dad; but I experienced church as too often being a stone cold, boring, austere thing that sometimes even seemed to bring out the worst in people rather than the best in them. I was strangely drawn to the whole concept of church even as a very young child. But most of the time when I was actually in church buildings, I would simply wish I was back at home with my toys.

In the midst of my early confusion about church, I treasure a single memory. My father was a Church of England vicar who led a church plant on a tough estate outside Leicester when I was very small. The tiny chapel we all met in was little more than a shack. In winter it was freezing cold and when it rained you couldn't hear anything because the corrugated tin roof acted like a drum. In that shack of a church aged three, I recall becoming very upset one Sunday morning, just as my dad began to deliver his sermon from the low dais at the front. I slipped from my mum's grip and bolted forward towards dad. I straddled his foot, wrapped my arms around his leg like a limpet and clung on for dear life. I expected my mum to come and prise me away from him but she stayed where she was and my dear dad didn't even try to shake me off – he let me sit there as he continued to preach and I sat on his shoe, hugging his leg, until he'd finished. My heart still melts when I think of it and I can almost smell the leather of his shoes, so powerful is that memory for me. That single moment probably saved church for me for the rest of my life. It gifted me with the instinct that church was not at all the negative things that it had often appeared to me to be; at its core, church was one big family where I could encounter the father heart of God. Unfortunately, many people have never had such a redeeming experience. Many have had almost no experience of church at all. At our ordination, Anglican priests like myself are called upon to profess the Christian faith, which we must 'proclaim afresh in each generation'. I dare to believe that we might now be seeing a new movement of the Holy Spirit in the UK whereby leaders across many streams of the church are taking up this challenge again.

When my big sister and I were kids my mum kept us still and quiet during seemingly interminable services by feeding us fruit pastilles. With a shiver, I remember one particularly cold church linked to my Church of England primary school. The church regularly welcomed the school and tried to convey something of the faith to us. It was actually a wonderful church and I now know only too well how hard and expensive it can be to heat an old, draughty, listed church building effectively. But I didn't know or care about that as a child. Neither did I understand that churches are not buildings but communities of Jesus' disciples. All I knew or cared about at the time was that we were made to sit on the stone floor, leading directly to a freezing bum and the deep desire for it all to be over. The priest there was a towering figure called Father Brian Taylor. Little did I realise the depth of his faith and compassion for children. Twenty-five years later when my dad told him I was considering a call to ordination, without batting an eyelid Father Brian replied, 'Oh that is wonderful! I've been praying for him and other children from those times for all these years, asking God that he might save all of them and lead some of them towards ordination.' Unknown to me as a child, hidden behind those cold stones existed a church of warm love with a leader of great faith. I have found this so often to be true: great leaders and congregations with hearts full of God's love find themselves in cold buildings and austere cultures that prove hard to change. I sincerely hope this book serves as an encouragement to leaders in church, whether ordained, staff or lay volunteers, to embrace change and to lead with courage, for the sake of reaching the vast majority of those in their communities who do not yet know Jesus.

Transforming church life for the better across the UK can be done. Indeed, it has been done before. I thoroughly recommend reading Nigel Scotland's great account of *Evangelical Anglicans in a Revolutionary Age, 1789–1901*.[2] He considers the vast impact that influences such as the Clapham Sect, Lord Shaftesbury and D.L. Moody had upon the UK and far beyond. In the education sector alone, the impact of that great movement was phenomenal: by 1850 three quarters of the poorest working-class population of England aged between five and fifteen were receiving basic education through Sunday schools. This period saw a huge growth in the church not at all restricted to evangelicals – far from it. Pioneered by groups such as the 'High Church' Oxford Movement, what might now broadly be described as Anglo-Catholic approaches transformed worship and mission in the UK during the nineteenth century. It became an audacious church-planting network. It sought to remain faithful to the historic beliefs and practices of the church while preaching the gospel in imaginative, multi-sensory ways, particularly to the poor. Between 1851 and 1875 2,438 churches were built or rebuilt including both our current Bournemouth sites at St Swithun's and St Clement's. Numbers of clergymen in the Church of England increased from 14,500 in 1841 to 24,000 in 1875.

However, once again we find ourselves at a low ebb, most notably among poorer urban communities, as was the case in the nineteenth century. England's population since 1875 has more than doubled but there are now about a quarter fewer active clergy – a number that is declining. Yet I am tremendously hopeful for the future of the church in the UK and the Church of England which is in a process of renewing and reforming (admittedly I'm biased as I find myself swept up in this wide movement). From unpromising beginnings that could have turned me off for ever, I now love the church. Thankfully, I've realised that, although great architecture can certainly be a form of worship and make a huge difference to the way we interact with God and one another, buildings are just buildings; whereas the church itself is what Bishop Graham Tomlin describes as a transforming community in which people's full humanity can be restored. Evangelism, therefore, 'is inviting people to the transformed life of the kingdom, lived as fully and as daringly as possible'.[3]

However strong our views about church are, even if like my own they're tinged with a powerful sense of nostalgia, they pale into insignificance compared with Jesus' view about his church. Scripture leaves us in no doubt: Jesus loves his church. The closing picture in the Bible is of Jesus as a bridegroom and the church as his bride (Rev. 22:17). Every day I am discovering more of God's jealous love and intent for his church, and I find myself remotivated to establish its beauty for the sake of the world he loves.

In Jesus' eyes, church isn't just beautiful, it's also powerful. We must handle this power carefully, ensuring that we embrace humility, suffering and vulnerability. Righteous ends never justify unrighteous means. Self-sacrificial love is the way of Christ. One might think that rejecting the world's ways of winning would mean inevitable failure as we resigned ourselves to some kind of noble, morally-superior, loss. This is not the case. The remarkable power of the church is its capacity to live sacrificially in God's love, following Jesus through the cross and in to the resurrection. Jesus said, 'I will build my church and the gates of hell will not prevail against it' (Matt. 16:18). I always used to believe Jesus was saying here that, although the power of hell would grow and besiege the church, we shouldn't worry because in the end we'll be okay. But Jesus wasn't saying that – he was saying the total opposite. The church's mission is not defensive; it's supposed to attack! We're not to cower behind a closed hedge of pastoral comfort, hoping that Satan won't strike against us. We are supposed to leave our imagined comfort zone and advance into the battle. Ultimately we will be far safer if we do this: it is often by hearing God's call but failing to act upon it that we present the devil with a dangerous opportunity to bring about the greatest damage and distress into our lives. Jesus is asking you and me to trust him and give him our lives through which he might build us together into his beautiful and militant church. Jesus was urging us onwards, confident that the very citadel of hell itself will not be able to resist the onslaught of invasion posed by his victorious church.

The muscular missionary C.T. Studd commented: 'Some wish to live within the sound of a chapel bell; I wish to run a rescue mission within a yard of hell.'4 I guess something of Studd's audacious faith has, somewhere along the line, got hold of me. If you're looking for an easy life, don't plant a church. Don't go anywhere near church. It will cost you dearly. Great suffering may well be involved in pursuing God's call whatever he calls you to. But it has been the best and hardest thing I have ever done. I can't imagine doing anything else. If you're looking for adventure and purpose in life, pursue God's call and you'll find it in spades. Studd also reportedly said, 'The best cure for discouragement or qualms is another daring plunge of faith.' That appeals to me because I'm a goal-oriented person; if I don't feel I've achieved something every day I get miserable. Even on holiday I need to achieve something. It drives my family crazy. I find that I have to go for a run, battle the ocean surfing, complete a crossword, finish reading a book – just about anything – in order to feel that my day has been worthwhile. So for me, having a big goal in life is important. Now I get up every day motivated that the transforming community I'm part of has another chance to give every single one of the 570,000 people living in Bournemouth the opportunity to encounter Jesus as he really is, alive and kicking, through his church.

Chapter 1

Every day is a school day

Start children off on the way they should go,
and even when they are old they will not turn from it.
Proverbs 22:6

I was raised in a loving, stable family home in the leafy middle-class town of Guildford. I went to decent schools. I had some fun friends and didn't hang out with the wrong crowd. I enjoyed church youth groups. I was fit and healthy and played a lot of sports. I was reasonably intelligent, although by no means outstanding. I did okay at GCSE and A-level without too much crisis. But at the end of my time at school I felt restless and hungry for a change of scene and decided to take a year out before heading off to university. I was in a group of friends who used to head down to England's south coast – Devon, Cornwall or even west Wales – to surf during the weekends and school holidays. One of them spotted a small advert in the back pages of *Surfer* magazine and dared me to apply. It was to go to Mexico for a year with a missions agency called Surfers For Missions International (SFMI).

The SFMI programme turned out to be a six-month Discipleship Training School (DTS) run by Youth With A Mission (YWAM).

I decided to go for it and wrote to several family friends asking for their help to finance the trip. Thanks to their generosity, at the end of a gloriously long summer in England and having said goodbye to school, I found myself on a plane to Mexico. I was looking forward to the surfing but not a little intimidated by the idea of what I might find. I've surfed ever since I was a teenager and was used to the slow, freezing cold waves on England's south coast, with the odd occasional trip to bigger breaks elsewhere. Mexico was very different though. Pretty much the first thing I did when I arrived at the SFMI house in Mazatlan was to go for a surf. Wherever we were in Mexico for the next six months we'd surf at least once a day, or more if we could. My first surprise was that the water was bath-warm, particularly when a late-afternoon tide came back in over the sun-scorched sand. Surfing in board shorts only was a far cry from the heavy, thick wetsuits used in the UK. And then there was the size, speed and ferocity of the waves. More than once I just about managed to paddle out on a rip into big surf that was way beyond my skill level. It's a terrifying feeling knowing that the only way to get back to the beach is to pick just the right wave, take a very deep breath, turn and paddle like your life depends on it, then ride a monster wave that will chew you up with utter disdain for your well-being. Pretty scary. And incredibly thrilling.

Hazards abounded: burning sun, vicious rip-currents, shallow rocks, reefs and all manner of animal life in the ocean could all turn a fun surf session into a world of pain very quickly. One afternoon I duck-dived under an innocuous wave and surfaced into the tentacles of a blue-bottle jellyfish. The stings seared right across my diaphragm and I began to have trouble breathing. (Apparently, I should have asked one of my friends to pee on me but neither I nor the guys knew of that particular trick!). My friends wisely took me to a Red Cross clinic, where, after fainting in the shower, I was given some kind of injection, although to this day I have no idea what it was. What I do know is that I had painful chemical burns all down my torso for weeks afterwards.

Despite missing out on the questionable experience of being peed upon, every day in Mexico contained an adventure. And it was the same in my faith. From the safe shallows of middle-class English Christianity, I found myself surrounded by people who were totally sold-out for God. We'd simply rock up at a coastal village, surf the beach, and start evangelising anyone we met. We'd play beach football or baseball, sing songs and perform puppet shows to draw a crowd, then share our testimony and ask for a response right there and then, praying with anyone who wanted to commit their lives to Christ. There are valid questions about the long-term effectiveness of such an approach, but we were young and cared little for anything other than what we believed God was asking us to do each day as it came to us. In hindsight, I see that I had become a little spiritually intense. But I was impressed with the authentic and courageous evangelists I travelled with and wanted to emulate them; they seemed to exhibit so little of the timidity and British reserve that had stymied my own attempts at sharing my faith up to that point in my life.

Somewhere near the coast of Southern Mexico between Puerto Escondido and Puerto Vallarta I met a boy, aged about twelve, who lived in a large orphanage run by Catholic nuns. There was something about this kid – he was just so happy. We spent several days playing games and a lot of football. We bonded. He was always great fun, did his chores and studied hard at school. He liked helping the other kids, he loved singing and prayed earnestly and beautifully during the nuns' simple chapel services. Everyone called him Chico.

On one occasion, I was talking to the sisters who ran the orphanage and they told me Chico's story. He had lived with his family in a remote village in the interior jungle in Southern Mexico. His father was a violent man and an alcoholic. One day, when Chico was at home with his mother, his father came home very drunk and started to beat his mother, as he had done many, many times before. As was his way, Chico hid under the kitchen table. This beating was different, though, and went on and on and on. Tragically, he saw his father beat his mother to death, right in front of him.

As his father continued to beat his dying wife, Chico's older brother returned home. Seeing what his father had done, the brother grabbed a kitchen knife and killed his father, there in front of Chico, still hiding under the table. Men from the local village, hearing his brother's howls of rage, ran to the house, whereupon seeing the older brother standing over the bodies of his mother and father, knife in hand and howling in rage, they shot him on the spot.

The villagers eventually discovered Chico hidden under the kitchen table, locked in silent fear, and took him to the Catholic orphanage. The sisters wept as they told me Chico's story, explaining that for the first few years at the orphanage he hadn't uttered a single sound, so traumatised was he. Yet as I listened, I simply could not reconcile the joy-filled boy I had encountered with the tragic tale they told. I couldn't help asking them, 'I don't understand. How can Chico be so joyful and caring now?' They replied, 'Jesus has done this. Jesus is everything to Chico. Chico's life is a miracle.'

After six months in Mexico the DTS was complete and God had changed me. My Christian faith was no longer a theory but a very real relationship with God. I was a braver evangelist (and a much better surfer). On one of my final days I took a bus ride into town and treated myself to a coke in the ice-cold air conditioning of McDonalds. I sat in the corner, journalling, reflecting on all that God had allowed me to be part of, and wondered what might be next. As I prayed, I sensed God saying that he wanted me to lead an evangelistic trip to the North of England and I simply agreed with God that I would do it. A few days later, rocking the surf-bum look, with a good tan, crazy blonde afro hair and two surfboards wrapped in Mexican blankets, I came home. From the heat and intensity of Mexico, I landed into a cold, drizzly day in London. I didn't want to lose what I'd found, so in the days and weeks that followed I called my friends, wrote to a church I knew in Ambleside, and two months later led a small team to the Lake District.

I was eighteen and didn't have the first clue about how to lead a team on a mission trip. I thought I needed a few badges of office to make it clear who was boss, so I borrowed my Dad's old briefcase to keep stuff in. I thought God would only move through us in direct proportion to our purity, effort and obedience, so I demanded that we drank no alcohol and travelled not a single mile per hour over the speed limit. I look back now and cringe, having made all the girls sleep in a tent outside as I didn't think the boys and girls should be in the same church hall we'd been told we could have as our base. The tent blew down on the second night during a thunder storm and I only just let the two groups set up camp inside, sleeping at opposite ends of the hall. I'd also never given a sermon and was horrified when the church asked me to preach on the middle Sunday, stammering my way through a horrific mess of a message. At the time, the church was thinking of planting to a coastal town called Whitehaven. We'd been there to pray and seen that the proposed site was opposite a multi-storey pay-and-display car park. My mind-blowingly profound and contextual instruction to the church was that they should 'pray and display'. I remember the whole church laughing at me, shaking their heads at my ridiculous, contrived and cheesy message. Despite all this, amazingly, some people did come to faith on that trip and God began something in me too.

Being young and zealous, I'd begun to develop a kind of intensity that might have looked spiritual but beneath the surface was a simple blindness to my weaknesses. God would have to reveal those to me if I was to grow as a disciple and accomplish anything of significance with him in my life. Self-awareness and emotional maturity are such huge factors in spiritual maturity. But I knew none of that back then. As I was to find out, intensity is not a gift of the Holy Spirit.

When I returned home I was naturally excited to see my girlfriend with whom I'd exchanged countless letters while I'd been away. She came round the day after I got home, promptly bursting into tears as she told me she had cheated on me while I was away. I couldn't reconcile the love she'd declared in her many letters with what she was telling me, even though she was truly sorry and, to be fair to her, hadn't tried to hide anything. I felt hurt but oddly numb. I didn't take the time to consider what I thought or felt about it; I simply ended it right there and then. I discarded her in a way that must have been wounding and now regret the way I reacted.

In the months that followed I went to university in South Wales. It seemed to rain every single day of my first term. Despite some good people and enjoyable times, on the inside I was becoming more miserable. I didn't really stop to think what I was doing when I met a girl who didn't share my faith at all. Her demeanour and lifestyle seemed to offer an intoxicating thrill. We hit it off and it all got serious very quickly. Deep down I knew she was the wrong girl for me but it was like an addiction I couldn't – maybe wouldn't – control. Our relationship thoroughly messed me up; she had another rich boyfriend who would turn up unannounced to whisk her off on luxurious trips, needless to say without me. Her own father had done much the same thing to her mother. They say hurt people, hurt people; and so it turned out. I loved her so I always took her back, not blaming her because I was complicit in this messed-up thing. I blamed myself. It took me years to forgive myself for that relationship, long after God had forgiven me.

Our relationship came apart at the seams when we were both on a European year in the middle of our studies: she was in Italy and I was in Spain. I was crushed by the emotional turmoil of losing her and choked with all the guilt and anger that our relationship had left me with. I was on my own and I had no money. I was thrown out of the shared flat of foreign students where I had a small room, and for a while I was at the mercy of loose friendships, sofa-surfing in a few different flats, teetering on the edge of rough sleeping. But in the naivety of my youth I didn't see it. I had an old, cheap guitar with me and I could play three chords, so I decided to start street busking to get money. The trouble was, I was absolutely terrible at it. I recall regularly setting up to busk opposite one particularly posh jewellery shop. I did so only because I knew the store manager would always come out and pay me to go and play somewhere else because I was scaring his customers away. When I look back on those times now, I'm aware how low my self-esteem had got; at the time I welcomed the rejection because it validated what I felt about myself. It was the lowest point in my life.

Weirdly, however, I remember those six painful, impoverished months on my own in Spain with a huge amount of gratitude. They were the making of me. All I had was God and I threw myself at him. I read in the psalms that 'The Lord is close to the broken-hearted and saves those who are crushed in spirit' (Psalm 34:18). That became no longer just a verse to me, or something I *believed* was true; it became something I *experienced*. For the first time in my life, my relationship with God stopped being something I could turn on and off. God became like the air I breathed. I didn't just want God for comfort, I needed God for survival and, in my angst-ridden, rather melodramatic way, would echo King David's prayer: 'From the ends of the earth I call to you, I call as my heart grows faint; lead me to the rock higher than I' (Psalm 61:2).

In *The Purpose Driven Life*, Rick Warren writes: 'You will never know that God is all you need until God is all you've got.'[1] My need for God wasn't heroic and it wasn't a considered decision reflecting mature spiritual discipline and knowledge. Quite the opposite: God was all I had. If I didn't talk to him, I didn't talk to anyone. If he didn't give me money, I didn't have any money. If I couldn't find hope or joy in him, I couldn't find it anywhere else. But in reaching the end of myself, I'd found the start of something that changed the rest of my life. In the words of the great Richard Rohr, I found myself 'falling upward'.[2]

The Apostle Paul knew all about falling upward. He believed that the Lord had deliberately weakened him, using the devil to do so. We recoil at the idea, finding it almost impossible to imagine why God would do such a thing. In the strengths-based culture of our times, choosing weakness as a strategy to progress is wholly counter-intuitive. Yet Paul wrote: 'In order to keep me from becoming conceited, I was given a thorn in my flesh, a messenger from Satan, to torment me. Three times I pleaded with the Lord to take it away from me. But he said to me "my grace is sufficient for you, for my

power is made perfect in weakness'" (2 Cor. 12:7–10). This reali-
sation had such a profound effect on Paul that he concluded, 'When
I am weak, then I am strong' (verse 10). God was helping me learn
to rely on him alone rather than what I imagined to be my own
ability.

Not that I knew it at the time – it took a good few years back in
the UK to figure it all out. Having made a complete mess of the
first two years of my time at university, I returned with a new focus
to make it worthwhile. I discovered that inner motivations to achieve
things are far stronger than outer ones. Success has to mean something personally to me before I get seriously interested in pursuing
it. My first two years at university hadn't meant much to me
personally, but when I returned I wanted to get a good degree and
studied accordingly. The final year went so well that one of the
professors who taught on the course hauled me into his office and
demanded to know why I hadn't applied for his PhD programme.
I was gob-smacked as I'd never even considered it. The professor
arranged a scholarship and so I carried on my studies, also working
as a researcher and tutor. Within three years, I'd completed a
doctorate in marketing and social psychology. Although I enjoyed
the study and loved the teaching opportunities, I'd ended up in an
academic research group that seemed more driven by ego and selfish
ambition than by the worthy pursuit of academic goals. The part
of my research that I'd enjoyed the most was spending time with
business owners and managers, trying to understand their world
and add value to them. So I changed track and began training as a
chartered accountant.

My personal faith grew throughout that time and so did my
involvement with church. I tried different congregations in various
denominations ending up with a tight-knit group of Christians who

met together as a community church, part of the Pioneer network. They loved me back to life. They tried to live without any disconnect in their faith between Sunday worship and normal life and that was tremendously refreshing. When I'd been studying for my PhD, I'd started playing five-a-side football with some of the other tutors and researchers. One night I fell against a wall and split my head open. I recall being notably struck during and afterwards that no one really seemed to care; certainly no one helped me. I drove myself to the hospital with blood gushing down my face. Playing football with the guys from the community church was a completely different experience; there was far more banter and laughter – honesty too and a willingness to confront one another when people stepped out of line.

Throughout my late teens and twenties I'd been involved in leading summer and Easter Christian camps for kids and teenagers. I've always loved outdoor adventure and water sports so it was a natural thing for me. One camp was called Sail and Surf where we'd teach fifty or so teenagers to sail and windsurf in the shifting, fickle winds of Lake Windermere in the Lake District. We tended to get either a howling gale and rain, or not a breath of wind and hot sunshine. I always preferred the windy days because that's what we were there for. But the becalmed, sunny days taught me much more about leadership; it was on those days that you had to inject some fun into proceedings. I had to be the first to don a cold, clammy wetsuit and the first into the water for the raft-building challenge or whatever other 'no wind' activity we'd lined up for that day. Periods of calm that stretched on for days also taught me to pray. The centre where we were based had a long jetty that jutted out into the water. Early in the morning before anyone else was up, I'd go and stand at the end and pray for wind and keep praying until I sensed some kind of breakthrough. It was amazing to me how often those prayers about the weather were answered. That said, I've been to plenty of Christian camps and events where our prayers for perfect conditions seem to have been ignored. More often than not, though, I've reflected back on how adverse conditions bring people together, so maybe it's not so bad.

The camps taught me too that miracles weren't just reserved for YWAMers in Mexico. One summer a fifteen-year-old girl called Kim came on Sail and Surf together with her friend Sarah. Kim's grandmother had paid for them to go, a faith-filled Christian woman who had neglected to tell the girls that she was sending them to a Christian camp. Five minutes after arriving onsite off the coach, Kim found me and explained that there had been a bad mistake: she'd opened her bag to find a Bible that her grandmother had smuggled in when she wasn't looking. Then she'd seen on the programme that each evening we'd have a meeting where we'd sing worship songs and hear a short talk based on a Bible passage. Her immediate family were not Christian and she couldn't imagine anything worse. I tried to set her mind at ease, but she didn't want to listen. In the end I agreed to take them to the station the next day to catch a train home, but during the night the whole team prayed and in the morning the girls agreed to stay just for the day's sailing, then travel home after supper. They had such a fantastic time that they confessed they could probably bear the evening meetings as the first one actually hadn't been as bad as they'd feared; in any case, it was worth it for the sailing during the day. They began to make friends with some of the other girls and we didn't hear any more talk about going home.

On the fifth morning Kim asked to speak to me later on. She intrigued me by saying that she knew she had to talk but didn't feel ready, and wanted to enjoy the day fully first. That evening she explained just why she'd been so resistant to the Christian bit of the holiday: her father had died horribly when she was younger, and she'd written in her diary: 'If I ever find out that God exists and I meet him, I'm going to tell him to his face how horrible he is for taking Daddy away. I'm going to tell God that I hate him.'

I didn't know what to say and started to mumble some words to express how awful that must have been for her. Kim wasn't interested in my sympathy and signalled for me to stop talking. She looked at me and said:

Here's the thing, though – last night I had a dream. I was lying in my bed when the door opened and in walked Jesus, who sat at the foot of my bed. I wasn't scared. I was furious. I tried to tell him how much I hated him for taking Dad but I just couldn't get the words out. He looked at me with such understanding, almost as if it had hurt him more than me. Every time I went to say I hated him waves of light and love came off him and went right through me. Joy and peace were flowing out from him and overwhelming me. I started to feel so safe and happy to be with him!

'Wow, that's quite a dream,' I replied, adding, 'Did Jesus say anything to you?'

'Yes,' Kim said, 'Jesus told me to come and talk to you.'

I admit it: I had not the slightest inkling that was coming. Jesus had not spoken to me to get me ready for that – I'm not sure I'd even given him the opportunity to do so that morning. I tried to keep the nerves out of my voice as I gently led Kim in a simple prayer to commit her life to Jesus. That night she wept through the entire evening meeting, but the next morning when she came down to breakfast she looked visibly more joyful; in fact, she was absolutely radiant. I guess her heart had been healed. That evening her friend Sarah gave her life to Christ too.

But I owe those camps even more than endless fun, leadership formation and spiritual development. The whole camp leadership thing started when a friend of mine invited me to join the kitchen team for a large kids' camp on a clifftop site at West Runton in Norfolk. I spent two weeks in a field peeling potatoes and making huge jugs of tea on which were written 'Ugh' for tea without sugar and 'Soapy' for tea with sugar. During the afternoons I tried to teach kids how to juggle and play crocker – a mixture of rounders and rugby. That first year I was seventeen and the kids were aged between eight and twelve. One of them, who was there with her little sister, was called Deborah Calvert. The girls were fun enough, with their thick Liverpudlian accents and matching shell suits (this was in 1990 after all). However, they were also incredibly annoying and absolutely hopeless at juggling.

Years later, when I was trainee accountant in Cardiff, I was still connected to the camps and agreed to join the team for a skiing camp in Switzerland led by a friend of mine. He invited me to attend the annual conference of the umbrella organisation for the camps and I merrily set off for a weekend in deepest, darkest Norfolk. As I walked in, there stood Debi Calvert – no longer a little girl but now at twenty-three a beautiful young woman. I was delighted to find that she was part of the team for the ski camp also and spent the whole of that Switzerland trip doing what I thought was outrageously obvious flirting, including, with a nod and a wink, buying Debi illicit, brandy-laced hot chocolates every lunch break. She didn't seem to notice, although I did overhear her saying how strange it was that she seemed to ski with so much more carefree confidence in the afternoon sessions.

Our first date back in London didn't get off to the best start. I was three hours late. In my defence, I was driving from Cardiff to London on a Friday night. But still, not good. We had decided on a Lebanese restaurant because Debi had spent her gap year at a Christian school for the blind in Beirut. She invited me to eat what she assured me were a Lebanese speciality of luscious sweet peppers but I declined, remarking that they looked a lot like hot chillies. You need to know that Debi is quite competitive – she looked at me with scorn, popped three in her mouth and started chewing. I've never seen a reaction quite like it. Her face went bright red. She downed her drink. Then she downed my drink. And then she grabbed the jug. She actually couldn't speak for ten minutes. Everyone else in the restaurant was looking at me with daggers in their eyes, assuming I'd done or said something so utterly evil to this poor young woman that I'd rendered her speechless and driven her to drink. Happily, just over a year later we were married.

By then I'd qualified as a chartered accountant and transferred within my firm to one of the big London offices so that I could more often be on time for dates with Debi. Debi had already found a great church at All Saints' in Peckham and it was a delight to join her there, although it took me a bit of time to get used to the idea of going back to a Church of England set-up. Fortunately, the vicar broke the typical clergy mould, not least by being universally known as 'Frog'. Frog Orr-Ewing and his wife Amy, a phenomenal leader in her own right, are passionate evangelists keen on overcoming secular society's disbelief in the claims of Jesus and its negative preconceptions about what church might be. Under their leadership the church had grown, gaining energy and a missionary mindset. The congregation reflected the area – a bustling, noisy mix of races, cultures and classes. It was a little chaotic at times but full of life. Debi and I absolutely loved it.

Chapter 2

The reluctant leader

We know that in all things God works for the good of those who love him, who have been called according to his purpose.

Romans 8:28

Debi and I had been married for two years. We lived in Peckham and we were happy. Debi was enjoying her first teaching job and I was working as an accountant in the City. But in the summer of 2006 we began to sense that God might be calling me to leave my job and become a priest. It was something we'd spoken very briefly about once when we first began to date and had that 'So what do you think God wants you to do with the rest of your life?' conversation. I'd realised that I was falling in love with Debi and my hidden agenda was to check that God's call on our lives wasn't completely incompatible. I didn't want to let myself imagine marrying someone who felt called to live in Antarctica alone for ten months of every year studying the penguins; or someone who had taken vows of chastity and felt called to remain single or something. I'm glad there are people who do those things, I just didn't feel called to the same thing and was looking for some compatibility. I found myself mumbling to Debi what I had not said out loud in many years: 'Well it wouldn't surprise me if one day I worked for a church or even led one, perhaps. But not for ages, obviously.' In reply, Debi showed little of my bashfulness: 'I've always said to myself that I'd never marry a vicar, but deep down I think I've always felt that I might do.' I seem to recall there was a rather long, painful, pregnant pause after that. We didn't talk about it again for three years.

I'd grown up with a father who was a vicar and knew that such a vocation could be very demanding, a little lonely, depressing at times, and tough on family life. On the other hand, I also knew that it was a meaningful role that could make a huge difference in the lives of many people. Although he was often very busy and out in the evenings, I do recall my Dad being around for the most part during my upbringing, whereas in the City, a lot of my bosses, whose jobs employees at my level were supposed to covet, rarely saw their families during the week. Several of them were on their second or third marriages. I didn't want that either. But it wasn't about the costs or benefits of each career, it was about my calling. Debi was enjoying life in a good school, teaching Geography to kids in East London and I thought myself reasonably fulfilled in my work too, in a good firm with great bosses and an invigorating set of clients. I was earning well by then and opportunities to climb the career ladder were coming my way. A two-year secondment to our office in New Zealand looked an exciting way of accelerating my promotion. Was that what God planned for us next? The fact was, I was confused about what God's purpose was for my life.

That summer, though, it seemed that everywhere we went people asked me about what I felt called to do. By this time, we had started to pray very tentatively all about it, although I can't say that I offered God any faith to work with. All I had was doubt, so that's what I poured out to God. We decided to hold it privately for a while, giving God the opportunity to speak through others we trusted, unprompted by us. As we headed out to spend time with friends, Debi and I would make each other promise to steer conversation away from the subject of our future or of church leadership. But more than once, at the end of such an evening, our friends would stop us leaving and announce that they'd felt led by God to ask whether I sensed a calling to leave my job, get ordained and lead a church? As we continued to pray, the possibility of a call got stronger, until we could ignore it no longer. We had to go public with someone.

My misgivings about the whole idea didn't reflect any lack of passion for the church. I just felt like a fish out of water whenever I considered it. I didn't think I was at all equipped for leading a church and so would be a very poor choice because it was not my gifting. Although I knew the church needed new leaders, I hoped God would call others to do it. I'm ashamed to admit that a deeper problem was the money: my bosses were earning an annual average of £600,000 each and that's where I wanted to get to. I told myself that this wobble I was having over my career was just nervousness at the idea of earning such vast sums and that my lack of confidence in my ability to do so, and to handle it well as a Christian, would pass. I reasoned that the City needed Christian business people and if I prospered there then I could put money back into the church. I certainly believe that those things are true for many other people and that is indeed God's call for them. But, in my heart, I knew that in continuing to pursue a City career I might just be running from God's call for my life.

I went to see Frog, my wise, godly and entrepreneurial vicar, to consider why God would want to call me out of a job that I seemed to be excelling in, and into one that I believed I was so poorly suited to. As always, Frog was very thoughtful and stumped me by asking if I believed the church of the future needed more of the same type of leaders it already had, or if God might be looking for different leaders with a fresh approach. Of course, Frog explained, leaders who might do things differently in the future might well look at current leaders and conclude they were not at all suitable at the present time. The feelings I had might actually be perfectly consistent with God's calling on me for ordination. That sort of argumentation is classic Frog and deeply annoying as he's invariably right – and lovely with it, so you can't even refute him on those grounds! I found myself unable to counter Frog's logic. Worse still, I spoke to several close, trusted friends who disagreed wholesale with my opinion that I was the wrong type of person. A few of them even said they were so relieved I'd finally realised it because God's calling on my life for ordained church leadership had been obvious to them for some while.

My last hope was Dad's opinion; he'd been uncharacteristically quiet on the subject whenever I'd raised it and I suspected he had some serious misgivings that would get me off the hook. He came up to London one sunny afternoon and we talked as we wandered through Borough Market and along the South Bank. Over a meal among arty types at the British Film Institute, I explained that I really wanted him to share his concerns with me, as he seemed very lukewarm about the whole thing. 'Oh no!' he exclaimed, 'That's not it at all! It's exactly what I think you should do. I just didn't want you to feel any hint of pressure from me, in case you felt obliged to follow in my footsteps or something.' That was the last straw. I gave in to God, entered the system by which clergy are selected, resigned from my job and became a student again, blinking wide-eyed at Oxford's sleepy spires in the late summer sun of 2006.

I share all this personal history to reassure you that I have never felt like a stereotypical vicar. Dawn French's *Vicar of Dibley* was a hilariously crafted role, as was Tom Hollander's character in *Rev*. Both are very well observed and played. Perhaps there are a few vicars who fit those portrayals; but although my friends might disagree with me just to wind me up, I don't recognise either character in myself nor in most of the other vicars I've met. Most vicars are good people, men and women who work incredibly hard for little pay, spending all their energy on the welfare of others, sometimes experiencing the pain of having their hands bitten by the very ones they are trying to feed.

It's tempting to become cynical about church, especially when we get hurt by its leaders. I know many people now who are still hurt by things that happened to them in church years ago. There's one guy who is selfless, kind, gentle and strong. He loves God and loves other people too. I'm convinced God still has a great call on his life; yet sometimes, when his faith-filled wife asks him to join her at her church, he asks with incredulity, 'Don't you remember what they did to us?', referring to events that happened in a highly dysfunctional church leadership team over twenty years ago. They hurt this wonderful man that badly. The church is missing out by not having this guy fully joined in.

Some people, gripped by past hurts experienced at church, are prevented from enjoying God's best for them today as a result. It's not their fault. Like the crowds in the *Jaws* movies they're simply afraid to get back in the water after disaster has struck. And with some justification: when church leaders mess up it causes devastation. I do not want to be that guy – no one does. Every Christian leader sets out wanting to be like Jesus and see those they influence experience God's best for their lives. To grow as a leader I became convinced that I needed to ensure there was no unresolved emotional pain from my past that might later cause me to fail to handle well the stress that future ministry would surely expose me to.

Early in 2013, I'd been the officiating minister at a wedding in a very posh location, for people I loved. I'd wanted to get it right for them and felt the pressure of the occasion and of famous people being present. During the final moments before the ceremony began, I suddenly felt very odd indeed and rushed out of a hidden priest's exit to the prestigious chapel that was our setting. I had to be alone and get some air. I leant against the rear wall with my eyes closed, trying to catch my breath and slow down my racing heart. I re-entered the chapel and struggled through the service. I managed to cover it up that day, but my inner world was in disarray. I simply couldn't figure why it was happening. I did at least know *what* was happening – it had happened once before when I was working in the City. On that occasion I'd escaped to the bathroom and locked myself in there until I felt better. I was having a panic attack.

A few weeks later, Debi and I decided I should go and see a professional counsellor about what was going on in my head. It was one of the best calls I've ever made. The counsellor, to whom I owe a great deal, agreed to see me and invited me over a series of sessions every other week for the next year simply to tell my story and reflect on it a little. He said that as we journeyed through my personal landscape we might discover some things I loved and some things I didn't – in which case we could accept or remove them. He was a brilliant listener who would help me grow in self-awareness and deal with my anxiety. He helped me learn that increasing self-awareness was key to personal growth, so that I might have a greater ability to choose my responses rather than simply react. He encouraged me to allow myself to thrive on God's love for me, to live out of the place where I had the maximum permission to be 'me'.

As you'd expect, we talked about my upbringing. My mum, dad and sister are all super-intelligent people. All three went to Oxford University and my dad then went to Cambridge to study theology on top. My sister, Katie, is very clever indeed and combines her intellect with a beautiful talent for all things artistic. Unfortunately, she was quite ill from a very early age and that continued into her teens and adult life. Love her as I do, my own experience of growing up sometimes felt like walking on egg shells as I tried not to upset her. She was sensitive and fragile at times and like many teenage boys, I suppose, I was not. My own temperament was so different, and I regret enormously not understanding and nurturing her own. As siblings we certainly loved each other, but it's also true that I didn't have as much compassion for her as I should have had and I didn't do as good a job of supporting her as I should have done. As a family we tended to muscle each other with superiority. It wasn't at all an unhappy home and to an extent all of us enjoyed the sparring conversations that occurred around our kitchen table. But they sometimes became fairly robust and if any one of us showed any degree of pride, the others were quick to make sure we didn't get ideas above our station.

Working for the church, my dad was a widely respected leader, but that brought with it a certain degree of pressure of expectation for us as children. I'm ashamed to say that for some of my younger years I was a little embarrassed at being a 'vicar's kid' and felt there was a negative stigma attached to it. Looking back, I'm not sure there really was and probably my shame was more self-inflicted for some reason still unclear to me. And then there was my colour-blindness. It may sound very trivial and, in all honesty, it is really

– it was not an enormous burden to bear compared to many people's childhood experiences. But as a kid I found it acutely embarrassing that I couldn't distinguish red from brown, green from orange, blue from purple.

To deal with this I did what we all do to avoid facing up to emotional pain: I developed coping mechanisms designed to suppress and hide my true feelings of shame, embarrassment, anger and jealousy. As a teenager I became somewhat arrogant and ridiculed anything I felt could be dismissed as 'emotional'. In fact, I probably over-developed an analytical intelligence and under-developed what the author Daniel Goleman refers to as emotional intelligence.

Years later, my lack of emotional intelligence became a debilitating problem. I was finishing my PhD and burning through my minimal grant funding too fast. An older friend in a senior City career invited me out for a meal at a classy restaurant where he often took his clients. As we sat down he said, 'Hey Tim, just for the avoidance of doubt, this is all on me.' One glance at the menu prices told me that I could do nothing but immediately accept his generosity. My friend took a look at the menu, asked the hovering waiter a few questions about two of the dishes, then chose one – very casual, all normal. He sat back now able to relax and looked at me with raised eyebrows signalling it was my turn to order. Trying desperately to maintain a calm exterior, internally I was in full panic mode, unable to decide between the many choices available. Sensing my dismay, my friend tried to help. 'Which dishes are you considering?' he asked. 'Errr, everything looks amazing,' I replied. 'Okay, well, what mood are you in? Fish? Game? They do a risotto here that's to die for.' By this time I was beginning to sweat. I found myself analysing the menu, trying to calculate which dish might be the best value or perhaps the most healthy. My friend looked at me more quizzically and the discerning waiter moved away to give us a little space.

Eventually my friend leaned forward and took the menu out of my hands. He said, 'Look, I come here all the time. Just tell me what you really like, what you're in the mood for foodwise right now and let me chat to them. We'll come up with a dish that you'll love.' I looked at him helplessly and muttered, 'Well that's the trouble. I just don't know what I really like. I don't know what I want.' He looked straight at me and said, 'You don't know what you want *right now*? Or you don't know what you want *full stop*?' I couldn't even reply – the answer by now was self-evident. I knew that my friend loved me deeply and therefore I also knew that he wouldn't let me off the hook easily. He said, 'If you don't know what you want *full stop* then you've got a problem. It's not because you don't want anything. We all have strong desires. But it seems to me that you don't know that bit of yourself well enough. It's like your emotions are speaking a language you don't understand.' He called the waiter back over and with smooth skill ordered something I don't recall but that I'm sure turned out to be delicious.

When I reviewed the memory of that meal with my counsellor, I recalled the insight it had helped me gain at the time, that I needed to relearn once again. No one lives by analytical prowess alone. It's our emotions, rather than rational thinking, that drive so much of our personal, social and economic decisions; even, it now appears, our voting. It certainly drives many people's approach to church, which is one reason why so many have rejected it.

As I reflected I found that as I grew up there were two safe spaces where I could be 'me'. The first place was the world of scouting where I could light fires, get lost on night hikes, shoot air rifles and skin rabbits. We had a brilliant local troop led by two selfless adventurers. The second was the world of sports – rugby in particular. I was quite tall and well-built for my age and relished being right in the thick of the battle in such a physical game. The feeling of being part of a well-drilled team working together with a single objective was immense. Controlled aggression wasn't just allowed, it was necessary and encouraged. Every match was a fast-paced, exhausting, muddy fight.

My counsellor helped me see that it wasn't just that I had a fear of failure – that's pretty universal. I also had a fear of success because my success in life didn't look that great against my sister's situation and that made me feel bad. As a family I felt we'd tended to amplify her successes and diminish mine in order to preserve some kind of level playing field. It wasn't my parents' fault. Now a parent myself, I fully understand their approach. It wasn't my fault either, nor was it my sister's. It's just what happened, or better still it was what as a child and teenager I perceived to be happening. But my sister and parents didn't want that legacy; they didn't want me to avoid success for fear of feeling bad about it. The more I talked to my counsellor, and subsequently to my parents and sister, the freer I felt.

I began to imagine what it would look like if I lived my life with a mindset that was closer to how I used to play rugby, or set out on a night hike. I decided to leave my fears behind and approach life as an adventure to pursue and a game in which to engage myself fully. As Debi and I went through all the setbacks we faced during the planning phase and on into the early years of St Swithun's, we tried not to hold back out of fear but to take on life for the great adventure it is, enjoying the challenge of battling to overcome it. I used to hike like that and play rugby like that; now I try and live life like that. Like Jacob having wrestled with the angel, I'm stronger for all the difficulty I've been through, grateful now for the limp that reminds me of how critical it is in Christian leadership to yield to God's grace-filled strength rather than to try and go it alone.

For all that, though, leaders need to handle power with great care. As a curate at HTB, I recall one clergy meeting where the vicar, Nicky Gumbel was talking us through his outline for a sermon he was due to preach a few weeks later and we were all chipping in ideas. The two-part sermon was about leadership, looking at the character of Moses. Nicky wanted to call his talk 'Time to Lead: Moses, the Reluctant Leader'. I tried to resist the idea that leaders should be reluctant but a quick check online of Nicky's archived talks at HTB will bear witness to the fact that I lost the argument. Nicky's point was that Moses was known for his meekness – immense power held in check by colossal humility. As a young man Moses had used his power to murder an Egyptian whom he'd seen beating a fellow Hebrew. Moses had let the red mist come down once in his life and he wasn't about to do it again. At the burning bush we see that Moses led not because he wanted to but only because God told him to. He didn't have any inner 'need to lead' that's often so dangerous. He would much rather not have endured all the trouble. But he led in order to serve God and other people because he loved them. In Exodus 32 we read that when the people again rebelled against God, God wanted to destroy them all and start from scratch, making a great nation from Moses himself. But Moses talked God out of it. Most leaders have a strong inner drive to action, but godly leaders must balance that with humility of character, love for people and total obedience to the God we serve.

Chapter 3

Repurposed for hope

Listen, I tell you a mystery: we will not all sleep,
but we will all be changed.
1 Corinthians 15:51

St Swithun's is in an area of high crime, mostly fuelled by the drug problem here. As a result, we've had a lot of break-ins and a fair amount of stuff stolen. The disruption and damage that such crime causes is a real thorn in our side and I get easily frustrated over it. I'd been taught that leaders keep hope alive for people experiencing difficulty, repurposing setbacks towards good purposes, but I've often found it's easier said than done. The time when thieves stole the lead flashing off the roof of our church hall was a particularly low point; we didn't even know about it until there was a huge downpour one afternoon and the ceiling caved in as water poured through. I must admit, it was hard to see the upside in that.

In our first year, thieves smashed a glass panel in an external door in order to break into the church and rip a TV screen off the wall. The police told us they strongly suspected drug addicts knocking over a soft target for crime to fuel their addiction. As I surveyed the damaged door, wall and carpet, my eye fell on a rock inside the back door. The police reasoned that's what they had used to break in. I picked it up and over the next few mornings turned it over in my hands as I prayed through my frustration, sensing that God wanted to somehow speak through this to us. It's hard to pray for hope when you're angry with people, so I confessed how I felt about the thieves who had caused all the damage. As I began to pray for them, though, I realised just how desperate they must have been and what a tragic situation their actions revealed. That Sunday I stood up and told the whole church that a terrible thing had happened: not the smashed door, ruined wall and carpet and stolen TV screen; no, the tragedy was that these desperate people had to break in the back door of a church at night because we haven't yet worked out how to welcome them in through the front door during the day. We took it as a sign from God challenging us to redouble our commitment to addiction recovery and our love for that community.

Thinking like this is not just empty spin. I have a friend who planted a new church in a UK city where churchgoing had dropped like a stone. The Church of England building he was appointed to was in a terrible state. The church congregation needed a lot of love and the building needed a lot of money. He didn't have much money, but he had a lot of love and the church immediately began to grow because of it. Just one month into the new plant, they were facing a major problem with the building: a section of floor just inside the doorway that suddenly collapsed. As he told me the story my friend winced with pain at how he'd had to start apologising to everyone for the upset and agonised over where they'd find the money to fix it. I found myself beginning say 'I'm so sorry for you . . .' then I stopped – that wasn't going to help. So I changed my approach and said, 'That's fantastic!' He looked at me with surprise and confusion. 'You mean to tell me that since you reopened that church, so many people have come in to feel the love that the old structures have collapsed? Get round that hole and shout and cheer the Lord, thanking him for this sign that due to fresh growth old things will give way and new things will be built!' I'm not sure if they literally gathered around the hole but, re-energised by the Holy Spirit, my friend spoke to the congregation much more positively. That church is still growing and redeveloping its dilapidated venue.

Without denying pain and suffering but embracing it, the Bible is relentlessly optimistic. Accordingly, the church has, on the whole, been a very affirming movement even though there have undoubtedly been many horrific episodes when, to our shame, the gospel of Christ has been used as a cover for oppressive rule and great evil. Paul told the persecuted church in Rome: 'We know that in all things, God works for the good of those who love him, who have been called according to his purpose' (Rom. 8:28). Whenever I'm in difficult circumstances I try to remember that God has not spared me from them because ultimately he's wanting to bring some good to me or others through them. Listening to the stories of people whose lives have been repurposed by Christ from much more broken circumstances than my own, I'm reminded that Christianity worships a God who is not immune to suffering but willing to embrace it entirely: Good Friday is named as such because the original meaning for the English word 'good' was 'holy'.

Waving farewell to the hustle of working life in London, Debi and I left for Oxford to study theology in August 2006. We were sad to leave, but excited about what lay ahead. I missed the buzz of my commercial work and felt out of my depth in Oxford, where intellect is revered. I felt forgotten and as I began to read academic theology also felt singularly stupid. Gradually, though, I realised that it didn't matter: God doesn't care that much how clever we are, but he does care how wise we are. One kind of wisdom is about knowing the right answers – the only kind of wisdom many people think exists. Luckily, there's another kind of wisdom, and that's knowing the right questions. I'm constantly learning to ask questions, then listen. Many leaders get stressed out because they feel as if everyone is looking to them to come up with answers to infinite problems. When staff or our ministry leaders at St Swithun's ask me what they should do about a problem, rather than rolling out a directive answer I'm learning to reply, 'I'm not sure. What do you think? What do you want to do about it?' Nine times out of ten they already have a good idea of what to do, even if you have to probe a little to get them to verbalise it. What they're usually looking for from me isn't direction, but permission and encouragement. It might feel so good to act like a magical leader who has all the answers, but whenever I fall into the trap of viewing myself as the expert star it doesn't last long before my family or friends burst my bubble. Thank God they do. Then I'm free again to view those I lead as the experts and to act as their coach. I've been amazed at the results of this approach. Now I know that for nearly every activity in church there's someone else who's better at it than I am. So I ask them to do it instead and support them to the hilt. My role as a pastor is to identify, release and empower others into ministry, serving them as they go about it.

But learning all that in practice came later. Oxford is a beautiful place and it's where our first son, Josiah, was born. Fatherhood changed me. I stopped hooning around on motorbikes for a start, as I became more aware that Debi and Josiah were counting on my being around for the long-term future. Motorbikes are fantastic fun and there's no feeling like sweeping around fast bends with the wind rushing around you, the exhaust howling and bars buzzing as you accelerate, but all it takes is one thing to go wrong and it's game over. Now I get my kicks from surfing, windsurfing and mountain biking. Although I've had some knocks doing those things too, they're a lot safer than motorcycling. I could tell everyone around me was relieved when I sold my motorbike.

Midway through my course all students were supposed to do a summer placement at a church. When the list of placements came out they got snapped up by others around me and I was the only one in my year left without a placement. I felt I'd been left unwanted on the shelf. It was then that one of the guys in the year above me, Adam Atkinson, suggested that I go down and meet his former boss, the then-curate at HTB, Archie Coates, to ask for his wisdom. Of course, it was a set-up – I was going for an interview – but I didn't realise it at the time. Fortuitously, Archie asked me to come to HTB for my placement that summer. Neither Debi nor I had been part of the HTB family previously, although many years before, in 1994, I'd been invited to their summer church family holiday called 'Focus'. That year there was a major move of the Holy Spirit and it had been a powerful week. I vividly recall some of the scenes after the evening meetings: everywhere I looked people were laid out in ecstatic encounters with the Holy Spirit, experiencing waves of God's love and presence, accompanied for some by laughter, electricity jolts, roars, shakes, clapping hands or peaceful, blissful rest.

I loved my placement at HTB. Debi was still teaching near Oxford, although she was pregnant with Josiah and suffering with terrible morning sickness. She was able to come down and visit several times, although her memory of those occasions is simply trying *not* to throw up all over Nicky and Pippa Gumbel. After a short, sharp grilling by the then-churchwarden Ken Costa, I was invited to serve my curacy at HTB if the bishops agreed. Debi and I, with our baby son, moved back to London thus embarking on my six very happy years as a curate at HTB.

There were so many highlights. My central role was to develop and support leaders to run the midweek discipleship and community groups that we used to call 'pastorates' and now call 'connect groups'. The idea was that they were larger than traditional home-groups and therefore a much better place to develop gifting and welcome in newcomers. And it worked. Groups like these are a critical hidden weapon in large churches where it's possible to remain disconnected and anonymous at Sunday services or other events. Connect groups are where friendships can form; where honest, practical discipleship can occur; and where church members can care for one another. When these groups thrive in a church every other ministry wins because there are more people around, with more maturity, skill and gifting, and more fire in their belly to love and serve the church. Running these groups at HTB I found myself up to my neck in messy, good old-fashioned disciple making – and I thrived on it.

But the best thing of all at HTB was seeing many unchurched younger people come to faith in Jesus through Alpha. Alpha is central to HTB's health and growth and it has been central to St Swithun's health and growth too. Beyond its undoubted effectiveness as an evangelistic programme, what Alpha really does, if you're prepared to swallow it whole, is set the culture of the whole church towards welcoming in people who don't yet know Jesus and aren't yet familiar with church. You learn to respect people's opinions and listen to them rather than preach at them. You learn to be informal and build trust. You learn to get rid of the barriers of churchmanship and impenetrable clouds of Christian jargon and religious antics. You learn to be hospitable and friendly. You learn to develop leaders. You learn to have fun and enjoy meeting fascinating people. You learn that it's better to be honest than right, and to have integrity rather than hidden agendas.

Alpha also gives you a pipeline of trained leaders with a strong, positive culture and skills; given time that overspills into all other ministries of church too. HTB's leadership team is impressive and at times I found myself intimidated. That's nothing to do with their approach and everything to do with my insecurity and pride. One of the four church sites run by HTB in South Kensington is called St Paul's Onslow Square. It's actually the church where my father served his curacy in the early 1970s when he was also the chaplain at the Royal Brompton Hospital. I was born and christened there. We lived in a basement flat in Neville Terrace. So it was an amazing feeling of homecoming to see my own three children christened at St Paul's, and to lead services and preach there. The building was often rammed full of young people for the evening service to the extent that sometimes I had to pinch myself.

I remember one event, celebrating the 150th anniversary of the site being dedicated as a church, with my Dad in attendence, an occasion when we'd just about squeezed in 1,000 people. Someone walking down the street outside, seeing crowds of people queuing round the block to get in, had said, 'What on earth are they all doing trying to get into that church?' This was mentioned to Nicky, who started the event by saying, 'They haven't heard the good news, have they? Jesus is alive!' I applaud and support the Church Revitalisation Trust's vision of one hundred new UK city centre resource churches by 2025 and London diocese's commitment to plant a hundred new worshipping communities by 2020 in our capital. Their publication *Buildings on Sure Foundations* says:

> Empty church buildings are 'like an empty palace of a long-forgotten king – people walk past and think that the king is dead'. Our mission is to show London that the King is not dead, he is very much alive, through the creation or renewal of one hundred worshipping communities. By reopening closed doors and renewing worshipping communities we are showing the community that Christianity is a living, renewing faith.[1]

This ethos reminds me of a story about Revd H.W. Webb-Peploe who from 1876 to 1916 was the third vicar of St Paul's Onslow Square, serving also as prebendary of St Paul's Cathedral. By all accounts he was a man of the people, passionate about evangelism and zealous about prayer. One day, arriving at the church appropriately dressed in Victorian clerical finery, he saw a workman right at the top of the scaffolding on site. He climbed up all the ladders simply to enquire of the man's soul. The man was so impressed that this distinguished clergyman had climbed up just to speak with him that he came to church the following Sunday and gave his life to Christ. As a great man of prayer, Webb-Peploe held the largest public prayer meetings in south-west London with 400 regularly attending in 1882.

Webb-Peploe had the kind of godly attitude that Debi and I want so badly. It's all too rare, which is why those who have it stick out by exception. Most of us get bogged down in the mire of life and allow ourselves to become cynical and joyless. I'll describe later in more detail how throughout my time at HTB, Debi and I tried over and over to lead a church plant out from there to restart a church in a new location. We faced endless difficulties and made countless mistakes. As time went on it began to get to us. I'd leave meetings with church leaders and staff feeling embattled, drained, hopeless and cynical. We knew we had to find a different way of reacting to our circumstances and knew we needed the ability to make our own emotional weather so that we could go 'sunbathing in the rain'.[2] We realised that if we were ever successful in planting a church we'd surely face numerous challenging circumstances and would need to resist the force of negative attitudes within ourselves and others. We felt we had a responsibility as followers of Jesus to have something more hopeful to offer when confronted by dismay; after all, we reasoned, if we didn't have something else to offer in challenging times we could hardly claim to know Jesus, who is 'a new and living hope'. (1 Pet. 1:3).

You may laugh at our pop psychology, but we decided to tape up some Scriptures and quotes on our kitchen cupboards so that every time we went into the kitchen we'd be confronted with truth that ran so contrary to our natural inclinations. We taped up James saying, 'Consider it pure joy, my brothers and sisters, whenever you face trials of many kinds, because you know that the testing of your faith produces perseverance. Let perseverance finish its work so that you may be mature and complete, not lacking anything' (James 1:2). We taped up St Paul saying, 'For Christ's sake I delight in weaknesses, in insults, in hardships, in persecutions, in difficulties. For when I am weak, then I am strong' (2 Cor. 12:10). And we taped up Joyce Meyer saying, 'Patience is not the ability to wait, but the ability to keep a good attitude while you wait.'[3] We practised, I guess, a form of meditation and, slowly but surely, it helped shape our attitudes and responses in more positive and hope-filled directions than would otherwise have been the case.

I have since seen how, with support, those who have been saved by Christ from desperate difficulty often become powerful teachers of reshaped attitudes and behaviours for others. Bournemouth is plagued by drug and alcohol addiction, and the town suffers all the social ills of crime, broken families and poor mental health that goes with it. In 2015, following the publication of Government statistics, it was widely reported that the town has the highest rate anywhere in the UK of people claiming welfare and disability benefits citing drug and alcohol addiction as the causing factor. Young people here are significantly more likely than elsewhere in the UK to be admitted to hospital because of drugs and alcohol. They're also more likely to be hospitalised for reasons of self-harm than elsewhere in the UK and that rate is rising at a frightening pace. I'll know that revival has hit here only when I start hearing news stories that these stats have collapsed.

One of the women who started the addiction recovery ministry in Bournemouth is called Emma. Her dad abandoned the family when she was fifteen months old, three days before her brother was born. Her mother worked tirelessly as a much respected Pharmacist providing for the family doing everything she could to give her children the best but it wasn't easy. Her younger brother reacted by becoming angry and aggressive in later life, fuelled alongside a sad journey involving drugs and alcohol. Emma blamed herself, developing a severe self-loathing that was encouraged by the cruel bullying she received at school and aggression from her brother at home. By the age of eleven she had begun to starve herself as an attempt to control her emotions leading to the twin tormentors we know today as anorexia and bulimia. She learned ways to disguise her internal pain and the physical bruises and black eyes, so she could live with an outer shell that appeared acceptable while secretly being grateful that her hidden wounds confirmed that she was right to despise herself.

As a young teenager Emma began to drink, in what she describes as 'a living hell' and spent the following seventeen chaotic years in a blur of alcohol addiction which at its peak reached two litres of vodka a day just to 'function'. She still managed to get a good degree at university, leading a double life as she lost her driving licence twice, was held against her will and tortured in a foreign country, suffered in an abusive relationship and was arrested for drink driving, subsequently being put on probation. Through her lonely journey of addiction she regrettably lied to people she cared about, manipulating people to feed her drinking, which as I know today is the total opposite behaviour to the woman that I have come to know and love. She lived with a constant inner pain that no amount of alcohol could obliterate. She cried most days and hated herself to the absolute core. She became suicidal and self-harmed. Longing for love, she settled for destructive and unhealthy relationships as a short-term substitute. She felt completely hopeless, unlovable and beyond help.

Remarkably – and as I now know, not unusually – as a person heavily involved in the deep cycle of addiction, Emma clung on to a deep inner faith in God. Her faith was her one inextinguishable hope, a candle in the wind. When aged twenty-eight the professionals took over and helped her into a rehab centre, Emma began to pray, asking God to forgive her and help her. It took a whole year to build her confidence to speak in group settings, so profound was her sense that she had completely lost the thread of her own identity.

That was ten years ago. She is now a highly regarded, professional woman and is one of the most powerful advocates for addiction recovery that I have been blessed to know, devoting her life to that cause, helping thousands of addicts to experience the same transformation that Jesus has won for her. She recently told me, 'I love being Emma, I walk in the light and am living proof that our scars can be moulded into our greatest triumphs! I truly believe now that I am blessed to be a blessing and can turn my battles into blessings.' Together with a team of dedicated volunteers, all of whom have experience with addictions, Emma started to help the many addicts who were turning up at church here in Bournemouth, looking for support from a compassionate community to support them get free. Along with several other churches in town we now have the privilege of doing exactly that through a twelve-step-based course called The Recovery Course that introduces recovering addicts to Jesus along the way. Emma has since become a trustee of the charity RecoveryTwo and is pioneering Christ-centred recovery nationally.

Emma's own mother had always known that there was very little support for the many who are the collateral damage of the life of every addict: the families and friends trying to love the unlovable. She began to tell her own story and now runs a programme for the family members and friends of addicts called The Recovery Support Group, also supported by RecoveryTwo. This ministry is phenomenally powerful and we've seen whole families restored as a result and the programme is also growing momentum around the UK.

Emma and her mother found the same thing that Debi and I discovered. Accepting the salvation Christ offers means much more than mumbling a reluctant prayer asking God for forgiveness to assuage our sense of guilt. That might be where we begin, but God is not content to leave it there. He wants much, much more for us. He made us for a purpose and wants to restore us to it. In Jeremiah 29:11–13 God says, '"For I know the plans I have for you" "plans to prosper you and not to harm you, plans to give you hope and a future."' The writer of Hebrews 12:1 urges us to 'run with perseverance the race marked out for us.' This is what the church is all about. It's a group of friends so inspired with the powerful message of God's self-giving love that they become determined to bring out God's best in one another and the world. At church the damage we've sustained in life can be repaired and we become repurposed to God's plan for our lives, a plan that fits us like a glove because it's what we were made for. Richard Rohr writes: 'Most of us were taught that God would love us if and when we change. In fact, God loves you so that you can change. What empowers change, what makes you desirous of change is the experience of love. It is that inherent experience of love that becomes the engine of change.'[4]

Chapter 4

The ones that got away

. . . though the righteous fall seven times, they rise again,
but the wicked stumble when calamity strikes.

Proverbs 24:16

For most of the six years I spent at HTB, I was trying to leave. Not because I didn't love HTB. I did. But I was hungry to plant out and I'd gone to HTB on that understanding and expectation. Sure enough, all around me the ordained leaders I worked so closely with one by one headed out on exciting church-planting projects. At the end of my first year, my phenomenal boss, associate vicar Archie Coates left to plant St Peter's Brighton. The following year in 2010 three of my fellow curates, Matt Hogg, Azariah France-Williams and Jerry Field, all left to plant churches elsewhere in London. In 2011 Jon March planted out to Kentish Town and in 2012 Jago Wynne planted out to Clapham. That year Libby Etherington planted a church in Hounslow and the outrageously talented Jamie Haith went to America. In 2013 David Ingall planted out in the Square Mile and Ed Dix planted out to Millwall.

Slowly but surely my confidence seeped away and I began to fear being left on the shelf. I felt like my eleven-year-old self at the school disco, when I stood alone against the wall, terrified of the girls who were deeply attractive in a way that I couldn't really fathom, yet utterly unreachable. I remember standing apart, watching all the other boys have fun all around me with such ease. It wasn't just jealousy, it was that sense of being ignored and unwanted. Likewise, as time went on at HTB, deep insecurity and pride within me seemed to dominate my thoughts and prayer life. I wish I could go back and speak to my younger self, sharing some of what I've since learned. Had I realised what was actually happening at the time the experience wouldn't have been so painful. I'd have asked my eleven-year-old self at that disco whether I really wanted the same thing as everyone else. I'd have encouraged him to be honest with himself and God, and then to go and pursue wholeheartedly the great thing that seemed most purposeful. That might have been growing in courage and asking that pretty girl in my class to dance. But more likely it would have been turning away from the whole set-up, leaving them all to it and going to ride my bike through the woods. The six years of waiting at HTB taught me to persevere, determine my purpose, and not be so bothered about what everyone else is doing but focus only on those things that God had for me. Trying to navigate life by looking at everyone else all the time is deeply dissatisfying and only amplifies our insecurity and pride, leading inevitably to purposelessness and alienation. I now count these lessons as so valuable that I wouldn't exchange the experience for anything.

Caught up in the HTB whirlwind of vibrant church life and a growing network, and despite our private pain as we waited for our turn to come around, Debi and I were catching the church-planting bug. During those six years we worked on at least twelve planting projects, none of which ultimately worked out for us. A church plant may not succeed for many reasons; but twelve times we had to go through the pain of seeing our plans fail. Each time we'd imagine moving our family into a new home, in a new area and into new schools; we'd research the projects and get all excited about the possibilities for mission in each instance; and we'd meet, be quized by and try to win over bishops, archdeacons, churchwardens, parish representatives, local councillors, PCC members, staff team, area deans and lay chairs of the deanery synod. The Church of England is getting better at facilitating church planting, but it's coming from a long way back.

There are myriad factors that have to come together in order to plant a church, certainly within the Church of England. There has to be an invitation from a bishop, the building and resources need to be in place, a team has to be built, and a leader has to be identified. Even when every human factor is in place, however, the heart of that leader sometimes just says 'no'. I've seen it happen to many others, and the first time a planting opportunity came round, that's what happened to me too. It's hard to disappoint others when you feel that way, but you have to be totally honest. My first church-planting opportunity was served to me on a plate after I'd been at HTB as a curate for just nine months. I was asked to go and look at a small church in a salubrious part of the London suburbs, opposite a leafy park and under the shadow of an historic castle. Nearby dappled shade fell on the sleepy upper reaches of the Thames and students lolled about in the sunshine. Over the bridge at the end of the road lay a large town centre and a station connecting straight into central London. Only millionaires would be able to live in local properties commensurate with the beautiful, well-appointed vicarage and there were great local schools for our children. The congregation were willing to welcome in an HTB plant and had plans to purchase the industrial site behind the church in order to make rooms available for offices, children's work and midweek mission. Everything seemed to be in place. The problem was me. As I looked around my heart sank at the idea of taking it on. I felt unprepared and not a little hurt at what I perceived as being asked to leave HTB so soon. So I convinced the leadership that I wasn't ready. As things turned out, it's a good job I did because the church planter who eventually took it on did a phenomenal job, as did his worthy successor, building up a thriving church that has had a profound impact in that community and continues to do so today.

The second opportunity came a year later and this time I was up for it. Right from the start, I felt incredibly positive about what could be done. The large church building was in spacious grounds on a very prominent site, right at the crossroads of a major arterial traffic route into central South London and a busy tube stop was directly opposite the church. Thousands of people passed through the grounds every day of the week and on Saturdays there was a thriving farmer's market leading from the church towards good cafés nearby. A large park was across the street, where in 1739 George Whitfield and John Wesley had preached to crowds of thirty thousand. The church building itself had an illustrious history but had fallen on very hard times and the congregation was ageing, declining and feeling overwhelmed by the needs of a significant minority battling mental health disorders, addictions and homelessness. I loved it and had a clear, strong vision for what could be done; I also knew that doing something new there would be attractive to a good crowd at HTB who would be willing to join a nearby plant to reach the local unchurched population. It was, and to my knowledge still remains, a prime site for a major church plant.

However, the church and diocese leadership were minded to pursue an open application process and consider our proposal against anyone else who might apply. That sounds entirely reasonable, but it can be the kiss of death for church-planting projects. And so it proved to be on that occasion. Among a field of more experienced candidates, who would come by themselves as a normally appointed new incumbent, our church-plant proposal seemed (and was) much more risky. Understandably, the congregation declined and went with a seasoned vicar instead. Debi and I were glad for him and the parish as we knew that he was a good man who had a missionary heart. But privately I was absolutely gutted. It had been a huge potential prize that I'd invested so much into and had such hopes for; to see all that come to nothing again led me to a good deal of soul-searching.

They say that you should never let people see how laws and sausages are really made. The reality of politics and butchering is not pretty and if we were to see it in detail then we might be put off the end product. Likewise, church planting requires a bit of back-room dealing too. Some people feel this isn't quite right and believe everything should be totally transparent, but I disagree. Diocese and local church leaders and decision-makers need our trust and often require a bit of cover. I'm not advocating they cover up anything – that's different. But suppose a bishop identifies an opportunity to do something new in a strategically important, under-evangelised area where the community is suffering because they do not have a thriving church to serve it and preach the gospel to it. Imagine there's actually a good building too that could serve as a base for this mission, perhaps a church where there is a small congregation, at least some of whom really do want to be led forward in mission. So the bishop (perhaps tasking his archdeacon) begins to approach various church-planting networks and bodies within the Anglican Communion, asking if they could help. However, imagine the questions that other local church leaders will have about that – it could easily be perceived as quite a threat. Or think of the congregation members not so keen on change – it could easily become a divisive issue just at a point where the church is fragile, often without a full-time priest taking care of it.

Bishops are busy people and, like all of us, might look at such a scenario and see it as fraught with risk if people feel they do not have a voice in what's happening. Even the most courageous bishop might well decide that a collaborative approach is a wiser option in such circumstances, giving all stakeholders a chance to input to the process and work through their views about it. That kind of approach is, of course, reasonable but inevitably lends itself to an open application process where the church-plant project would be considered alongside other mainstream candidates. Perhaps it can work if the church planter is the bishop's clear preference, but it's asking a lot from the patrons and parish representatives. They're being forced to compare a high-risk church-planting project against a lower-risk normal appointment of new priest. Seasoned, safe applicants at interview would be expected to perform better than young church planters, priests who have probably never led a church outright before, and who are proposing to arrive with a new team, new congregation members, new ideas, some new money, and who are asking for a full mandate for radical change. Unsurprisingly given that choice, representatives might look at the planter and say, 'Err, no thanks', and choose the safer option instead.

That was the case at another parish that came and went. At the time it was one of London diocese's largest parishes, home to well over thirty thousand people, about thirty of whom went to the parish church. The first time I visited I thought I'd found the church when I came across a prominent site directly on the main road. I should have known better: that was sold off a long time ago, having been thought extraneous to mission. However, just around the corner lay a large facility in obvious need of repair and maintenance but basically sound, shared through a Local Ecumenical Partnership, whose partners were very keen to see new life and mission through a church plant. The actual parish church was small and lay hidden away in a surprisingly quiet and secluded quaint enclave in the midst of the largely poor conurbation.

The parish church and small parish office and meeting rooms next door were all run by one lady, who lived just opposite and was also employed as the parish secretary. She was also one of the parish representatives. Every conversation I had with church members there talked about this lady as the central, dominant feature of the church and she controlled (and made happen) nearly everything that went on there, so that all others deferred to her. She deserved to be heard and honoured, and it's completely understandable that she had a very high sense of ownership – after all she had served and worshipped there for many years, did everything and lived right across the road. The problem was that she didn't want change at a moment when it was desperately needed both for the church itself and the wider mission in the local area. Knowing how key she was to the whole thing, Debi and I were pleased to feel that we had made a good connection with her when we'd met. I liked her and saw that she would flourish within a church plant as the burden of carrying the church on her own shoulders was very heavy. She also had a real faith and wanted others to be able to experience the love of God. But I knew it would be asking a lot from her to let go of things and to welcome in change in order to achieve what, deep down, I was sure that she wanted.

The parish had already failed to appoint a new leader twice already, so we stepped very carefully through the process with the bishop and invested an awful lot into trying to win everyone over to the idea of change through a church plant. We offered everything we could think of to overcome any problems that were raised and tried to exercise as much grace as possible to counter any defensiveness that we encountered, taking time to listen and understand the fears that, quite naturally, various people had about the project. Since there was a traditional Anglo-Catholic worship tradition at the church, I offered to retain a regular expression of worship in that style alongside the new contemporary services that the bishop was looking for us to begin.

The bishop had decided that there should be an open application process because it would create total acrimony to try and force a scheme for change upon the church. In fairness, he didn't have many other options and he also wanted to protect me – he didn't want my first appointment as outright leader to be into a situation of warring hostilities. Quite rightly, he felt that any new leader would need some kind of mandate for change from the small congregation. Only two other candidates applied, one of whom the parish representatives and bishop agreed would not be appropriate. But even then, at the end of a long discussion after both interviews, the parish representatives refused to appoint me to bring in a church plant, nor the other candidate to initiate a much slower, measured change. Apparently, the bishop asked the parish representatives if they had been prepared to appoint either candidate before they'd started the interview process and they admitted they had not. The bishop was so cross he even got cross with me! I've forgiven him –he's a very good guy indeed – but even he couldn't make it happen. It was a crushing blow for us and deeply sad for the parish – even for the woman who was at the heart of it, because I genuinely believe that she would have been loved and honoured if we'd gone there. She wanted a thriving church; she just wanted it to be all on her own terms, and none of us is going to get that. Ever.

Over time, resistance to any change at all in a church will lead to its demise. Even small, stable congregations will eventually age and die. We live in a society with a fast rate of change. Of course some aspects of those changes are negative social, economic, ethical or moral ones that the church must combat or resist, as it always has done. But many of the changes are merely cultural and pose little or no threat to the gospel; in fact, they may present perfect opportunities for it – one thinks of changes in technology, music or design perhaps – and these need to be reflected in church life so that it can keep pace with the society it's called to reach. Resistance to change can be overcome by prayer, an honest appraisal of the real situation and bold leaders who love those they lead. As faith is shared, truth understood, vision seen and loving trust built, even ardent resisters can become powerful and enthusiastic advocates for change.

Nevertheless, church planting is a tricky business. I guess many congregations contain some people longing for change, while others are more resistant. Maybe the answer really lies in mobilising the silent majority in the middle. This seemed to be true at another prime parish church that came and went, in the busy heart of a fast-changing neighbourhood in London. The parish had two churches, one a very large, prominent facility near the tube stop in the centre of a small park, the other buried in the centre of high-density council housing. Both were hubs for their immediate communities and offered a great platform for increased mission to a fascinating local population becoming younger, more cosmopolitan and international by the day. Once again, we felt it would make a fantastic HTB plant. I still believed it could happen, even when they opted eventually for an open application process, because the people within the congregation who most wanted to welcome a plant were confident that they had the broad backing of the majority of the church. Perhaps they did and what occurred was really that I failed at interview. Unfortunately for me, and against the expectation of the archdeacon who had thought it unlikely that the post would attract other quality candidates through open applications, several strong candidates with years of pastoral experience had applied. I had just four years of curacy as experience to offer, and that within a very different context at HTB. I also carried with me the offer (or threat, depending on a congregant's point of view) of a group of enthusiastic newcomers, loud worship music and radical ideas about change. That proved a tougher sell to the wider church than anyone had anticipated, even for the representatives who wanted it. The bottom line is that even for the bravest and most visionary of parish represent-atives, the risk profile will determine their choice, and it's human nature to opt for safety. I had to admit to myself that I'd misman-aged the process, taken too much for granted, and failed to equip those who had most wanted change with all that they needed, to reassure and mobilise the majority.

Soon after we'd got over the mess and disappointment of our latest ill-fated attempt to plant out, I was approached to apply to another parish in a major UK city. An open application process was already in operation, and the suggestion was (not from within HTB I should add) that I might be appointed and then welcome in a plant afterwards. I think the phrase used was to 'church plant by stealth'. On reflection, although I'm ashamed to admit that I didn't realise it at first, the scheme was questionable in its integrity, the most basic of all requirements. The instigator of the scheme was, in fairness, trying to walk the church to a much better place out of faithfulness to God and great love for the church and its surrounding community. Of course we made an absolute commitment not to lie to anyone during the application process, but there was a certain deviousness in concealing the ultimate aim. For example, I was urged to ditch all language around church planting in order to get appointed. The instigator's plan was to secure for the parish a leader who would support it in approaching HTB to welcome in a plant retrospectively, as it were. I'm not at all sure that would have been a successful strategy, not least because full Christian integrity is fundamental to everything that HTB would even consider being involved in. However, the instigator was a godly and persuasive figure himself and was confident that a large number of people in the church, as well as other interested parties around it, were desperate to see new things and change occur. He was in a tough spot and was trying to do the right thing, and knowing the church was strongly influenced by a powerful minority resistant to change, he was trying to be inventive as to how they might see some kind of fresh start emerging.

The parish profile produced to advertise the role looked impressive and emphasised how open the parish was to change and new ideas, seeking a leader to help them discover their missional purpose and then to pursue it. I was told that the patron of the parish was also onboard with the intended aim, which was good news: in the Church of England the ultimate right to recommend or appoint a priest lies with a patron, who is sometimes a private individual, or charitable trust, archbishop or Crown. Bishops act as patrons for about half of all parishes in England. We had to move quickly, so there wasn't much time to meet people, but we were told that was probably for the best. A visionary, influential clergyman within the deanery was a constant source of encouragement and had arranged things behind the scenes in dialogue with the bishop and patron. I laboured long over our application letter and all seemed well.

I wasn't even selected for interview. In fact, I never even received a response to my application letter, which I know was received. The furious clergyman who had tried to mastermind proceedings tried desperately to mobilise the patron to become more actively involved but he was rebuffed. Embarrassed and ashamed, he had to tell me it was all off. It wasn't his fault: either those with influence simply hadn't been bold enough, or else they'd very wisely intervened to stop a compromised scheme. You be the judge. My first angry thoughts concluded the former . . . but I'm now sure it was the latter and thank God for their action (although a letter in reply would have been polite!). I learned further valuable lessons through this experience. First, I'd have to have the utmost integrity in order to participate in what God was involved in. I couldn't pull a fast one on God. Second, in the future I would need to demonstrate to all stakeholders that I was a trustworthy leader and my fully honest conduct would be fundamental to that. Third, and there's no way around this, to make renewal happen in the Church of England we're all going to have to be much bolder. We must pray for planters to have integrity and for decision-makers to be brave. We must also pray for the trustees of the large, somewhat hidden trusts and societies that hold thousands of patronages to become more actively and positively involved in the process of change.

Whenever I look back at my failures I'm always tempted to blame everyone and everything else. I find it so easy to become cynical about people who disagree with me or prove difficult, and frustrated by institutions that are bureaucratic and backward. Of course, leaders need a sense of holy discontent to drive them forward to grasp nettles and wrestle things towards a better future. And I really do believe that the future we face in this country urgently demands radical change in our approach to both urban and rural ministry, including radical changes to the institutions and processes of the church. But having experienced so many failed bids at planting, I've had to face the harsh reality that I am the common factor in my failures; most of the mistakes in the cases I've mentioned, as well as others that came and went, were all my own.

Although failure is painful, it can teach us invaluable lessons. This is another dimension of the process of 'falling upward'. Apparently, when Thomas Edison was inventing the lightbulb, he experimented again and again over the years, using different materials and designs. Nothing worked. But he kept on going. He is often quoted as having said: 'I have not failed. I've just found 10,000 ways that won't work.'[1] On my worst days I find it extremely hard to retain that kind of attitude and even get annoyed when others try and point me back to it. But in the brutal world of leadership it's an essential quality to live by.

Behind the scenes of even what might appear to us to be the largest and most successful churches in the world, I guarantee the daily story will really be of pain, difficulty and setback. Looked at objectively, one might conclude that there is an insidious dishonesty in our social media streams and websites that display happy, shiny people living victorious, fulfilled, problem-free Christian lives. At worst a total lack of authentic depiction of the Christian life is an evil deception, but while I've no doubt that's sometimes a fair accusation, it's a mistake to become cynical about every online offering by churches striving to provide hope. There's enough discouragement and bad news in the world and we should be glad that many churches are trying to counter that.

Having now had the chance to meet some of the leaders of large churches, I'm often struck by their humility. Humility is an essential trait of Christian leadership and is a very valuable quality that our failures can help us to obtain. Without humility you might momentarily impress others until you fail, as sooner or later you surely will, but you won't encourage them. It doesn't encourage people to go around posturing and pontificating as an expert. The truth is there are no experts when it comes to leading churches; we're all winging it. If your church is going well, then rejoice! Encourage others with some of the stories by all means. But make sure you season your account with plenty of truthful tales about how badly you've actually messed it up – the success is the result of God's grace not your expertise. I hope that when I talk with people about church, or even when you read this, you walk away thinking, 'What an idiot! But if God can do it even through him, maybe he could use me.' He can! Biblical wisdom tells us over and over again that God will humble arrogant and proud people but lift up those who are humble and lowly. James and Peter both write, 'Humble yourselves before the Lord, and he will lift you up' (cf. James 4:10; 1 Pet. 5:6). The Bible defines humility as 'the fear of the Lord' that yields great wisdom, honour and life to those who have learned it (Prov. 11:2; 22:4).

There is of course a distorted sense of fearing God, which occurs when we misjudge his character. Jesus once told a story of a king who entrusted three servants with his money, giving them crystal-clear instructions to 'put this money to work until I come back'. Two servants did exactly that, gained a return and were rewarded for their faithfulness, but one did not, explaining to the returned king: 'I was afraid of you because you are a hard man. You take out what you did not put in and reap what you did not sow' (Luke 19:21). There's no indication in the story that the servant was correct in his view of the king's character; in fact, there's every indication of the exact opposite when one looks at the trust and reward that the king extends to the faithful servants. The unfaithful servant, despite having been entrusted with his master's wealth, distrusted his master's motives and actions and even assigned evil characteristics to him. Those errors of judgement paralysed him with fear and kept him from investing what the master meant for him to steward.

The attitude of the unfaithful servant, with its inevitable result, is a terrifyingly easy error for church leaders to make. I find it a constant challenge. We have been given a crystal-clear commission by God to go and make disciples of all people. This is no empty call, because God has also entrusted us with huge resources to use as we carry out this mission. Furthermore, just as in Jesus' parable, we know we are stewards only for a short time and that the Lord will soon either come back, or else we'll die and appear before him. Either way, we'll have to give an account of how we've invested the resources we were trusted with and what kind of returns we've gained in terms of the extension of his Kingdom. God has given church leaders today so much opportunity: the Church of England runs around sixteen thousand church buildings in thirteen thousand parishes covering every square inch of the UK, along with forty-three city-centre cathedrals. It educates one million children in the UK every day, through its 4,700 schools, eighty per cent of which are rated good or outstanding. We can build God's Kingdom at the heart of every community. God has also richly entrusted the Church of England with great wealth to resource this work. We spend around £900 million annually and possess an investment fund worth £8 billion. So why aren't the returns higher? Like the wicked and lazy servant who failed his master so badly, is it possible that we squander wealth and opportunity because we have misjudged our master? What are we so afraid of?

Chapter 5

Your Macedonian moment

After Paul had seen the vision, we got ready at once to leave
for Macedonia, concluding that God had called us to
preach the gospel to them.
Acts 16:9–10

President Josiah Bartlett, in Aaron Sorkin's *West Wing* TV drama
series, doesn't dwell on either successes or failures for very long.
He's always asking, 'What's next?' Most of us are tempted to try
and bask in glory for a while when things go well, or to give up
and grovel in the dust when they go wrong. When I'm feeling low,
I find cheerful people can be annoying as I like to wallow in my
misery for a bit. But Nicky Gumbel taught me, 'Don't stay down
too long.' He's right. Although I initially resist colleagues, friends
and family pulling me off my high horse, or out of my emotional
nose-dives, that's exactly what I need them to do. Queen among
everyone who does that for me is my wife, Debi. She is unfailingly
encouraging, but has certainly pulled me out of more self-inflicted
pain and emotional quagmires than anyone else. I consider myself
very lucky to be loved by her.

February 2013 was a particularly low point. We'd been trying to plant into yet another urban parish with a huge population but only a tiny number in church. Debi and I had tried to woo and befriend and build trust, while also being authentic and honest with the mandate for change that the bishop wanted us to pursue. I felt we'd done everything we could and followed the bishop's lead every step of the way. Nevertheless, in the end the parish turned us and the bishop down and there was nothing we could do. I felt rejected and not a little angry at having been taken for a ride for nearly half a year. I sensed the bishop's sharp frustration too and thought I'd let him down as well as the HTB family. It had happened to us before and I was sick and tired of it. I wanted to be left alone to sulk.

At that time, I was part of a leadership development programme run by the then Bishop of Kensington, Paul Williams, for emerging church leaders across London. The cohort had really bonded; I trusted and respected them and Paul was an effective coach. I went along for one of our bi-weekly gatherings, still sulking and sore about what had happened. Tearfully, I shared it with the group. Several of them had experienced something similar, so they set about encouraging me and praying for me with great empathy. One friend, Ruth Bushyager, said, 'Tim, you're having a Macedonian moment.' I had no idea what she was referring to, so asked her to explain:

It's from Acts 16. The Apostle Paul had a great personal desire to get into Asia and start ministering there, but the Lord prevented him over and over and he didn't know why. But then he received a clear call to head into Macedonia instead, where he had huge success. You're in the first half of that story right now, being prevented from going where you want. It's a godly ambition but God has something else in mind. Be patient and trust God; he knows what he's doing. You're stuck in the frustration of the first bit – all you can see is where you *can't* go. But sooner or later, you'll see the second half of the story and hear a clear invitation to go where the Lord wants. It will be to a new place you can't see right now, where he has prepared everything for you.

Ruth's word really comforted me and I went home and shared it with Debi, but we decided to keep it to ourselves.

The next day Nicky Gumbel, knowing full well how low I felt about crashing out from the previous planting project, said to me, 'I've just got off the phone with Bishop Tim Dakin, who's talking about a plant in Bournemouth. Would you like to think about it?' I love Nicky and respect him enormously. I'd lie down in traffic for that man. But at that moment, my perspective was so skewed by my frame of mind that I thought him hugely insensitive for offering me this new hope and nearby exploded with rage. Inwardly I counted to ten, bit my lip, and replied through gritted teeth that I'd go home and talk to Debi. That did nothing to lift my mood; Debi was hurting too and since she's a lot braver than I am, I thought she might not exercise the same restraint. Grudgingly, I admitted to Nicky that my only acquaintance with Bournemouth was through some very happy memories of its sunny beach life, having surfed there a few times as a teenager. 'Excellent!' said Nicky, 'Why don't you and Debi pray and go down there to see if you like the place?' He was right. I was wrong. It's amazing to look back and see that I was so focused on my hurt, shame and rejection that I very nearly missed what God had in store for us. Self-pity always keeps us from God's best. Somewhat annoyingly, Nicky's right: don't stay down too long.

My mum and dad offered to look after our kids for two days so that Debi and I could go down to Bournemouth, simply to see what it was like. Debi's aunt and uncle had run several hotels down there and her grandparents had lived there too, so she knew it better than I did. We found a cheap hotel room in the town centre and decided not to put any expectation on to the trip other than to see if our hearts fell or rose at the idea of living there. Bournemouth was not at its best for us. The hotel was pretty grim: the room's much-vaunted 'sea view' could only be obtained by standing on your tip-toes while squeezed against the wardrobe, and the wind rattled the windows at night. The weather was frigidly cold. But as we walked around we made an instant connection – I still can't put my finger on it. That night, chomping on spicy fajitas, we began to laugh at the funnier side of things we'd experienced over the previous year. The wind swept through us as we walked down the beach, cleansing us of disappointment. The relentless crashing of waves reminded us of God's unceasing grace and the beautiful views offered us new perspectives. We returned home healed and excited. Nicky put us in touch with Bishop Tim, and the ball started to roll.

I find it so encouraging that even the Apostle Paul found it hard to discern God's guidance. That's true for all of us in the Christian life. Sometimes we have an apparently good desire that gets frustrated. Paul wanted to preach the gospel in Asia. What's wrong with that? God had a plan to get the job done that involved Paul going elsewhere first, however. Paul did all the right things; he persevered. But before he went East, God wanted to send him West. He wasn't doing anything wrong, it's just that God had a different way of doing things that wasn't obvious to him. God isn't limited by human wisdom, so the way he makes things happen will often appear inscrutable to us. Isaiah 55:7–8 says, '"My thoughts are not your thoughts, neither are your ways, my ways," declares the Lord. "As the heavens are higher than the earth, so are my ways higher than your ways and my thoughts than your thoughts."'

Paul's Macedonian moment consisted of four factors that helped me as I reflected on Acts 16, following Ruth's word to me. First, Paul was up for a challenge. He tried over and over to get into Asia and do what was in his heart – to preach the gospel to people who hadn't yet had the opportunity of hearing it. That was a good desire and God blessed him for it. When you stand back and look at Paul's ministry, he faced challenge after challenge and never seemed to lose heart. I think he was energised by it. I once heard a preacher describe him as, 'The apostle of confrontation'. He liked being up against it and having to rely on God.

No church should spend too much time trying to do things that are humanly possible without God. The New Testament makes it abundantly clear that the church is not like a secular charity or Non-Governmental Organisation. We might carry out some of the same activities to reach and save the lost and to alleviate poverty, suffering and injustice, but our gifts are spiritual (1 Cor. 1:7; 2:13) and so is our battle (Eph. 6:12). We work way beyond the limits of human power because we work in a totally different way, drawing instead on the spiritual power of God's love (Col. 1:28–9). Jesus said, 'I will build my church' (Matt. 16:18). Not us – he will do it. And he invites us to work with him if we want to. But that requires faith and trust and what we might perceive to be outrageous risk, occasionally bordering on the irresponsible. This is the faith that Paul had in spades. Too often I take matters into my own hands. God and others have had to intervene to help me stop and learn whenever they've seen me trying to do great things *for* God, but fundamentally trying to do them *without* God. This is potentially disastrous. In this mode it's so easy to fall into the trap of thinking that godly ends justify ungodly means. They don't. I've had to learn that God's things can only be done God's way. And that means doing things with him not just for him.

Second, Paul had a holy discontent. He was frustrated, and frustration can be particularly dangerous, tempting us to make rash, unwise decisions. But it can also be empowering, as Paul goes on to prove when he frees a slave girl possessed by an evil spirit (Acts 16:18). It can be God's way of energising us to take the actions required to change something. Inertia takes a lot of energy to overcome. A 'righteous frustration' comes from the tension between what you see today and a God-given unrealised ambition for what could be tomorrow. It can give us enormous energy and provokes breathtaking creativity. Carefully, so as not to cause division or discouragement, I often *mine* for appropriate discontent and encourage it, not only within overall church leaders elsewhere, but also amongst our own leadership teams.

Third, Paul's Macedonian moment helped him to see that he had an unexercised compassion and possessed an undeployed gift. He saw in his vision the man of Macedonia, 'standing and begging him, "Come over to Macedonia and help us"'(Acts 16:18). The vision shifted the focus of Paul's compassion from Asia towards Macedonia. He heard their cry in a new way and knew he could do something about it. He had what they were begging for – the gospel. Paul realised he possessed an undeployed gift that they were begging him to come and put into play.

I love Paul's response here: there's not an ounce of pride in it. He's sure he's heard from God and senses he's being sent on the basis of God's compassion to meet the needs of others. He and his travelling companions immediately move to action. Luke recalls, 'after Paul had seen the vision, we got ready at once to leave for Macedonia' (Acts 16:10). I'm not suggesting for a moment that Debi and I are anything like as holy as Paul! But on this point, we've often felt mystified as we've seen what's happening in and through the church we lead. Most of the leaders of the large churches and ministries that I know feel inadequate for the task, just as I do. The hilarious and wonderful visionary Mike Pilavachi champions the truth that God doesn't call the equipped. He equips the called. As Mike often explains, on this he speaks from first-hand experience: from a small youth group in one church in the early 1990s, Soul Survivor has grown to reach, convert and disciple hundreds of thousands of young people all over the UK and elsewhere in the world. Many have planted churches and run huge city-wide missions that have mobilised countless Christians in acts of service and evangelism.

Finally, Paul concluded what God was calling him to do. Luke tells us that after receiving the vision they immediately prepared to leave for Macedonia, 'concluding that God had called us to preach the gospel to them' (Acts 16:10). It's vital that at some point or other we reach a decision about what we believe God's purpose is for our life at any given stage. The Bible makes it clear that God has a universal purpose for all of us to become children of God, to follow Christ and to become Christlike. But for each one of us, God also has a specific purpose unique to our life alone – a 'race marked out for us' – he is even able to work our mistakes and sufferings into this unique plan: 'we know that in all things God works for the good of those who have been called according to his purpose' (Rom. 8:28).

In my office at home I have a picture cut from a newspaper that my dad sent me years ago. It is a dramatic photograph of a huge high-performance racing yacht towing a tiny figure behind it on a wakeboard. Dad had scrawled on it, 'Tim – fancy this? Love Dad'. It has always spoken to me since I first saw it and eventually I put it in a frame along with an Oswald Chambers quote that I love: 'Complete weakness and dependence will always be the occasion for the Spirit of God to manifest his power.' At St Swithun's we talk about something being 'God or bust'. Whenever we're considering something big or new, sooner or later someone will mention it. It's shorthand for 'We have no idea how we can overcome this challenge. There's no way forward but to trust that God's going to help us do it.' That sounds clueless but, when you think about it, why would we want to do anything that doesn't involve such faith? It's the only way of knowing that we're doing God's work and not trying to engineer our own agenda – however godly it might seem.

We are all just tiny figures, towed along for the ride of our lives, behind an almighty God who loves us. The calling and power are his; all we have to do is hold on. However good a leader you are, church planting and revitalisation projects will stretch you to your limit. I imagine the same is true for leadership positions in education, healthcare, media, business, charitable works or politics. There are thousands of times when I've looked up and wondered whether I really am doing the right thing; I'm so grateful that thousands of times I've been able to say, 'Yes. This is tough right now. But I know this is God. I can rely on his call and power.'

In the early summer of 2014 I attended a series of meetings in Bournemouth with local clergy to discuss our plans for the church plant. Several of these meetings were chaired by the bishop or archdeacon and one of them particularly sticks in my mind. It was a full meeting of our local chapter and all clergy who could had shown up for it. Bishop Jonathan (Southampton) chaired the meeting. We discussed the vision for the plant and dealt with practical issues such as finance and where we'd got to on the site. We also sought to allay some natural fears around so-called 'transfer growth', whereby those who are already Christians switch between churches, and we discussed how to minimise that in practice. Bishop Jonathan brought the meeting to a close by telling us all in no uncertain terms that while any fears and problems would be listened to and addressed, no one was to be in any doubt that the plant was going ahead. I was obviously elated to hear that, but what he did next blew me away. He jumped to his feet, waved his arms as if beckoning me over, and said, 'Listen Tim, we love you and trust you and appreciate all you bring. We want you to join us in bringing the gospel here. I suppose we're like the man of Macedonia in Paul's dream saying, "Come over to Macedonia and help us!" Tim, we're your Macedonian moment. Come and help.' There is no way he could have known about Ruth's prophetic word given to me a year-and-a-half previously.

Chapter 6

My big but

> ... but I am a man of prayer.
> Psalm 109:4

These are often the first words in my mind when I wake up, driving me out of bed and into my study to pray. I don't say this to impress you with my virtue. I don't do it out of holiness but out of need. That 'but' in Psalm 109, verse 4 is a huge single word. It doesn't matter how big the challenges and obstacles are that I'm facing or that others around me are facing, that 'but' is the start of the answer. When I feel the panic rising within me, that 'but' calms me so that I can focus. When I'm really up against it, when things are going wrong and when I feel like giving up, I pray. My own prayer life is more often driven by failure than faith, and more often motivated by desperation than by drive. I only began to understand why the psalms are so powerful once I began to pray them as the cry of a drowning man. Dietrich Bonhoeffer, the German pastor and theologian who died in prison at the Nazis' hands shortly before the end of the Second World War, preached, wrote and spoke relentlessly about the psalms, saying in one of his earliest lectures, 'There is not a single detail of the piety and impiety of the Christian church that is not found there . . . The only way to understand the Psalms is on your knees, the whole congregation praying the words of the Psalms with all its strength.'[1]

Church is not a human idea; it starts in the mind of God. So the only place any church can be birthed is in prayer. During my curacy I spent many hours in the HTB 24–7 prayer room praying for other church plants, as well as a church plant that I could lead. These prayers circled around many sites and places but from the spring of 2013 began to focus on Bournemouth. For well over eighteen months, the only place that St Swithun's existed was in the place of prayer. I also began to go down to Bournemouth for prayer walks, picking up things as prayer triggers to help me continue to pray from my home in London. Once, after a prayer walk trudging around Bournemouth in the rain in the late summer of 2013, I ended back at the St Swithun's site. I felt the Lord telling me to march around the site seven times, following the pattern of Joshua and his army at Jericho. I shuffled around in the pouring rain like the drowned rat I was, feeling pretty self-conscious. On the last circuit, I took my sandwich box out of my bag and filled it with the pine-scented, sandy soil from the church ground. Back home in London during my quiet times I'd lift the lid and smell it as I prayed. Often I'd tip it out on a sheet of paper, take off my shoes and stand in the soil to pray. In this way, I prayed every morning for a year. I still have that box with the same soil in it; now when I pray using it I'm reminded of God's faithfulness and ask him for a deeper confidence in his call, strength in perseverance and a lot more patience than I naturally possess.

St Swithun's had been sold off by the Church of England in 1998 as a problem-child building that was thought to be no longer of any use. Fortunately, it was handed over to an enthusiastic bunch of free-church Christians who over the next fifteen years built up a sizeable church at the site, completely refurbishing it. However, by the time we came to see it they'd already moved out and the sense of emptiness and dereliction was hard to beat. It was the most unlikely of all the sites we looked at and undoubtedly the hardest to obtain. We were repeatedly warned off it. At several points along the journey it was about to be sold off to the private sector for development. The empty site had become a magnet for homeless people, pimps and drug dealers. We had to clear many syringes, needles and improvised bongs and pipes from the site before we opened and the day before we had to stop two teenage girls shooting up heroin in the grounds. It was heartbreaking and we felt so impotent to help them. That same day I also had to stop a pornographic photo shoot happening in the grounds – that's the kind of thing the site had become infamous for. But we didn't want St Swithun's to stop being a magnet for those types at all; in fact, we wanted many more of them to come – albeit for a different reason. One staff meeting when we'd just started, after we'd hoovered and cleaned as we always did, I gave each team member a bottle of olive oil and a container of salt. We all trooped outside and prayed around the entire site, scattering salt and pouring oil everywhere as a prophetic act. We knew the site had to be cleansed spiritually, not just physically.

I mentioned previously that I've kept the rock that thieves threw at one of the church windows in order to break in and steal a laptop and TV screen. When I hold that rock and pray, I cry out for those we know, love and see who are poor, addicted, unloved or who in some way have lost hope. When I hold it I sense their desperation. The burglars didn't hurl that rock through our windows because they really wanted to. They hurled it out of the pain, loss, poverty and anger they feel towards a church who they believe is not helping them. As I pray I ask myself whether they'd be justified in feeling angry at my hypocrisy for preaching Christ but failing to be more like him? So my prayer becomes that God will help us reach people who feel like throwing rocks at the church – as, to be honest, I do sometimes – so that they can experience our love, and as they do, to encounter God's life-changing love for them too.

In the planning phase I was advised to develop a group of inter-cessors that I asked to pray for me, by emailing them regular updates. You have to take responsibility to mobilise prayer. I'm having to relearn this now that the project is further down the road. Prophetic words from friends at HTB during the build-up were so important to us. Very soon after Nicky first mentioned the invitation to plant in Bournemouth, I prayed with someone after a service at HTB Onslow Square and they turned to me and said, 'I can see a huge wave and I feel like God has told me you will know what that means.' I certainly did. Bournemouth isn't a classic surf spot but on its day there are plenty of waves here, the two piers helping to shape sandbanks that provide a decent break. The picture of a 'wave' has been a recurring motif in so many words and pictures given to us. In fact, for a while the working title of the whole project was 'The Wave'. It has come up over and again in our leadership meetings, at our weekly 7.00a.m. prayer meeting, and at our 'Kingdom Come' nights of prayer and worship.

The idea that there is a large approaching wave of God's love which will soon crash upon our town makes sense to us and encourages us on. In Luke 12 Jesus asks his audience why they are able to tell a change in the weather but unable to discern a change in a spiritual climate. He asks, 'How is it that you don't know how to interpret this present time?' Out of all the prayer and prophecy we've received has come a deep conviction that the spiritual climate in Bournemouth is changing; there is a new period coming when the church won't be defeated and downtrodden but will be militant and alive! Out there in the vast ocean of God's love, there's a swell building and approaching the shore: I'm utterly convinced that there's a new wave of God's love coming which we're to prepare for.

As much as excitement began to build about the idea of planting to Bournemouth, I was nevertheless troubled by leaving my church family at HTB, particularly those at St Paul's Onslow Square. Owing to my family's personal connection there it seemed a huge wrench to leave and I asked for God's help as I wanted to face forward and not look back. On one occasion after we'd started St Swithun's I remember thinking about St Paul's while driving into Bournemouth. I was tired and at that time we were facing so many challenges; I had a bit of a wobble and began to wonder if I'd done the right thing. So on the way I'd been praying for guidance and some kind of comfort and assurance that I'd been right to leave St Paul's. I asked the Lord to speak to me. For some reason I had the car satnav switched on, even though I knew the way. As I turned off the motorway that takes you nearly straight into the heart of Bournemouth, my satnav said to me, 'Leave St Paul's Road heading straight ahead south on to St Swithun's Road.' Those are the actual names of the roads leading to our church! God doesn't usually speak to me so clearly and I've never heard of him speaking through a satnav before, but that was pretty clear! Sometimes, I still put the satnav on at the same point now when I'm coming home, just to remind myself that God knows what he's doing. Only God puts stuff together like that.

Like a yacht on a windy day with no sails hoisted, without prayer the church is purposeless, powerless and totally pointless.

With prayer, though, it can prosper through the storms and travel to the very ends of the earth. And, for sure, storms are coming. In John 16 Jesus warned his disciples all about it and concluded: 'I have told you all these things, so that in me you may have peace. In this world you will have trouble. But take heart! I have overcome the world' (John 16:33). Since starting St Swithun's we've welcomed many Christians visiting from other churches in Bournemouth and beyond. I've noticed a tendency for a tiny number of them to come up to me after the service and, with a warm smile, tell me how they're a very mature Christian who is deeply gifted in prophecy and that they've been sent by God to warn me that we're just about to enter a very dark period of satanic attack and difficulty. The third time it happened I replied: 'Thank you! That must mean we're on track as that's just the normal Christian life, isn't it? Don't worry, it's okay, we've prayed.' The lady was not very happy with my answer. But I meant what I said. And anyway, church planting is hard enough without that kind of 'encouragement'!

Most visitors, whether Christian or not, have shouted us on. Each year one visitor is a personal hero of mine – the ex-banker, now philanthropist, author and speaker, Ken Costa, who was also the churchwarden at HTB when we planted St Swithun's. He comes to speak each year and we always go for a walk together in the afternoon during which I share with him all my problems and he gives me his wisdom and encouragement. (I try to encourage him too but for the seasoned deal-maker that he is, the balance is by far in my favour.) On the day that Bournemouth's local football club gained promotion to the Premiership, Ken tweeted '@timjmatthews plants a church in Bournemouth and in the same season their football club joins the Premiership. Spiritual power at work.' I don't know whether Ken was referring to my planting a church or AFC Bournemouth's amazing story as being the more miraculous – he clearly thought both were virtually impossible and he was right! Having said that, Ken's a Chelsea fan, so his wisdom does have limits after all.

I was raised a devout Tottenham Hotspur supporter and I'll never stop supporting Spurs, but since coming to Bournemouth I must admit that I have taken up supporting AFC Bournemouth too. The Cherries' story is a famous football fairytale. During the 2007–8 season the club were forced into administration with debts of £4m they could not repay. They suffered a ten-point penalty and were relegated at the end of the season. The next season, further point penalties followed and the club narrowly avoided disappearing from the leagues altogether by winning their last game, their best away win in thirty years, scoring 4–0 at Morecambe. Then, under new ownership, former player Eddie Howe was appointed as the youngest manager in the Football Leagues aged thirty-one. Despite one stint away from the club, by the end of 2014–15 season, Howe had guided Bournemouth to the Premiership.

Far less well known is that at the time of Howe's appointment another new person arrived at the club to help behind the scenes: club chaplain Revd Andy Rimmer. Andy is pure gold and spent at least a day a week at the club and training ground, as well as most match days, 'loitering with intent – to help people in any way I could, to reassure them, encourage them, give them hope, instil in them determination, and to pray for them.' There were only a handful of staff when Andy was first appointed. He judged when to make himself invisible and disappear from view (which was often) and when to step to the front – as he did establishing the club's annual carol service, a great family event inside the stadium each

Christmas. Most of the time all he did was shuffle around and pray, for the club, for the manager, for the players, for the staff, and for the fans. For eight years. In the brutally short-term, performance-oriented world of professional football Andy is a gentle, constant man who gained trust behind the scenes and has been able to help a great many people there. The results of his prayer and presence on the values of the club, the resilience and wisdom of the manager, and on team morale, fitness and on-the-field performance speak for themselves.

At St Swithun's staff meetings we often remind one another that unless God's going to show up and do what only God can do, then whatever we're planning will be a total waste of time and money and will most probably fail anyway. We constantly seek God's power in prayer and his wisdom on how we can align ourselves with what he's doing. Our 'It's God or bust' ethos means that we pray from the very real assumption that without God's direct involvement we *can't* and *won't* succeed. Jesus said to his followers, 'Without me you can do nothing' (John 15:5). So often I think I can do quite a lot for God without his direct involvement and without a total reliance on him. I have a godless tendency to rely on planning and project management rather than on prayer. Just for the record, planning and project management can be deeply spiritual activities but the risk is that we don't give God much opportunity to inform our plans. We get his vision, then say to him, 'I've got it from here.' When I fall into that mindset I quickly become stressed-out because I feel as if I'm doing too much and I'm on the hook if it all goes wrong. If I succeed, I feel as if I've made it happen, so I deserve the glory. Jesus sees it all very differently. Clearly he has a word to describe the category of activity where we try to do stuff without him: he calls it 'nothing'.

I spend way too much of my life trying so hard to do, as it turns out, nothing.

On the flip-side, Jesus also said to his followers, 'With me everything is possible' (Mark 9:23; 10:27). Before starting St Swithun's I'd often read that statement, but tended to gloss over it. Maybe I'd written it off as Jesus being a bit exuberant, indulging in some Hebrew comedy that frequently uses hyperbole. I don't think that any more. During one or other of my difficult moments in the planning phase, Archie Coates had said to me: 'At the end of the day, Tim, you've got to decide whether this is God or not. If it's not, then get out now. You don't want to be part of a human vanity project. But if it is, then persevere, believe, trust. Keep moving forwards. Keep sharing the vision with boldness. Keep praying with faith.'

I've since learned that this was how the Apostle Paul operated. We don't know for sure if he ever visited Colossae. A church was planted there from Ephesus, where Paul had spent a lot of time and he had certainly travelled through the general area; but perhaps most of his knowledge of the church was indirect, through leaders like Epaphras (cf. Col. 1:7). And yet Paul's letter to the Colossians shows he held a very special place for them in his heart. He wrote to them, 'Since the day we heard about you, we have not stopped praying for you' (Col. 1:9). Notice that Paul then goes on to tell the Colossians exactly what he prays for them. Sometimes people ask me how they can pray for us as a church plant and Colossians 1:9–12 is the best answer I can think of. If this was what Paul considered to be important when praying for church plants, then we should pay attention. He singles out ten things all church plants need prayer for and continually asks God to:

1. fill you with the knowledge of his will
2. . . . through all the wisdom and understanding that the Spirit gives
3. . . . so that you may live a life worthy of the Lord and please him in every way
4. . . . bearing fruit in every good work
5. . . . growing in the knowledge of God
6. . . . being strengthened with all his power according to his glorious might
7. . . . so that you may have great endurance
8. . . . and patience
9. . . . giving joyful thanks to the Father
10. . . . who has qualified you to share in the inheritance of his holy people in the kingdom of light.

Try it. Stop reading this right now, think of a church that you know and love, then pray this list of ten things for them. Think what that church would be like if God started to answer your prayer and make this stuff happen! You can pray in the same way for the organisation you work in or the family or friendship group that you're part of. Wherever you have influence, think how you could work with God to become the answer to that prayer. If every family, church and organisation where a Christian had influence prayed and lived like that we would soon see revival across the UK.

While I do try to keep a habit of starting every day with an hour or more of Bible reading, silent reflection and prayer, I often feel that my most effective prayers are not spoken during those times. Usually, the times when I feel I've had some kind of 'breakthrough', or 'heard from God' on something, or 'realised' or 'seen' or even 'heard' something new, come from raw prayers uttered when I'm walking, running, cycling or surfing when I really and truly let my guard down.

Other powerful prayer moments have come at times of utter desperation. In the early summer of 2012 Debi and I headed off for a bank holiday weekend camping in the Purbeck hills just west of Bournemouth. Our daughter, Rebekah, was about four months old, Josiah was four, and Caleb was two-and-a-half. From an early age it was clear that Caleb loved adventure, as do we all. A friend in London leant me his car for the trip: a fully-loaded, jacked-up, 4x4 Land Rover equipped with every kind of gadget you could imagine, including a fold-out safari tent on the roof. It was epic. To my young boys it was like riding in a giant Tonka-truck toy. Actually, that's how it felt to me too. We escaped London, met our friends and set up camp at a great site, cooking supper, settling the children after seemingly endless games, and happily drifting off to sleep.

The next morning the kids woke early and were excited to explore their new surroundings in the daylight. Caleb was at that delightful stage where he just wanted to climb everything. I put him up in the high back of the truck where the huge tailgate was swung open while I tidied up – Caleb laughing at the excitement of it all. With my back turned, he attempted to climb out of the back of the truck, down a ladder that reached only half way to the ground. All I heard was a clatter, a dull thud and an agonised squeal. I whipped around to see Caleb dangling in mid-air from the bottom of the ladder he had clearly fallen down. It seemed that one of his legs had trapped in between the last two rungs as he'd fallen, and my stomach dropped inside me as I realised that his leg was horribly twisted, completely bent the wrong way between the rungs.

I rushed to Caleb and took his weight in my arms. With distraught urgency I freed his leg, which just dangled helplessly, apparently with no muscle control. He seemed mute with fear. Involuntarily, I fell to my knees and cried out, 'Jesus! Help!' I think my whole heart went into that cry. Even writing this, I'm terrified by the memory, or I would be but for this: at once, Caleb seemed to shudder in my arms, then wriggled out of my grip and simply ran off to play with the others. He had been instantly, miraculously and completely healed.

Whenever I'm in doubt about the power of prayer and feel desperate – which happens far more often than I'd like to admit – I think back to cradling my son in my arms after he'd fallen out of that truck. Of course, part of the reason I recall the episode so powerfully is because it was unusually dramatic and emotionally intense. Certainly, the answer I received that day is not my normal experience in prayer; on many other occasions I have prayed for healing – including that of my children and wife – without apparent success.

So often I pray without any concrete answer forthcoming. Why do bad things happen to good people? Does not the existence of human suffering run contrary to the existence of a good, faithful God? How long should we keep praying for something before accepting that God may have decided not to grant our request? I fully acknowledge that such questions are real, profound and powerful. Nothing I can say here could begin to answer those questions, nor address the depth of pain that we all feel occasionally – and some of us feel daily – at what appears to be unanswered prayer regarding intense human suffering. Personally, I have found Pete Greig's amazing book, *God on Mute*,[2] to be the best I've ever read on this dimension of prayer, together with many other aspects of prayer along the way. Pete writes from the experiences of suffering he and his beautiful wife Sami have experienced, so his wisdom has cost them dearly, but you and I can access it for the equivalent of a few cups of coffee.

All I know is that when I feel helpless or in difficulty or pain, prayer always helps me feel better. That's because often I don't really pray to get answers; I pray simply to relate to God and talk things through with him. Sometimes prayer is just a matter of enjoying life with God; sometimes it's pinning my inner ears back and allowing him to teach me something, even if it's a painful revelation of what I've done wrong or a part of my character I need to work on. God is a good father who simply loves to spend time with his children being in his conscious presence. There is no limit to his love and nothing he is uninterested in. Prayer is basically doing life with Jesus. I also fully believe that sometimes prayer seems to result in remarkable occurrences that can change the course of people's lives, even that of nations.

My grandfathers both fought in the Second World War. On my mother's side, Corporal Albert Hare-Brown drove trucks and motorbikes all around Europe. He was rescued off the beaches of Dunkirk, a miracle he struggled to talk about his entire life, such were the horrors that he saw and his relief at being rescued. By May 1940, the British Expeditionary Force (BEF) was in full-scale retreat from the Nazis as they swept through Europe, fighting rearguard actions as the BEF withdrew to Dunkirk. The German High Command boasted that the British army was encircled and its troops were proceeding to its annihilation. Well over 300,000 were stranded and under relentless attack. Initially, it was estimated that just 45,000 troops could be rescued. General Brook, the British Corps Commander, wrote in his diary, 'Nothing but a miracle can save us now.'

Acknowledging the dire situation, King George VI called a National Day of Prayer on Sunday 26 May. At least three miracles then occurred. First, Hitler overruled his generals and halted the advance of the Nazi armoured columns, the head of which was only ten miles away from the BEF. History has yet to explain this decision. Second, violent storms erupted over the Flanders area on Tuesday 28 May, grounding the Luftwaffe and enabling ground troops to make their way to the coast by foot in relative safety. Third, despite the storms just inland, the sea state remained unnaturally calm, enabling a fleet of 900 ships, many of them small private vessels, to make repeated trips back and forth with minimal attack from the air. In the end 338,000 troops were evacuated. According to Churchill, it was a 'miracle of deliverance.' Having been rescued off the beach at Dunkirk, Grandad later returned to mainland Europe shortly after D-Day to play his part in securing victory. My mother was conceived after the war had finally been won, so in a way, I owe my own life to the 'Dunkirk miracle' too. Prayer works.

Chapter 7

No turning back

'I'm going out to fish,' Simon Peter told them, and they said,
'We'll go with you.' So they went out and got into the boat, but
that night they caught nothing.

John 21:3

Everything had gone wrong. It looked as if St Swithun's wouldn't
be happening after all. There was a lot of local resistance to the
idea of a new church plant, especially moving into a building that
the Church of England had sold off such a long time ago. We had
no money to buy it and its owners were in conversation with a
property developer who had seemingly unlimited funds. None of
the Church of England's houses in Bournemouth was available for
us to move into and there were no school places for our children.
The diocese couldn't agree on the legal structure of the new ministry
and seemed to be getting cold feet. I was getting demoralised and
we'd had no joy recruiting a team to come with us. Understandably,
given all this, the HTB leadership began to doubt the project was
ever going to happen and started to ask if I should look elsewhere.
It pained me to admit that they might be right.

It all came to a head when HTB was invited by another diocese to plant into a major city centre where everything appeared ready to go. Nicky floated the idea of my having a look at it and I didn't react well. That led to a meeting with the HTB leadership to review the Bournemouth project. I was tired, worried, overwrought and, to be perfectly honest, a little angry – never a good mix. In my angst-ridden delusional state, I had even begun to doubt the motivation of those in the HTB leadership who had done so much for me over the years. Yet the difficulties could not be ignored and Nicky was absolutely right to confront the general state of discouragement around the project. Debi and I had been praying like mad but against every good reason to give up pursuing our dream we felt God say one word only: persevere. That left us in a bit of a tight spot because citing 'I think God's told me so' as the only reason to continue feels inadequate. Under pressure I felt like a child, getting overly melodramatic and assuming the worst is going to happen. It felt as if the whole world was against me, so I turned up at the vicarage in an embattled mood.

The meeting didn't start too well. Nicky asked for a recap and I stuck to the facts of the project, which were all pretty demoralising. However, I was careful to highlight two essential truths that remained: first, that the underlying rationale for a church plant in Bournemouth had not changed; and second, that I felt called to do it. Nicky listened respectfully, as he always does. He then turned to Rebecca Stewart, the then CEO of HTB/Alpha International – a phenomenal leader with the gift of discernment among many others – asking for her objective view on the project. Rebecca knew and loved me well enough to be no-nonsense and honest in her reply: 'I'll eat my hat if it happens.' Nicky turned to me, 'Tim, I agree. It's over. It's dead in the water. You have to move on.'

I was crestfallen, caught between bursting into tears and exploding in anger. Nicky could see I was having a hard time dealing with it and said: 'Tim, it's confusing and upsetting now but one day we'll look back and think all this hard journey was worth it for the church plant you eventually lead.' Although I was shaken, in that moment a steely calm came over me. I looked straight into his eyes and replied from my heart, surprised at the strength of conviction I heard in my voice: 'Nicky, *this* is that church plant.' I remember him sitting back, somewhat exasperated that I wouldn't let it go, asking, 'Well, what do you want me to do?' I asked him to call Bishop Tim Dakin for a simple yes or no as to whether or not we should proceed to plan a plant at St Swithun's. Three days later Nicky and Pippa asked me to have some tea and toast with them before an evening event. They sat with me at their kitchen table and Nicky told me: 'I've spoken with Bishop Tim. It's a no.' Although they were so tender with me that evening, I left considering my limited options. If I couldn't move on, then should I consider leaving the Church of England for another network, or forgetting the whole thing and returning to my former work in the City as an accountant?

At this point in the St Swithun's story I didn't know that everything was going to turn out well in the end. I spent some time reflecting on how Jesus' disciples must have felt in the days following his death; they must have been so confused and distressed. Jesus' words to them just before his death must have seemed at such odds with the events of the cross. And then, just a few days later, there was such wild talk among some of them claiming that Jesus was alive again. Back from the dead? If it was true, Jesus' resurrection meant the biggest point of no return in history. His disciples had a decision to make: did they check out of following him and go back to what they were doing before they met him? Should they forget it all, chalk it up to experience and turn back? Or should they believe in what really did seem to be the case – that Jesus had come back from the dead and was still wanting to talk about their future?

Like most, if not all, of Jesus' episodes with his disciples, the one about the miraculous catch of fish is a set-up (John 21:1-14). It happens around ten days to two weeks after the resurrection, the third time in John's account that the risen Jesus has come to them and spent time with them. The first time Jesus met them was on the evening of the first day of the resurrection – what we'd call Easter Sunday. Jesus talked with them, showed them the nail marks in his hands and the spear mark in his side, and prayed for them to receive the Holy Spirit (John 20:19-23). One week later he did the same thing, allowing his disciple Thomas, who hadn't been there the first time, to see for himself, to stop doubting and to believe (John 20:24-29). So after the first two occasions, there was no room for doubt: Jesus was alive and they all knew it. The big question was: what now? The outpouring of the Holy Spirit at Pentecost hadn't yet happened; the disciples had got the vision but they hadn't yet received the realised power to effect that vision. So frequently the Christian life feels just like this: we want to live in the power of resurrection, but often things are plain confusing. What should we do?

For one thing, we don't turn back. When you know Jesus, but you don't actually know what to do, it's very tempting to retreat back to familiar ground, returning to what we previously considered our 'normal life'. That's what Peter and six other disciples did, leaving Jerusalem, travelling back to their home town on Lake Galilee and returning to their previous trade: fishing. Old friends, in their old place, resuming their old way of life. The trouble is, they found that they couldn't even do that well anymore. They fished all night and caught absolutely nothing.

Is that not so much like the Christian life? No sooner have we put our trust in Jesus than our faith is tested. What used to be our purpose in life becomes empty and fruitless. Jesus once said: 'No one who puts a hand to the plough and looks back is fit for service in the kingdom of God'(Luke 9:62); usually for us, when Jesus calls us to follow him, there are some things we do that are sinful and need to turn away from and never do again, but there are many others that aren't sinful in themselves and that we can certainly keep doing. We may remain in the same line of employment, the same family, the same school, or living with the same flatmates. Things may not change on the outside, but we will have changed on the inside and we mustn't turn back.

This principle is definitely true when it comes to getting married. Being a priest in the Church of England, one of my greatest privileges is to conduct marriage services. I love a good wedding. Usually a day or two before the service, there's a wedding rehearsal. Often couples are more nervous about this than they are for the real thing and sometimes you can see the penny dropping about what's going to happen, what they're actually signing up to – that from this point onwards, nothing will remain the same. During the couple's preparation, after we've established they're actually in love and ready for marriage, Debi and I always make sure that we talk about three things.

First of all, we check that the couple understand that the decision they're about to make is permanent and binding, that as far as it depends upon them, they're prepared for it to be non-reversible. Marriage only works if there's a very high bar on exiting it. Mutual commitment is the key to a long-term healthy relationship. Every marriage goes through tough times when believing you're both still utterly committed to one another and to healing your relationship makes a huge difference. With that secure foundation and honest communication, love will thrive over time and the couple will flourish. I know one wise vicar who in every wedding sermon turns to the couple and says, 'The time for decision-making is over. Never revisit that choice.'

Second, we ensure the couple understand that in the marriage ceremony there's a leaving as well as a cleaving (meaning to join together and remain faithful). In the service itself this is often acted out by the groom leaving his seat with his family and stepping out to stand alone before God, while the father of the bride brings his daughter to the same point. God then gives the groom and bride to each other: both leave their families to cleave to God and to one another (Gen. 2:24). In making their declarations and vows before God they are forming a new entity, a new bond, a new family that takes precedent over their previous one. In order to form a new home, they have to leave their old home – if not physically then certainly emotionally. Of course, both partners must always honour their parents and siblings however they can; but their new husband or wife must take precedence. Sadly, I've seen marriages break up because one or both of the partners never left home. This is a picture for us all, whether we're married or single: once we've committed to Jesus, we mustn't turn back.

Third, to get married is to begin a new journey but it's surprising how many people go into that new journey expecting nothing to change. Maybe that's because many people now cohabit together before they get married, but there's a very big difference between living alongside one another and approaching life as a single unit. The Bible talks about married couples as 'one flesh' (Gen. 2:24). A newly married person no longer thinks of themselves in purely individual terms; now there's someone else involved in 'me' too.

So the Bible tells husbands – and if they're one flesh this principle is going to apply to wives too – 'He who loves his wife loves himself' (Eph. 5:28). That's a big change from the former way of life. I'm not sure you can ever really be ready for that change but you can certainly determine to be open to it, open to a new future.

The love between husband and wife in a marriage is of course a picture for us of God's love for the church. Paul's teaching on marriage in Ephesians 5 concludes: 'a man will leave his father and mother and be united to his wife, and the two will become one flesh. This is a profound mystery – but I am talking about Christ and the church.' All three of our deal-breakers for readiness for marriage apply to the disciples as they realised the stranger on the shore was, in fact, Jesus. Their reaction is epitomised by Peter's response when he recognises his friend and master: he jumps off the boat and wades ashore, leaving behind the former way of life he was tempted to return to, to be utterly united to Jesus from that moment onwards, even unto death. Although he'd seen many things with Jesus already, over the weeks, months and years that followed, Peter and the others had some serious surprises coming their way: the outpouring of the Holy Spirit, Gentile inclusion, the abandonment of food laws, and on and on it goes.

Back on that shoreline, watching the weary disciples still in their boat, I imagine Jesus smiling to himself, knowing what he was about to teach them. The disciples were exhausted after a long, frustrating night having caught nothing; yet Jesus stands on the shore and shouts a friendly, 'Hey, friends! You haven't got any fish, have you?' I actually think John's being a bit generous to the disciples in the boat when he records their answer as simply shouting back 'No!' I'm sure they muttered much stronger words under their breath, if not out loud. Some commentators argue that the scenario of someone on the shore seeing shoals of fish not visible to people in boats wasn't unusual – some trick of the light perhaps. Well maybe, but it sounds to me as if Jesus might be taunting them, albeit in a friendly way. He could make fish appear or disappear at will. Knowing the disciples think him a stranger, Jesus lays down a very simple challenge and we're now in the realm of pantomime as Jesus shouts out, 'Behind you!', testing whether they're still open to something new.

Perhaps the real miracle we're seeing here isn't that Jesus can make a very large shoal of very large fish appear – that's easy. The real miracle is that with one sentence he's able to get seven totally disillusioned and frustrated fishermen, tired after a long night catching nothing, to obey him and try again! Was there something in his voice that carried challenge, authority and respect in just the right balance? He is trying to help them after all. The disciples face a simple choice: to obey or not. Are they willing to risk looking stupid in order to gain a great reward? You have to love them for the fact that even at this point they're open to the miraculous, to God blessing them, to something new. They swallow their pride, accept they need to change their approach and go for it, thinking, 'What have we got to lose?' Bible scholar Bishop Tom Wright notes, 'we must always be ready to be surprised by God . . . When God ceases to surprise us, that may be the moment we have ceased to do business with him.'[1]

At the lowest point in the project of St Swithun's, when it looked as though everything was over, I thought a good deal about the disciples during the period between Easter and Pentecost. They had travelled past the point of no return and so had I. Against common sense and the desire of the great people I worked for, loved and respected, I refused to take 'no' for an answer; by this stage I was simply too deep in – I'm sure others thought that it was not altogether in a healthy way. I prayed and prayed, poring over all that I'd seen to date, reviewing every prophetic word piled up in my battered journals. I re-examined the reasons for a new church in Bournemouth and concluded we had a cast-iron case. Debi and I talked to a few other people about it but mostly between ourselves, reaffirming that this really was the one project to put our necks on the block for. Eventually, we reached a conclusion before God. Since we were sure he was asking us to plant a church in Bournemouth, we agreed with God that if we couldn't do it through HTB or Winchester diocese then we'd find another way. With enormous apology, I told the HTB leadership the same thing. It wasn't pride and I wasn't trying to manipulate; by that stage I was pretty broken and didn't have any leverage anyway. Debi and I were simply convinced that it was what God wanted and we couldn't unconvince ourselves. We couldn't turn back.

To break the deadlock I knew I had to find an edge. First of all, I went back to Nicky and assured him I was trying to resolve things one way or the other and wouldn't take too long over it. I knew that HTB would never consider planting to a place without being invited by a bishop, so I checked whether, if such an invitation were forthcoming, HTB would still be up for it. 'Yes, absolutely!' came back the unequivocal reply. Okay, good, that was something. I then went back to the archdeacon of Bournemouth and the bishop of Winchester to investigate what might be at the root of the impasse and my findings from these conversations were encouraging. Did they believe there was still a case for a new church plant located somewhere in central Bournemouth? Yes. Were the various key people and committees in agreement about that and prepared to back it? Yes. Would the bishop still be happy with my leading it as an HTB plant if a way forward could be found? Yes. Did they still have the basic finance in place to make it happen – meaning, in reality, funding for three years' worth of my stipend and housing? Yes. So what was the 'no' really about? The answer to that was the site: the building of St Swithun's was the problem. So if we could find another great site we could still go for it? Yes. Suddenly, the plant seemed back on track: we agreed I'd continue to plan for a September 2014 church plant and reconsider all the other possible sites. Privately, I vowed to keep praying and probing for an opening at St Swithun's but I was more than happy to put that to the test, knowing that it might well be simply my stubborn nature at work. If God wanted the plant to be somewhere else, then I was open to it; and if God wanted it at St Swithun's, then we'd need a miracle. I could live with that.

Fast-forward several months, after much research and many meetings, I remained convinced that St Swithun's was for us. The owner of the site – a large church in town that had since moved to purpose-built premises – was trying to sell it on the open market. Their problem was the restrictive covenants that governed the use of the building, preserving it for Christian worship. Although land-bank investors might be prepared to take the risk, if we could convince the church commissioners and bishops to stand on those covenants, we'd effectively rule out any other buyer. I didn't feel bad about doing that, not least because the owners had a strong Christian ethos and wanted us to take it; but I also became convinced that we were their best hope of recovering the £700,000 investment they'd put into the site since they purchased it from the Church of England in 1998 for £18,000. Of course, we didn't have anywhere near the money to buy the site at that value and no one seemed prepared to lend it to us.

I began to enjoy the prospect of cutting a deal. The buzz of commercial deals was something I'd missed since working as a City accountant and I leant on my experience, calling on a few experts. Wheeling and dealing is actually quite fun and a very useful skill when it comes to planting churches within the Church of England! Plus, I was past the point of no return and convinced that God would somehow make things happen. I was looking forward to seeing how he was going to do it.

First things first: could I get those in power to stand on the restrictive covenants? I knew it wouldn't be easy. They were the last thread of any kind of ownership rights that remained on the site and I'd have to convince them that we were serious and able to execute our plan to plant a new church there. I needed a big gun. Once again, I prayed to God, laying out the situation he already knew inside out. At that time there was a very large leadership conference organised by HTB at the Royal Albert Hall and I'd done my homework on who the key gate-keepers and decision-makers were, knowing that several of them would be present. Triangulating between them all, I felt nudged by God to approach a very high-ranking bishop to step in. My problem was I had no access. I knew someone who did however: the leading City of London banker Ken Costa, who at that point was also the warden of HTB. When I put all this together in my head I was deep in the bowels of the Royal Albert Hall on the opening morning of the conference. Having already established that Ken was to be seated next to our senior bishop but that both men were only there for that morning of the conference, I knew I didn't have much time. I had no phone signal to call Ken and was lost in the rabbit-warren of corridors and rooms underneath the auditorium – I couldn't even find the exit. 'Come on, God!' I remember muttering out loud in desperation, 'You know I really need to speak to Ken right now!' By now frantic, I ran down one tunnel and turned the corner at the end. I found myself face to face with Ken. He was delighted to help and one by one, everything came into line.

The second issue concerned how we could afford the site. We needed the site before we could afford to buy it, but not before we could afford to rent it. So the obvious solution was to try to negotiate a short-term lease and purchase option. After a knowledgeable advisor helped me to meet with the owners, we established that if we could sign a lease that transferred most of the costs and rewards of ownership on to us, then they would be able to treat the income we gave them as funding they could spend rather than hold in reserve. They'd be happy with that situation for two years if we could then purchase the site outright; if not, they'd try to sell it elsewhere again. We were happy with the deal as it gave us two years' use of the site at a fixed cost we could afford, while also lending us some breathing space to grow and raise funds to buy the site. It was a win–win situation.

All that remained was to agree the details and values of the lease contract and purchase option: the owners would retain responsibility for the roof, gutters and drains as well as the onsite trees and we'd look after everything else. They were all linked, actually, because the trees were all protected but their roots had ingressed into the drains and were causing problems (in truth they still do). Finally, we commissioned a detailed survey of the site and agreed the price of the purchase option. Here, having prevented the owners from selling the site to the private sector, I'm proud to say we were able to help them. Some felt that since the Church of England had previously sold the site to them at £18,000 that should be the starting point for negotiations to repurchase it. My advisor and I found ourselves in the odd position of arguing that we should price the purchase option at the full value of all the funds the previous church had invested into the site. We were pushing on an open door as we all agreed that there was a much wider Kingdom issue at work here – our brothers and sisters in Christ had done a great job while based at St Swithun's and had planted out many churches from it. Together we agreed that getting £700,000 back into their hands would be one of the best things we could possibly do for the Kingdom. Here was a church who knew how to spend that kind of money to spread the gospel. Where was I going to find £700,000 from though? That was a can we kicked down the road in order to get started. We planned to get to the end of the first year renting the property, then see where we were and whether it might be possible to raise the money we'd need to buy it somehow.

At our final meeting we sealed the deal and agreed the share of risks in the lease, along with various aspects of the deposit and rent, and agreed a £700,000 purchase option during the second year of the lease. We'd shaken hands all round and were putting our coats on. At the door, my advisor hesitated and addressed the room, saying, 'There's just one more thing. You'll all think I'm crazy but if by some miracle we were able to purchase the site during the first year of the lease, would you discount the price?' I remember us all laughing at the absurd scenario that during our first year we'd be able to raise such a large sum. 'Of course,' said the chair of their trustees, 'You could have £25,000 off the price.' Thank God for wise advisors. In the end, we were able to do exactly that.

Chapter 8

It's snowing money

Opportunities come infrequently. When it rains gold, put out the
bucket, not the thimble.

Warren Buffett

Then Peter said, 'Silver or gold I do not have, but what I do
have I give you. In the name of Jesus Christ of Nazareth, walk.'

Acts 3:6

In July 2014, Matt and Laura Clayton, a young, newly wed couple
who were both on staff at HTB, took a wild leap of faith and agreed
to join the fledgling plant team. Matt was in training for ordained
ministry and was passionate about reaching Bournemouth's large
student population; Laura became our administrator and immediately set about organising the ramshackle project into some
semblance of order. One of her first tasks was to draw up the list
of items that we needed to find before we launched. The St
Swithun's site was nothing but a very big, old, empty box. We had
no chairs, no children's toys, no lecterns and no loo rolls. No nothing.
We hadn't completed all the legal documentation so we had no
charity vehicle, which also meant we had no bank account.

We found an old table and a couple of ripped chairs that had been missed in the site clearance when the previous tenants left, so we reclaimed them for our 'office' – a small storeroom that every week for the first six months we packed away so that it could be used as a kids' room on Sunday. A major problem we faced was that the building had a hard wooden floor without a carpet. That was a nightmare for sound and made sung worship really challenging: every note, cough, footstep and cry of a baby blended together in an impenetrable, resonating cacophony that gave me a headache. I knew that a carpet the size of our main meeting venue would be outrageously expensive and was far beyond our wildest hope at that stage. Salvation came in the shape of a few rolls of discarded event carpeting from HTB's summer Focus festival. Designed for use in outdoor marquees, we were told it might get us through the first ten weeks and that we could have it for free if we came and picked it up. We were ecstatic! We'd prayed for a carpet and here it was. I thought it was a miracle: I longed to see miracles of healing and deliverance once the church started, but at that point all we needed was a carpet – and now we'd been given one.

Matt and I rented a van and drove to collect the carpet rolls from HTB, having stopped off at my old house in Oxford to collect some other bits and pieces. It was a blisteringly hot and sunny day in August. As we drove into London on the A40 near Northolt Airfield I began sharing with Matt how concerned I was by our continued lack of money. I rattled off all the items on our list that we didn't possess and, frankly, had no hope of getting before the launch. There's probably a good time for leaders to be vulnerable with their lieutenants and voice their inner doubts, but that wasn't it. Matt and Laura were leaving secure jobs in London to come down to

Bournemouth and I was giving them zero reason to have confidence in their choice. Matt was taking all of this in, I suspect silently asking God to give us some money and to shut me up. Suddenly he leaned forwards in his seat, stared ahead of us and said, 'Tim, slow down, I think it's snowing ahead.'

As we got closer I struggled to make sense of it. My brain was screaming at me that it could not be snowing on one of the hottest days in August but my eyes couldn't deny the scene either. It appeared that Matt was right. As we got closer to the blizzard ahead of us, though, we realised the 'snow' was really small bits of paper fluttering about in the wind, blowing out of discarded rubbish in a skip behind a fence at the side of the road. By now we were travelling much more slowly in line with all the traffic and as we drove into the cloud of paper itself, a single piece fluttered down and lay flat against the windscreen. It was a £5.00 bank note. And then another £5.00 note landed beside it. In fact, there were a lot of £5.00 bank notes blowing all around us. Matt and I stared open-mouthed at one another as it dawned upon us it was literally snowing money. I stamped on the brakes, punched the hazard lights on and shouted at Matt, 'Get out and grab as much as you can!' We joined several other foolhardy drivers who were doing the same, leaping around at huge risk in the passing traffic, trying to catch £5.00 bank notes billowing in the breeze. We stuffed them in our pockets, down our trousers, inside our T-shirts, anywhere. Realising we were at risk of causing a major road traffic accident we jumped back into the van and drove off.

We were hooting with laughter as we peeled the by-now quite sweaty bank notes off our legs and torsos and counted them up. We'd managed to grab about £200 in total. We felt like bank robbers but remembered we were in fact ministers of the gospel – we should involve the police. When Matt called them and tried to explain, they thought it was a hoax caller at first but eventually advised us either to bring the cash into a police station and surrender it, or take it with us and if anyone asked them for it they'd redirect them to St Swithun's church in Bournemouth. We chose the latter, so if you're reading this and lost a lot of cash near the A40 at Northolt during August 2014, all I can say is thank you – please do come and visit and meet some of the people we spent it on.

Back in the van, once we'd come to our senses, we began to reflect on what had happened and what God might be saying to us. The message seemed so clear: we remembered how easy it is to get lost in worry about money and felt sure that if we could resist that temptation, and have faith and courage to pursue what God was calling us to do, then he was promising to provide us with what we'd need. And that's exactly what has happened. Nevertheless, I won't lie to you: every step of the way has been fraught with difficulty and last-minute rescues. Many, many months we've had to hold back from all expenditure so that we could be sure of paying our mortgage and payroll commitments. We've begged and borrowed all we can. Several people, including Debi and I, have put last-ditch cash injections into the church account to make sure we could pay our outgoings.

Quite a few church leaders spend a lot of time fixating on money. We all tend to think that we could lead amazingly successful and fruitful ministries if only there were more money, as if that's the one thing we really need. We become obsessed with the cost of things and lack generosity, contributing to our own downfall. I have found the truth that finance follows vision very hard to swallow. However, when leaders have a crystal-clear notion of what God wants them to do and they give their lives to it by example, communicating the vision in compelling ways, others begin to invest. It's essential to focus not on money but God, who knows what we need before we ask him and who, having not held back from giving us his own son, will surely, graciously give us all things (cf. Matt. 6:8, 33; Rom. 8:32). I write this aware that every day I have to choose to believe that rather than worry about how much money we *don't* have. Every time I'm tempted to doubt, I cast my mind back to that hot day during the summer of 2014 when God made money literally fall out of the sky.

Scroll forward three years and I stood motionless in the church office, having opened an envelope with my name on it, handed in with the offering that Sunday. I'd laid out the vision of the church once again and been honest about the audacious plans that I and the leadership had together discerned as being God's will for us. The congregation had responded enthusiastically but we were still way short of the financial target we'd set. Inside the envelope was a sheet of paper with a photo of someone's front door keys, on which a single sentence was handwritten: 'I pledge to the church one third of the value of the house that these keys open upon completion of its sale.' There was no name. Shortly afterwards, £101,500 was deposited into the church account. In the interim I had discovered who the mystery giver was – the last person I or anyone else would expect. I was, and remain, greatly humbled by their faith and generosity. I was in awe of the good, faithful God we serve. There had been quite a few months since we started where we didn't have £101.50 in the account, never mind a thousand times that amount.

I've found it hard to ask people for money in the past, but I'm learning to be less timid. I no longer see encouraging giving in the church in terms of simply asking for money but as presenting others with an opportunity to join me and get in on something through which they'll experience God's blessing. Generous giving opens a huge door for the Spirit to disciple and bless anyone who is willing. Of course, giving does not cause or secure God's blessing in some kind of transactional way devoid of a genuine relationship of love in worship to Jesus. My own experience is that church has certainly cost a lot of money but, as Debi and I have given to it, it's turned out to be more like paying into an investment fund from which we're reaping huge rewards. I truly believe that giving generously to fund Jesus' kingdom is quite simply the best possible thing we can do with our hard-earned cash.

The Apostle Paul and his apprentice Timothy went around building up the early church, planting and establishing leaders. Later, Paul wrote to Timothy as a new leader, advising him on how to lead young churches. Paul told him not to be timid. *The Message* translates Paul's instruction to Timothy as 'Don't be embarrassed to speak up for our Master' (2 Tim. 1:8). Timothy must have been a lovely guy, a very talented young leader, a gentle, good man who it was hard not to like. He loved and served everyone he met. Maybe he was a very sensitive guy too, a little anti-confrontational, risk-averse, perhaps a little bit anxious. Paul encourage him not to underestimate the influence he had, but to use it boldly. Some people think way too much of themselves – that's misguided superiority. Whilst others think way too little of themselves – that's misguided inferiority. Paul seems to say there's a sweet spot of truth in the middle that we should all aim for.

My dad's a very discerning man with deep spiritual insight. Wisely, he keeps most of it to himself and uses it to pray. Nevertheless, over the years he's passed on one or two pictures and words of knowledge to me. He once gave me a simple word of knowledge he'd heard for me one morning as he'd prayed. It was this: 'Don't be anything less than God is calling you to be.' That stopped me in my tracks: I can still remember exactly where I was when he told it to me over the phone (my bathroom in London, if you're interested). I hope it stops you in yours, because most of us, for most of the time, settle for way less than who God is calling us to be and far, far less than what he's calling us to do.

Every church has a slightly different model for promoting giving. My own approach changed when I began to see that Jesus spoke about money all the time, viewing it as a key matter in our ongoing discipleship. Currently at St Swithun's we hold two back-to-back 'Vision Sundays' twice a year as a chance for us all to review where we're investing our time, relationships, skills and money. These Sundays act as a health-check for us that we're staying on-task with the vision that God has given us. Each time they come around, Debi and I review our giving and try to stretch it a little further. We give a one-off offering and try to increase our regular monthly bank transfer to the church. Personally, I don't preach the *rule* of tithing, although plenty of leaders for whom I have enormous respect do. To me, Jesus doesn't seem to teach tithing as a *rule* in the New Testament but as a principle. If giving the first ten per cent of income is what the law required, the era of grace should not result in anything less. Debi and I apply this teaching to our own finances and use ten per cent of our net income as the minimum guide for our giving. I have to self-assess my personal tax each year, so I know exactly what percentage of our income we're giving. Each time we review it and pray about it, we try to stretch beyond the ten per cent level; some years it has been very tight and other years we've been able to give much more.

Debi and I also try not to let a request for an offering go by us in any church setting or conference without contributing at least something. I have to confess that Debi is often more generous than I am. At one of HTB's Leadership Conferences we were standing in a box in the prestigious Royal Albert Hall, praying about what we should give into the offering to help with the costs of putting it all on and subsidise those who otherwise wouldn't have been able to attend. I leant across and asked Debi if she sensed any steer from God about what we should give and she whispered a number in my ear that nearly made me fall out of the box. But we've never regretted giving on these occasions either. It's amazing to me that although we have seen God provide so much for us in myriad ways, every time I'm asked to give I have to allow God to reconquer the part of me that wants to cling on to money rather than him. This is another good reason to give regularly.

When leaders get a vision for their giving and make it personal, applying whatever they preach to their own lives first, then invariably good things follow. I'm aware of some Christians whose giving as a proportion of their income is way higher than whatever Debi and I have as yet achieved; unsurprisingly, they're some of the happiest, blessed people I know. God has certainly blessed us financially beyond anything we could have imagined when we were first married. We want to invest our lives doing what Jesus commanded: clothe the naked, heal the sick, feed the poor, cast out the demons and raise the dead. In St Swithun's we've found a big family who want exactly the same thing and who are prepared to put their time, skills and money where their mouth is – or, as Jesus put it, where their heart is (cf. Matt. 6:21; Luke 12:34). That's one reason why I keep an eye on who is giving what into the church. I want to know who's got skin in the game as they're the people I want to make sure I listen to. Many leaders don't want to be party to this information in order to avoid favouritism, whereby larger donors have undue influence. That is of course a very valid approach and in many contexts may be hugely wise. But I worry that in our context, and given my own personality and those of others on our leadership team, a different kind of favouritism might then kick in, whereby those who shout the loudest and try to throw their weight around will get listened to above others. My experience so far is that those kind of people, sometimes even quite wealthy individuals, are rarely the ones who have invested the most money – relative to their income – into the church. Of course, there are many ways to give into the church apart from money and I try to apply the same approach to my consideration of how everyone in our big family of church contributes their time and skills – myself included.

Among our most precious treasure at St Swithun's are our poorest members, those of us fighting severe addictions. Those caught in such horrors sometimes come in really broken, full of guilt and shame, feeling they have nothing to give. With love, respect and support, however, we challenge their low self-worth and learned helplessness, encouraging them to serve on our teams and find different ways of giving, even if they're not able to give financially. God loves us and helps us. Our worth is equal to Christ's, who was given in exchange for us. And we are not helpless because we are called by God and filled with his Spirit. No one is discarded or becomes obsolete in the Kingdom of God.

Jesus' teaching on our giving to others urges us to have faith in God's giving to us. Accepting God's miraculous provision for us in the form of Jesus leads us towards generosity in our giving, integrity in our actions and purity in our motivations. One day, Jesus decided to really blow his disciples' fuses and took them to the temple, where they could watch people giving money into the treasury. Mark is careful to record a single difference that revealed so much more – the manner in which they gave. The rich came and 'threw in' large gifts, betraying an attitude of not really caring too much about it. Many of us give out of what we have spare; our giving rarely costs us that much. There's nothing wrong with such offerings of course, but compare it to the poor widow who came and 'put in' two small coins, just a few pence in value. To me, her manner seems so much more careful and deliberate. What she gave that day meant something valuable to her. Jesus told his disciples that the poor widow gave more than all the others. How can that be? It seems that not every pence or pound given to God is of equal value. The world doesn't distinguish between the value of one person's pound or another's: they're all the same. But not in God's financial system, which works very differently. In God's Kingdom, the amount we give relative to our overall wealth, the thoughts of our heart, our attitudes and demeanour, even how we actually give money, all affect the Kingdom impact of our giving (cf. Mark 12:41–4). So watch out when faith-filled poorer people start giving, because they can unleash wealth of Kingdom value beyond rich people's wildest imagination.

I recently received a note and generous donation for the church from an amazing couple in the church called Mark and Mandy. They are both on the prayer team and Mark has served on our addiction recovery team too. They became caught in a benefits trap after Mandy suffered a debilitating illness that forced her to retire from her job in nursing and also confined her to a wheelchair. Mark had to take on lower paid shift work so that he could be around more to care for her. Mandy wrote to me saying: 'Love is a verb. After a lot of thought and prayer I request this money to be set aside for those who genuinely can't afford to pay the money to use the church. Church = home, the people = family, family = rich, poor, young, old, all together.' I was deeply impressed at the generosity in the light of their own pressing circumstances and gently asked how they had been able to remain so generous even when they had urgent needs of their own?

They told me they had always considered tithing important and so gave away ten per cent of their income. It was easy to do before Mandy became ill and their income radically changed. Although Mandy was eventually considered eligible for disability benefits they had a year of uncertainty and could do little but watch in horror as their small savings accounts emptied. They went to their bank to ask for help and spent three hours there going through their personal finances cancelling insurance policies, direct debits, reducing pensions and readjusting their mortgage payments. When they got to the monthly direct debit to St Swithun's (their tithe) the bank suggested they cancel that as well but Mandy and Mark resisted; they felt God was promising them directly and specifically that he would provide for all their needs to enable them to keep giving as they desired.

Shortly afterwards Mandy went back into hospital for another round of painful treatments. When she came home Mark realised they had no food in the house and set off to the supermarket. On the way home their car broke down and was later declared to be a write-off and beyond repair. That afternoon Mark walked home with all the shopping, heavy bags cutting into his hands, and when he walked through the door he stepped into water and found the kitchen was flooded with foul water from blocked drains. He had an immobile wife in pain, no transport and a flood. He felt confused and angry. Had God forgotten about them? Mark cleared up as best he could, cooked the family a meal and, thoroughly dejected, cried out to God.

A couple of days later there was knock at the door. It was a plumber, explaining that someone had paid him and sent him round to fix the drains. Later that day a friend called, explaining he'd just lost his driving licence and offered Mark his car, asking only a very small amount in return. Although it was a small amount, Mark knew they couldn't afford it, but miraculously the money turned up in his bank account a few days later. Losing his licence also proved to be the kick up the backside that guy needed to sort out his drinking habits so Mark got him into a recovery programme. During the following months, over and over again, money turned up when Mark and Mandy needed it. But Mandy's benefits situation continued to be complex and a long waiting game through different appointments and long, complicated forms. While they were incredibly grateful to God, they knew that long-term they desperately needed her benefits.

After eight months they were still tithing, but now in dire straits. Desperate to avoid getting into debt, they were referred to a food-bank and went to pick up one of the invaluable box of supplies that so many rely on. When they returned home they opened a letter informing them that Mandy was entitled to full benefits and free car tax; the award had been backdated eight months too. They were overwhelmed with relief and joy. In celebration, Mandy decided to do an online shop to stock up their bare cupboards. As they unpacked the delivery they discovered they'd received someone else's shopping. It was far more than they'd ordered and contained lots of luxury goods – chocolate, biscuits, expensive tea and coffee. They rang the supermarket to rectify the error, who said they'd refund their original shop and that they should keep the delivery they'd received. One week later, the supermarket was back on the phone telling them they had won a stack of vouchers in a prize drawer and had enough to purchase a new dishwasher and microwave.

Mark told me: 'God's timing is great! It's not easy but we will still carry on giving to God as time and again he has been faithful and provided for us, often at the eleventh hour! I sympathise with people saying that they can't afford to tithe or give. But as someone who has struggled in that situation, I can give testimony to how God blesses those that give who have very little.'

Chapter 9

Budget for coffee

I no longer call you servants . . .
Instead, I have called you friends.
John 15:15

I work hard. But I also surf, windsurf or paddleboard whenever I can and spend a good few hours each week meeting people and working in local cafés. The permission to feel good about deliberately spending working time in cafés all over Bournemouth is something I owe to my former boss at HTB, Archie Coates. Archie and the church he planted at St Peter's have been a model for us in so many ways. Just before we started, I went to see Archie, with a long list of all the issues over which I needed his wisdom. One of them was what to do about our lack of a church office. He laughed and told me to work out of cafés, which was where I'd not only get to meet the people I wanted most to connect with but also get to know the place where God had sent me. That was a brilliant piece of advice. In truth, I often feel my time on the water or in cafés has greater impact than whatever it is I do at the front of church or sitting alone in my study. There have been times when I've caught myself trying to build the church by sitting in front of a computer all day, pastoring by email and texts. It's absolutely futile. Getting stuff organised is important as is processing email effectively – it's like a fast-growing lawn that has to be mown daily. But I feel driven to keep getting out there and meeting people.

For Debi and me, church has always been a noun referring not to a building but a group of our friends. Over the years in London we'd developed some wonderful friends such that our number one fear in leaving London was that we'd be lonely. We needn't have worried: for one thing, all our London friends seemed quite excited by the idea of coming to stay with us at the seaside – and we've loved receiving them; more importantly, we began to see that God had prepared some great local friends for us here too. We now have a budget line in the church accounts for me to buy coffee for the people I meet in cafés and, for such a small cost, we've got some very big returns as a church. Some people I've met this way have given their lives to Christ; some have also joined the church and become our most committed volunteers, contributing hours of skilful time towards serving others.

The first two people we met in Bournemouth remain very close friends. Tom and Lizzie Redman had lived there for ten years and knew the place backwards. They were also great fun. A mutual friend in London had connected us and we agreed to meet in one of the many bars overlooking the beach. Debi and I had spent the day driving around looking at houses and trying to set up school places for our children. It seemed there were no suitable houses and no school places either. We'd just had a depressing meeting with a council officer and received a call from my dad back in London who was looking after the children; somehow he'd managed to lock himself out of our house and had made the decision to smash a window to get back in rather than get the spare key from our neighbour. I'll love that man to my dying day but it wasn't the kind of childcare we'd imagined. Anyway, by the time we got to the bar it was late afternoon. It was hot and sticky, and we were fed up, tired and hungry – not ideal conditions to reach out to new people.

Tom and Lizzie greeted us with big smiles and hugs and shoved drinks into our hands, proffering delicious snacks. I sat back and surveyed the scene. Sitting in the warm sunshine, cold drink in hand, I looked out over a beautiful stretch of beach with some promising waves rolling in, being entertained by lovely people. Maybe the day wasn't quite so bad after all. I turned my attention to our hosts. Tom was a warm, positive, easy-going guy who was impossible not to like; he seemed to find the fun side in everything – laughing harder at himself than anything or anyone else. Lizzie shared his sense of humour and immediately bonded with us, so naturally putting us at ease. I remember her wearing huge sunglasses that she whipped off when she met us so that we could see her eyes and make a connection. She asked us if it was all right to put them back on before she did so, not wanting us to think she was hiding behind them. Together Tom and Lizzie were genuine and huge fun and, as we talked, it became apparent that they also shared a deep commitment to Christ and a burning desire to see Bournemouth's unchurched younger generations reached with the gospel.

We ended up staying with Tom and Lizzie a lot longer than we'd planned to. Somewhere during the conversation more drinks had been ordered along with delicious pizzas baked in wood ovens right there. I thought it was pricey but worth it for this important first connection. We eventually prised ourselves away for the long haul back up to London. I was sure that Debi had paid for the whole lot when I'd gone to the loo before leaving and, bracing myself for the worst, asked her how much it had all cost. She replied that she thought I'd paid. We stared in horror at each other: we'd just left Tom and Lizzie with the whole bill. Panicked that we might have ruined God's provision of our first friendship in Bournemouth with such amazing people, we immediately called them. Fortunately, they couldn't have been more gracious about it and claimed not to have been offended in the slightest . . . although Tom has still got that bill somewhere and keeps threatening me that he's going to frame it and then hang it in their home so that everyone can see how I treat my friends.

Another good friendship came about through a conversation with a café owner in Cornwall. It was raining and custom was slow, so we got chatting. He was interested in my hope to start a church in Bournemouth. Other customers came in and he returned to work. But later he came over to me, mentioning he'd recalled that one of his regular visitors actually lived in Bournemouth and he offered to put me in touch. I readily accepted. So it was that during my first week in Bournemouth I sat in a café opposite Andy Bye and his wife Beryl. We bonded over windsurfing – he's a fantastic windsurfer and we go out together regularly now. He's a lot better than I am, so he'll sail up to me and give me some tips to help me improve. I confess I get frustrated when it's not happening right – windsurfing is a technical sport and exhilarating but difficult; I guess that's what makes it feel so good when it all comes together. Unfortunately for me, that doesn't happen very often. When I fall off repeatedly, I have been known to swear at myself and, I'm ashamed to say, at God too. I guess it's cathartic and I don't think God minds – in fact, I think he might enjoy it because I'm not hiding from him but letting him into that aspect of my life. I usually sense him laughing at me and that makes me smile too. Andy wisely sails away when I'm getting worked up. It's invaluable to me to have good friends who aren't going to think I'm a terrible person for venting any pent-up anger in safe ways.

The sun was shining and the coffee was good. Andy and Beryl chatted about where they were at in their lives and I shared why we'd moved down to Bournemouth. It was obvious that they were interested, if naturally a little cautious. I wasn't trying to recruit them away from any other church involvements and was thankful simply for the encouraging conversation. However, as they got up to leave Beryl turned round and said, 'If there's anything Andy can do that's practical, do ask him – I call him Handy Andy, because he's good at stuff that involves power tools and he loves feeling useful.' I agreed I'd call him when I needed some help in that way and the next day I thought of just the thing.

I remember once hearing one of my heroes, Rick Warren, recommend that if you're looking to set a new culture then make one highly visible change: repaint a wall; think of a new group name; redesign the branding; meet in a different place or at a different time and get some new faces involved. So for a while, I'd wanted to have something visible inside the building that would give anyone who walked in an instant visual steer as to who we were and what we were trying to do. I shared the idea with a friend who's a wedding photographer, and she mentioned that at one recent wedding the bride and groom had their initials made up as large, free-standing letters in the entrance to their reception venue. We had a light-bulb moment: we could do something similar inside our building. But what should the letters say and who could make them?

My first thought was to try and make them myself. I've always struggled with that – it's a terrible combination of arrogance, thinking that no one else can deliver quite what I'm imagining, and self-pity, suspecting that no one else will want to help me if I ask them to. Leaders have to deal with both of those impulses or they'll achieve very little and miss out on so much. I now firmly believe that for about nine out of every ten things that I could do, there's someone else who can do it far better and much quicker than I ever could. Not only that, but those people actually want to do it and would love to be given the opportunity; they're waiting and longing to be asked. And that's how it was with Andy: I swallowed my pride, called him, and asked for help.

But what would we spell out? In the planning phase of St Swithun's I'd drafted many documents for all the different decision-makers, outlining what I felt God was asking us to do and how we were going to do it. They were fairly standard business plans and I knew that a section on our core values would need to be included. I reasoned that we didn't have any machines or proprietary technology, we were a people business. And people care very much about values. I also felt that the Kingdom of God is about pursuing God's aims using God's means. I knew that without strong values to guide me I might otherwise be tempted to achieve godly goals in any way and at any price.

Having researched many different lists of the values of churches I respected, along with major values of the churches in the New Testament, I ended up with my own list of about twenty-two core values. But that's ridiculous, I thought, you can't have twenty-two 'core' values; there must be overlap. So, in conversation with others, I whittled them down first to twelve, then seven, then five, then four – I could just about remember four core values. I wrote them down like this:

- **Famous for love** Everyone was made by God. Everyone is loved by God. So we honour God's creation and image in everyone too. We want to be famous in Bournemouth for our love. Hospitality is important to us. So when we meet we eat. Anyone who visits us will be offered something to eat or drink within three minutes of being onsite. We 'get' grace and extend it uncon-ditionally. Whether people reach a point of faith or not, everyone is welcome and will find friendship, understanding and compas-sion. It also means everyone is open to being loved and to recovering the person God has made them to be, recognising that this requires us to challenge one another. Jesus summarised the whole Christian message as loving God and loving others. He also made the strength and authenticity of love among his followers the acid test of the true church to a watching world. We are creative and generous in our love. We spend time together, we affirm and encourage each other, we give gifts to others, we hug a lot, and we love through actions that serve others.

- **Flowing with life** We're here to have fun, to encourage everything good, and to see everyone's life flourish to be everything that God intended it to be. We will seek to build up every child and rebuild every adult so that they can enjoy the full, purposeful life God has for them. We believe that full new life is only possible with Jesus. Although we take the truth about Jesus seriously, we don't take ourselves too seriously. We laugh and party a lot. We are honest and authentic. We honour one another with honesty and believe that spiritual maturity requires emotional maturity. We offer buoyancy to one another when we're in pain.

- **Focused on Jesus** He is perfect theology. We are passionate about worship and are devoted to prayer. We live by grace and are committed to holiness. We believe the Bible is all about Jesus and our life with him. We seek justice and we extend mercy. We are confident in the life-changing power and presence of the Holy Spirit. We are a supernatural church not trying to do what is possible without God, but what is only possible with God. We pray like we mean it and are expectant for the miraculous. We believe we owe everyone living in Bournemouth an opportunity to meet Jesus – not just the chance to hear about him, but the chance to meet him in his living person, present with us and powerful for us.

- **Fully committed** We will work together as a team and partner with others. We will win together and persevere through adversity. We will defend each other and honour one another's unique skills, seeking to harmonise our own with them. We will keep the faith and keep hope alive. We are utterly committed to unity. We respect authority and exercise our obligation to dissent. We listen to one another. We are loyal. We're a battleship not a cruise liner – so if you're on board you're a member of the crew; we don't take passengers. We do take patients though, so you could say we're a hospital ship too. However, very respectfully, we will disagree with learned helplessness and seek to empower each other. We will appreciate vulnerability and not dismiss or despise weakness, but seek restoration, healing and wholeness. In practice this means that every member of the St Swithun's family prays, everyone serves, and everyone gives. We are one. We will invest everything that God has given us to put it to work in his Kingdom. We are motivated by vision and driven by compassion. We have an audacious faith, are relentlessly positive and enjoy doing things well. We are committed to raising up and deploying lay leaders at every age, life-stage and level of activity.

Around that time, the local newspaper called me and asked for an interview to talk about the new church we were starting up. The reporter seemed incredulous that we were doing it. They told me that the general feeling in Bournemouth was that church was a thing of the past that modern, young society was at long last leaving behind. In reply, I found myself focusing in on our first core value: love. I said that it was the core nature of God. The Bible says, God *is* love, personified in Jesus (1 John 4:8–16). I argued that love is also the universal core need of every person, so there's a match between our core need and God's core attribute. We were made to know God's love in Jesus. The trouble was, I explained, not many people would associate the word 'love' with the word 'church'; most people's experience of church, particularly the younger generations, didn't connect God's core attribute with their core need. That's what we were going to have a go at changing. Church has to be all about love because God is all about love. At St Swithun's we want to be famous for love.

Napoleon famously is believed to have said, 'Alexander, Caesar, Charlemagne and I have built great empires. But upon what did they depend? They depended upon force. But long ago Jesus started an empire that depended on love, and even this day millions will die for him.' We're not building an empire that can only be held together by force; Jesus is building a kingdom and it's held together by love.

I asked my new friend, Andy, if he could make us some letters to put up inside church that spelled out L.O.V.E. Three days later

Andy's surf van rolled into my drive. He'd been working on the first of the letters and wanted to check on progress before he made the others. As he pulled the 'L' out of the back of his van, it was so much better than anything I'd imagined: it was awesome, much bigger than I'd had in mind and beautifully crafted. I can't think of anything else that's made as much of an impact as those simple letters that a guy I met in a café knocked up for us in his garage. We were amazed when *The Times* newspaper wanted to use it as a powerful image of something new that God was doing. It's not new – it's the oldest thing in the book.

We have a vision to break younger generations' negative preconceptions about what church is, who God is, and what life is about, as soon as they get on to the site. For us, loving people who don't like church is a core aspect of what it means to be a church. A visitor's initial experience of church plays a huge part in determining whether or not they're open to revising their negative preconceptions about who God might be. I still regularly stand up to open a service and say that if any newcomers weren't befriended and offered something to eat and drink within three minutes of entering the building, then I'm truly sorry and if they introduce themselves to me at the end of the service I'll take them out for coffee myself to make it up to them. It's a great thing to communicate and it also sets the bar for our hospitality teams. Despite our best attempts, over four years I've had a handful people take me up on my offer. Without exception they've been phenomenal people. I do shudder occasionally, though, thinking who God has sent our way but we've allowed to slip through our fingers.

Sometimes I walk outside our building, close my eyes and put myself in the shoes of an unchurched young person; then I walk back in and notice the first things I see, smell and feel. I ask myself whether they reinforce negative preconceptions about church or dismantle them. Try it. This gives you the list of things to change. In the Anglican church today, we need change. Most people in the UK now think that the church is not designed with them remotely in mind – they feel it's simply not aiming at them. For most people the name of Jesus is little more than a swear word. Through what we in the church do and say in the name of Jesus, we have to change that opinion.

Last year I exchanged a few tweets with a guy on Twitter about who Jesus really is. He was trying to goad me by using the hashtag '#hokum'. I had to look it up: 'hokum' means 'something apparently impressive or legitimate but actually untrue or insincere; nonsense.' This guy was expressing what most people think: that all this stuff about Jesus is a load of nonsense. It's exactly what most of the people of Jerusalem thought about Jesus in his day too. Jesus was crucified by a baying mob, utterly despised and rejected, with scorn heaped upon him by the public. Jesus had become rubbish. The name of Jesus was, and for many remains, synonymous with the unholy, unacceptable, rubbish of life. Not with the glory of God.

The Beautiful Gate formed the main entrance to the temple of Jerusalem in New Testament times. A massive pair of Corinthian bronze gates, seventy-five feet high, towered above worshippers on their way into the temple. The Roman historian Josephus recounts his tour of Jerusalem and notes the outstanding magnificence of these spectacular gates, the main entrance to the temple from the town. He wrote that their beauty, 'greatly excelled those that were only covered over with silver and gold.'[1] That's some entrance. The gates had been built to impress, to point to the glory of God within them. However, they were a barrier of exclusion for many people; only the righteous could enter. To enter through those gates you had to be racially pure, ceremonially clean and faultless in your obedience of Scripture so only those utterly confident in their own piety could enter. Actually, the fact that Peter and John continued to enter through the Beautiful Gate in the book of Acts is in itself a tremendous prophetic act. By entering they were declaring that belief in Jesus as the Messiah was not heresy but the very fulfilment of all the law and prophets.

Outside the Beautiful Gate languished those who were not invited, who weren't acceptable. They were excluded because their minds or bodies did not conform to the standards of the law. It was imagined that the beauty within would be tarnished by them. The Beautiful Gate was a busy thoroughfare and the begging outcasts there offered worshippers an opportunity for a display of Jewish piety by exercising charity on the way in and out. The Beautiful Gate marked a dividing line the rejected could not cross.

Jesus ended such divisions. The good news about Jesus is that everyone is invited. I believe that Jesus had the Beautiful Gate in mind when he proclaimed: 'I am the gate; *whoever* enters through me will be saved' (John 10:9). and he said, 'Come to me, *all* you who are weary and burdened and I will give you rest' (Matt. 11:28). The Bible states that God, 'wants *all people* to be saved and to come to a knowledge of the truth' (1 Tim. 2:4). Everyone means everyone. The Bible makes clear about Jesus, 'In him and through faith in him we may approach God with freedom and confidence' (Eph. 3:12). Jesus is the embodiment, fulfilment and personification of the people of God: we are all invited and accepted through him.

The Beautiful Gate was where Peter and John found a beggar, an unholy, unacceptable outcast who had no hope in life beyond a fleeting appeal to worshippers on their way into the temple to exercise some charity as a last fling of self-righteousness. The guy was in desperate need, longing for love. It's unlikely he was on his own. Peter and John had been through this gate many times and he was probably a regular there. But one day they somehow see him in a new and specific way – 'look at us', they demand. To look someone in the eye is to make a soul-level connection, to communicate that you value that person by giving them your full, undivided attention. That's where something new started for Peter, John and the beggar. And that's where something new will start for us too.

Peter and John knew that the Beautiful Gate was actually a prophecy, a picture of Jesus. They knew that in his life and death, Jesus had become like the outcasts, in order to bring them in. They knew that Jesus often referred to himself as, 'the stone that the builders have rejected, which has become the cornerstone' (cf. Matt. 21:42; Mark 12:10; Luke 20:17; Acts 4:11; 1 Pet. 2:7). They knew that Jesus was a redeemer – one who rescues and restores, one who seeks and finds what is lost and breathes into it new life and purpose and value. They knew that far from being a name of scorn, Jesus is the only name by which we might be saved and healed. And so they decided to turn the Beautiful Gate into a reclamation yard. They looked at that guy and gave him the only thing they'd got – and everything they'd got – the name of Jesus!

Just up the road from where we now live in Bournemouth is an architectural reclamation yard. One of my guilty pleasures is going there and hunting through all the stuff, seeing what can be found. It certainly proves the saying that one person's junk is another person's treasure. The prices on some of that old stuff are almost unbelievable. I think the reason I love these places is because my dad used to take me to the local rubbish tip with him when I was a child. I simply loved it. Dad would pick up old bikes and bring them home to repair. Once we made a go-kart from an old pram – it was brilliant! He still can't walk past a skip today without looking in it to see what he can salvage and I do the same.

The wonderful truth is that God will never throw you away. The world will. But when you're rejected, consigned to the rubbish heap of life by those around you, God will find you, pick you up, bring you back and make you beautiful again. Church is the means by which God does this. The leader of the Hillsong movement, Brian Houston, writes about the scene at the Beautiful Gate with Peter, John and the lame beggar: 'The Gate is beautiful because in it we see the power of the name of Jesus – no longer condemned, excluded and damaged, but through which we may be forgiven and reconciled and healed. That's his mission. That's our mission.'[2]

St Swithun's hadn't been going that long before the local press began to sniff out that something unusual was happening as hundreds of people began to come. I received one call from our regional BBC radio station, who wanted to visit and interview people. Somewhat naively I welcomed them to come, although I did take some advice before I did and I'd caution anyone else to do the same. In the middle of her interview with me, the reporter tried five different ways of getting me to name and shame other churches in the area who she was trying to caricature as having failed in some way. I'm so glad that I refused to do so. That's not a good way to think and it's certainly not a good way to speak.

We laugh about that ridiculous interview now, because in their final edit that was aired the most radical thing they remarked on repeatedly was that our café was open *before* the service! Will wonders never cease? As though witnessing the dawn of some great ecclesiastical revolution they remarked that at this café we served coffee *and biscuits*. In point of fact, I want to state right here that we've never served a single pathetic biscuit at St Swithun's and while I'm here, we never will. They're not good enough. Biscuits don't shout about God's limitless power and extravagant love. Biscuits scream mediocrity. Give me fat cookies and delicious pastries but, Lord, deliver me from stale church biscuits! While you're at it, God, please purify us from all unrighteous instant coffee served in dirty crockery and flimsy cups held in plastic holders from the 1970s. Amen.

Chapter 10

Relational intelligence

One who has unreliable friends soon comes to ruin,
but there is a friend who sticks closer than a brother.

Proverbs 18:24

We launched St Swithun's Bournemouth on Thursday 11 September 2014. All three of our staff were in the worship band along with friends from elsewhere. The bishop of Winchester laid out the vision for the church and led us all in prayer. The only thing I said was to invite everyone to our first service that Sunday. Then we served drinks and food and had a party. In a side room just before the service, the bishop had asked me what I wanted prayer for, other than my family which was uppermost in his mind. For a moment I didn't know where to begin, so long was the list of things that we needed. But then my mind cleared: we had to pray for God's presence at St Swithun's. The bishop agreed, and then asked Debi and me what our personal needs were. I was tempted to ask for something that would sound impressive and spiritual, but I knew that the bishop was far too smart to fall for that, and I felt the sincerity of his personal interest. I found myself sharing my heart: the thing we really needed in Bournemouth was some good friends. Loneliness had been our greatest concern about leaving London to lead a new church. We needn't have feared. God had gone ahead of us.

As the bishop prayed for us with great love and power in that side room, I heard the excited hubbub of people gathering in the church for the launch party. Debi and I had invited everyone we'd met in Bournemouth and some of them had clearly invited their friends, because about two hundred and fifty people had shown up. But we were under no illusions – most of them were visiting family and friends from out of town or were well-wishers already well plugged into churches elsewhere in Bournemouth. I'd invited all the other church leaders in town whom I'd met during the planning phase and was so thankful that many of them came to shout us on. I was very uncomfortable with the idea of anyone blowing a trumpet fanfare announcing our arrival: imagining St Swithun's as some grand project to rescue the Kingdom of God in Bournemouth would be ludicrously arrogant and highly offensive to other church leaders there who were becoming my friends. I've never thought of it that way. We had no idea at all what we were doing at the beginning. So instead, I genuinely begged others for their friendship, help and wisdom. I'd say, 'I'm stuck. I don't know what to do. The bishop has asked us to do this, but without your help I don't know how it can happen.' Several of them almost visibly shook their heads at my ignorance and naiveté the first time we met, but took me under their wing none the less and have offered me guidance, practical help and encouragement ever since. A group of us have become friends and now meet every month to support each other and pray.

As launch day approached we had found a carpet but still had no chairs for the night or for our first Sunday that would immediately follow it. The day before the launch event, I was still frantically ringing around all the other local churches trying to find some. One old church leader who had been so encouraging to me during the planning phase offered us some of their ancient chairs that had been stored in a loft in their church tower and were covered in pigeon poo. We hired a van and collected them. Sure enough, they were in a terrible state, but beggars can't be choosers, I reasoned, so we got to work. I can still remember all those chairs lined up along the church drive, us with buckets and brushes in hand, scrubbing several years' worth of crusty bird poo off them.

On our second Sunday we realised that the number of pigeon-poo chairs we had wasn't enough. Almost unbelievably, we feared that we might have more people turn up than we had chairs to sit them on. It was a nice problem to have in one sense, but it was still a problem. Once again, I turned to my new friends who had offered to help. One of the other vicars in town took pity on us and only minutes before his own service was due to start on the Sunday morning, he was stacking chairs into his own car and driving them across the city to our building, making two or three round trips to make sure that we had enough.

We were growing in depth of friendship with our fledgling team too. Jamie Matthews with Matt and Laura Clayton were our staff. Friends Pete and Gill Drysdale with Tien and Charlene Tran had moved down from London to help us, as had Nikki Cross. Tom and Lizzie Redman had committed to come, together with Steve and Jo Coates who had been commissioned by their existing churches in Bournemouth to join us. A larger group had come to our three pre-launch gatherings but we knew we couldn't yet count on their long-term commitment, although several of them had already given and served very sacrificially just to get St Swithun's started.

When we first arrived in Bournemouth, Jamie, Matt and Laura were living with Debi and me and our three children as we had no other housing to offer them. We shared a four-bedroom house with one shower and some of the largest spiders I have ever seen in the UK. It was hardly third-world poverty, but it didn't afford much private space either. We all lived hand-to-mouth during those first few weeks of St Swithun's. I wasn't sleeping much and felt the heavy weight of responsibility. At church we were all working in a small room with one rickety trestle table and four mismatched chairs with ripped cushions we found by the bin. We had no legal charitable entity, no bank account, and no office equipment other than what I'd raided from HTB's stationery cupboard before I had to give my staff keys back. It was all a bit stressful.

Something had to give and, sure enough, one day it did. I'd spent the day with my team, who needed all kinds of resources I didn't have and answers I didn't know. And now they were my housemates. I'd been out early, had missed lunch and was hungry and low on energy. In blind selfishness I even recall being frustrated that Debi (who had been doing everything else in my absence) hadn't prepared an evening meal. Our middle son, who had just started a new school, was struggling to cope with all the change and was playing up a lot; our eldest child hadn't got a school place so was being home schooled by Debi, while she also juggled her attention with our young pre-school toddler. Tea time, bath time and bed time had been hard work and I lost my temper with our eldest son – the exact reverse of what he needed from me. In short, I completely failed my wife and family, not to mention God.

The moment we finally got the children into bed I walked downstairs and thoughtlessly chose that very moment to suggest to Debi that we needed to exert harsher discipline on our eldest child. She looked at me in disbelief and said that she disagreed. By this stage, Jamie, Matt and Laura had disappeared to their rooms as they saw the storm clouds gathering. Before long we were embroiled in the worst argument we have ever had. Quite rightly, Debi explained to me that our son was finding all the change a challenge and that we needed to reassure him of our love, and provide security and stability for him at home. She urged me to be patient. But I was so locked down in my fear and frustration – I cringe at this memory – that I reacted to it in the worst way. I shouted and generally behaved in an appalling manner. Thank God that Debi had the wisdom not to let me get away with it: she looked at me with hurt and anger and talked to me in no uncertain terms. I don't quite recall what she said, but I do remember the telling off was severe! And quite right too.

A few weeks later we were invited for a long weekend away to go through a marriage course hosted by HTB's associate vicar and his wife, Nicky and Sila Lee. Nicky and Sila are global authorities on the subject and have produced many materials and courses to enhance family relationships all over the world, so the idea of spending a weekend with them and a few other couples at a sixteenth-century mansion in West Sussex was very tempting. Having just started a new church, however, our first thought was that we couldn't possibly leave it in the hands of others so soon; then again, we knew that it was God's provision for us and that it was right to go.

Slowly it dawned on me that we had to go for three reasons. First, our marriage was more important than the church. We needed to get away and invest in our relationship. One of the best things Debi and I can do for the church is keep our marriage in good shape. Second, it would do our team and small congregation good to see right from the word go that church did not depend on us, or revolve around us. The Holy Spirit was running the show, not us, and he could do that through many different people; the fledgling team was strong and would see it as a huge vote of our confidence if we were to leave it to them. Breaking any sense of dependency on us at the outset would be very helpful to the future. Third, by going away to focus on our marriage we would be teaching other married couples in the church by way of example. I decided not to hide the fact that we were going away but made sure that the guys who were leading the services announced to everyone where we were. The team did well, and the importance of investing in marriage relationships was a message that went out loud and clear.

We had an amazing time that weekend. Our kids barely gave us a second glance as we dropped them off with my Mum and Dad, knowing they were about to be extravagantly loved and indulged for a whole weekend. When we arrived at the country estate, we drove through the grounds towards a beautiful old castle that was to be our home for the weekend. We were shown up to a huge, lavishly decorated and furnished room that more usually accommodates visiting dignitaries and ambassadors. The spacious ensuite had a deep, full-length double-ended bath that we promptly filled with piping hot water and all manner of oils and bubbles. As I recall, we fell into the enormous four-poster bed before we'd even opened our cases to unpack. It was time to reconnect emotionally and physically. That weekend was glorious, although not every conversation was easy. The sessions made us look at our communication again, at how we handle conflict, at the quality of the time we spend together, and so on. It's a cliché to say it I suppose, but we really did fall in love all over again. We'd never stopped meaning to love each other of course; but the stress and strains of life had cut in on us and it felt so good to reset our marriage as our priority in life, second only to our individual relationships with Christ.

Forget strategy documents, budgets and meetings with donors and decision-makers. They're all necessary in due time, but if I were to start a business, charity or church out of those things alone, I'd be done for. I have found that the two greatest factors that determines success over the long term are the health of my personal relationship with God and the vitality of my core relationships with those I love. This is God's call and command for my life too. My daily, hidden quiet time of prayer and Bible study is of the utmost importance and my core relationships are the next thing to focus on, ahead of the work place. As I'm married, that's my marriage, and as I have kids, that's my parenting too. But it's no less true if you're single, in which case it is your relationships with your closest friends and family. Our ability to connect with and love others well is known as relational intelligence. Intellectual intelligence is useful and emotional intelligence makes a big difference too; but relational intelligence matters even more. There's a lot of truth in the old adage that 'It's not what you know, but who you know', which doesn't have to be a bad thing. Many of us never think about our core relationships and friendships as something that we could either be good or bad at, but I firmly believe that this is an area of life where competency can be learned if you have the inclination to do so.

It's very telling to me that right at the start of the St Swithun's project early in 2013, my bosses at HTB, Nicky Gumbel and Nicky Lee, made it clear that what Debi thought of the whole project was the one deal-breaker. Whether I thought I was ready for it, or the various pros and cons of different locations, could all be debated as long as Debi and I were together in it. So the very first thing they did was to send us to Bournemouth for two days, just to be there, walk around and pray together. That's the value they put on our marriage and the value they put on the project.

Look at what happens to churches when the leaders' marriages fall apart. It causes devastation because it's so fundamental to leadership. Writing to Timothy, Paul asks, 'If anyone does not know how to manage his own family, how can he take care of God's church?' (1 Tim. 3:5). If love is to be truly the core value of the churches we lead, it's got to be the core value of our marriages, parenting and friendships too. My kids are still relatively young, so Debi and I have a long way to go in our parenting and still have a lot to learn. Frequently we don't feel we're doing very well, but we hold on to the fact that while the Bible certainly tells us to expect times of difficulty and suffering in our core relationships, ultimately it promises us that, 'Love never fails' (1 Cor. 13:8). The wisdom at the heart of relational intelligence is the golden ethic that when we don't know what else to do, we act in the way we sincerely believe to be most loving.

Obviously, that's not the same as the most indulgent course of action, and nowhere is that clearer than in parenting, where in all manner of situations it's much more loving to say 'No' to a child than to give in and indulge them. They may constantly nag us to watch TV, eat sweets, buy products, and stay up late but we have to steel ourselves and, with an authority that still carries warmth, say 'No'.

Often church-plant leaders put so much time into planning documents and meetings and phone calls and emails – all of which end up making very little difference. Most of our plans went out of the window during the first couple of weeks. But even though we know our core relationships are in theory more important and will be a greater determinant of success, we invest little time or effort into our marriages and family relationships during the planning phase. It is terrifyingly easy to become so busy and preoccupied producing all the stuff of lesser importance that we fail to invest sufficient effort into the very things that will make the biggest impact.

Most church leaders will acknowledge that, second only to our personal relationship with God, our marriages and families are where we really lead from. When those relationships are strained I, for one, find it nearly impossible to lead well – it's as if the air is thicker. It's a constant battle not to prioritise anything over these relationships. Not bishops, not congregation, not leadership team, not staff, not pastoral crises. Nothing.

Debi and I have learned the hard way that the quality of our relationship depends on the quality of our communication. Every week we have two unbreakable commitments in our diary. The first is every Thursday evening: we have a 'date night' where the rule is that we don't talk about leading church. The second is a 'business' meeting where we both sit down with my assistant to go through everything to do with leading church. Of course, sometimes it's not such a clear distinction, but the intention is there and if we stray too much into business chat on our date night we call each other on it and change the subject. Equally, it doesn't help if we bring too much of our personal relationship into the business meeting as it clouds our decision-making about what's right for the church, as well as for our family. Having a good assistant who's able to work with us on that as an objective, yet understanding, third voice has been invaluable.

Debi and I had first attended a marriage course when we'd been married three years and were expecting our first child. We thought it would be wise to check the health of our relationship before we became a family. We realised that there were quite a few subjects we'd studiously avoided talking about since, whenever they came up, tension would mount, even though we didn't know why. We struggled to admit those conflicts even existed, much less actually confronting and resolving them. The main subject causing tension between us was our different family backgrounds. We'd each assumed the values, beliefs and behaviours that we grew up with were the universal norms for everyone to live by, even though we each thought 'normal' was something very different. Debi and I both had good parents, but now I have three children of my own I know that every parent is flawed. I try my best to be a good father, but I'm doing well if I haven't messed it up by the end of breakfast. It was so freeing for us to think 'What kind of marriage and family life do we want?' We didn't have to settle for what we had received as being 'normal', nor for what we currently had. Together we could decide to pursue the best things from both our backgrounds and add our own new ideas and practices as well.

Both Debi and I tend to avoid conflict. Whilst it is of course virtuous to seek harmony, we've learned that it shouldn't be used as a cover to simply keep the peace at all costs. Without raising hurts and airing disagreements, no real resolution and reconciliation can occur. We've learned the hard way that we can't really experience true harmony in our marriage unless we're prepared to speak courageously, honestly and vulnerably when we've felt hurt or have disagreed with each other. We've got to be able to trust that we'll each listen rather than react defensively when we try to raise such matters. Without that kind of commitment there will be no real intimacy in any long-term relationship.

After all, if Debi and I can't do this with one another, how can we hope to do it with our leadership team and the wider church? From the start I was determined that the core leadership team making the biggest decisions wouldn't become larger than a group of friends sitting around our kitchen table, somewhere between eight and twelve people perhaps. All our leadership meetings happen only after we've sat down and eaten a meal together. At the end of the day, we're friends and we've stuck with one another through a few tricky things now, so there's trust there. We're able to listen when we say 'no' to each other and can disagree without spilling blood. When we get a little heated or strained, it's not too long before someone will chip in some banter that we can all laugh at. Because our marriage is like that, our senior leadership team is like that, and therefore the wider leadership team is like that too, and so on, until I think a newcomer might well conclude that's the culture of the wider church whenever we meet. By no means do we have a perfect marriage; our aim as leaders, however, is that over time, the priority we place on our core relationships spills out into everything we do as a church.

At HTB Debi and I spent six years pastoring young professionals and preparing young couples for marriage in London. I firmly believe that relationships should be a huge area of strength for the church; in fact, we should be experts in it. Secular society's approach to dating is failing so many people. Many in their twenties and thirties might have lived through their parents' divorce or grown up with a parent who had several different partners of their own, assuming this was normal. Social media can certainly help our relationships, but the danger is that it encourages us to develop relationships based on carefully manicured public profiles rather than reality. For similar reasons, secular dating models are leaving many people damaged and alone. To show that we don't regard this as a taboo area, we hosted a massive Christian speed-dating event one Valentine's Day. It was quite a risk and a lot of work, but it was also huge fun. We had three hundred people – equal numbers of men and women – dating and partying that night in church. I don't see it as inappropriate or sacrilegious at all; I see helping to get every young person who wants it, into a healthy, godly dating relationship as one of the most important aspects of their discipleship. Some people might regard that kind of thing as too risky for a church – I certainly hope so. But if you're going to do risky things you need wise friends to call on to ensure that you're not doing anything really stupid.

Having worked for Nicky and Sila Lee at HTB, I was utterly convinced of the strategic importance of relationship ministry in the mission of the church. It seems clear to me that a strong, healthy society depends on strong, healthy families, and that strong, healthy families depend on strong, healthy marriages. Why do politicians not get this? Undermining traditional family values is just about the worst thing you can do for the people you're called to lead.

Many church-based ministries in social justice are about responding with God's compassion to people whose lives have become messed up. A great many churches run addiction recovery programmes, foodbanks, homeless shelters, and so on. These ministries are essential if we are to behave as Jesus did. Nevertheless, the old saying about pulling people out of rivers is also true – after a while you want to go upstream to find out who's throwing them in. I've been in full-time Christian leadership ministry now just over eight years, but even in that short time I've had plenty of opportunity to observe that the root cause of people's lives going off the rails as adults is very often their upbringing. Of course, that's not the only cause and sometimes tragic things happen beyond anyone's control. Also, we all have to take responsibility as adults for our own decisions. But I'm not talking about having generally loving parents who make many mistakes, as we all do; I'm talking about genuine neglect, desolation, abuse or constant discouragement. These issues are way too prevalent.

I've seen the beauty of church community, within which real healing can occur and people can start to flourish once again. Around a third of all the individuals and couples who come to various relationships courses that we run at St Swithun's do not come from a church background and are not currently churchgoers. In this way, these courses fuel church growth, because many of the guests subsequently go on Alpha or start coming along on Sundays. A further third come from (and return to) other local congregations thus strengthening other ministries in the area. The final third consists of our guys – and there I get to see very closely the life-changing difference to individuals, to marriages and families, which has a dramatic impact throughout every aspect of church life.

So when we were planning St Swithun's, we knew that we wanted both to enact rescue and restoration ministries where life goes wrong and gets extremely tough for people, while also enacting preventative ministries to eradicate the upstream causes. Even back in the planning stage we'd determined not to step forward with any ministry until we'd identified the right leaders. We felt that would be one crucial way in which God would clarify what he was calling us to do and when he wanted us to do it. Right now I've got a folder of projects and ministries I'd love to see happen and I believe God is calling us to do them, but until we've found the right leaders, they'll stay on the back burner. The more church goes on, the more I understand that deciding what God is *not* calling you to do is critical: only then do you have the capacity and resources to respond to what God *is* calling you to do.

One of my joys at HTB was leading its smallest Sunday service: a traditional 9.00am Communion at St Paul's Onslow Square. Although we didn't wear clerical robes, we had a choir and an organist and we sang hymns. The preaching each week was a ten-minute talk on the lectionary readings and our liturgy was from the Book of Common Prayer. When I started at HTB, I wasn't keen to do it, having gone there precisely to get away from traditional-style worship. But looking back, I'm so thankful: the small congregation, including many older people, decided to take me under their wing and train me up. And as I began to respond to their love by loving them, I began to love what they loved. I'm convinced that one of the reasons HTB has thrived and that St Swithun's and many other church plants now exist is a result of the faith-filled prayers of those gracious older saints. Some of them would take my hand at the end of a service and ask me to pray for them, but it soon became clear to me that what they actually wanted to do was to pray for me. They would pray with the kind of trusting simplicity that only comes from years of friendship with Jesus. It's very humbling to take the funeral service of a faithful prayer warrior who has held you before God constantly in their prayers, and I've had that honour a few times now. I can't wait to get to heaven, sit down with them, and tell them all the trials and tribulations of my church-planting story – maybe they'll know them already.

Just before Christmas 2013 after one service, standing at the back of St Paul's Onslow Square drinking coffee and chatting with everyone, I fell into conversation with two people I'd grown to admire very much – Pete and Gill Drysdale. Pete and Gill were team members on both the marriage course and marriage preparation course and I knew they'd helped many couples over the years. Pete was an IT project manager and Gill was a teacher. They asked me whether Debi and I were getting away for a Christmas holiday with the children, and I replied that we were looking forward to renting a cottage in the Purbecks, just the other side of Poole Harbour near Bournemouth. I hadn't breathed a word about my motivations for spending more time in the area.

Pete and Gill both looked at me, dewey-eyed: 'Oh, we love it down there!' they enthused:

> We've always had a sense of connection with that area. In fact, to be perfectly honest with you, we'd love to take early retirement and go and live there to establish some kind of ministry to get these relationships courses going. But the one thing stopping us would be our deeper sense of connection with what God is doing through church here at HTB. Tim, if only someone would plant a church from HTB down there!

They laughed heartily at such an absurd thought and I choked on my coffee. 'Why don't we both pray about that and then meet up in the New Year?' was all I could muster. But I knew it was God. After the holidays we met and I shared with them that the bishop of Winchester had invited HTB to plant a new ministry in

Bournemouth and that Nicky was ready to send me to lead it. We prayed with great excitement, and began to dream.

Pete and Gill made some brave decisions. They spoke to their employers, with the result that Gill resigned while Pete was able to transfer to an office that his company ran near to Bournemouth. They rented a house and moved down. Like us, they didn't know anyone down here. It cost them a lot of time, energy and money, but they were full of joy. They were exercising faith and that always feels good.

The prophet Zechariah warns us, 'Do not despise the day of small beginnings' (Zech. 4:10). Well, nine months later, we were all together at the launch of St Swithun's. Three months after that, Pete and Gill ran the marriage course. Eighteen months later, Pete and Gill had six relationships courses running at the same time, all with fully trained teams. They've since raised up leaders who are running the marriage preparation course, the marriage course, parenting courses, 'Restored Lives' (a course for anyone separated, divorced or going through a divorce) and the 'Bereavement Journey' (a course for those working through grief at the loss of a loved one). With their help and a capable team around her, Debi has run a parenting children course in our local school twice now. Quite apart from all that, Pete and Gill have also trained up teams in other local churches to begin running similar courses with their support. Pete has retired so that he can devote more time to leading the work and has also taken on vital behind-the-scenes administration for a local charity that works in secondary schools to help teenage girls battling insecurity, anxiety and low self-worth.

Pete and Gill and many other couples, families and friends here are proving that a professed love for God must immediately result in a love for others around us. It's no good my saying that our church has a core value of love if our marriages are in tatters, our families in disarray, or factions and friendship groups are at war: we must practise what we preach. What do we really have to offer to the world unless we can make the love of God known through our human relationships? The Church should be famous for love. Indeed, Jesus made it the acid test of authentic faith by which unbelievers can judge any church: 'By this everyone will know that you are my disciples, if you love one another' (John 13:35).

Chapter 11

Worship like you mean it

It's who you are and the way you live that count before
God. Your worship must engage your spirit in the pursuit of
truth. That's the kind of people the Father is out looking for:
those who are simply and honestly themselves before him in their
worship. God is sheer being itself – Spirit. Those who worship
him must do it out of their very being, their spirits, their true
selves, in adoration.

John 4:23–4 (*The Message*)

One Sunday one of my favourite messed-up homeless alcoholics
came in. When he's sober he's a lovely guy; when he's drunk he's
aggressive, difficult, emotional, loud, foul-mouthed and disruptive.
He's a very big, intimidating man who used to be in the army and
was universally known as 'Big Tim'. He had stayed in our homeless
shelter the preceding winter and had dipped in and out of Alpha
and the Recovery Course. I was speaking from the stage when I
saw the door swing open and Big Tim stagger in, barging one of
our team aside. He marched right down to the front and sat on
the floor, directly before me. I could smell the alcohol. One look
at his glazed eyes and inane grin told me that he was absolutely

smashed. I smiled and tried to remain calm but inside I was panicking and saying, 'Oh God, no, I beg you, please don't let him kick off'!

Big Tim – and I now like to think God too – had other ideas. He had come to church to worship God and that's what he was going to do; no one was going to get in his way. He started shouting out, 'I love you, God. I love you, Jesus. I love you, Pastor.' I smiled at him and motioned for him to be quiet, but he kept on, in front of everybody, totally oblivious to my acute embarrassment. He looked around at everyone and back at me very earnestly, as though not comprehending any possible reason why I wasn't appreciating his help. This time he stood up and took over; if I wasn't going to preach with force, then he was. 'I love this church,' he shouted, looking around gravely. 'You all want to know why I love this church? I'll tell you why I love this church. I love this church because you give a f***!'

It was the nicest thing that anyone had ever said about St Swithun's. Big Tim, in his bombed-out, worst state, was articulating – in his own style – the very thing we were aiming for in our worship. I loved it so much that the week afterwards I actually drew up a big joke poster for the wall of our office, making it our church's tag line: 'St Swithun's Bournemouth – the church that gives a f***.' I would still love to see that slogan on a T-shirt.

St Paul writes, 'Therefore brothers and sisters, in view of God's mercy, offer your bodies as a living sacrifice, holy and pleasing to God – this is your true and proper worship' (Rom. 12:1). Worship is everything. So at St Swithun's we put all our eggs in one basket: worship. The first team member we hired was a full-time worship pastor – for a church of eleven people. Having signed the lease on the building, the first thing we spent the remaining cash on was production kit. We purchased speakers before we bought chairs. Or even Bibles.

However, none of us can afford to delegate our worship to a pro with a guitar. There is certainly a shortage of worship leaders in every church that I know of. But far worse than that is the lack of uninhibited worshippers who are unafraid to lead a congregation by example from the front row, by demonstrating how to respond to the glory of God. At St Swithun's we're trying to implement this learning but it's not easy. Most Church of England churches have this terrible social disease whereby there's a kind of radioactive zone around the front two rows so that no one sits in them; it's awful for times of worship and terrible for preaching. We try to fill from the front to the back and not the other way around. The posture of a congregation is so important. When they lean back as if to say, 'Entertain or interest me, then I'll respond', they rarely get anything worthwhile from either the worship or the preaching. But when they lean forward as if to say, 'I've come to participate, I'm going to get the best out of you', then invariably church becomes the highlight of their week, they learn and grow fast, and their lives are quickly transformed for the better.

I recall occasions back at HTB when, at the 6.30pm evening service at St Paul's Onslow Square, Al Gordon and I would look around and wonder what was wrong. The service was packed with hundreds of people, the environment was warm and atmospheric, and the band were playing their best. What was missing was the sense of the presence of God among his people. On those occasions it wasn't unusual for us to grab a few others, head down to the front, and really give ourselves to the time of worship. I'd take time to check my motives before God on such occasions, to ensure that I wasn't being manipulative in influencing others around me by providing a lead in worship. I'd screw my eyes shut, raise my hands to heaven and give my entire focus to the Lord, thanking him, praising him, confessing sin to him, asking him to send his Holy Spirit to be with us. The enthusiastic and largely young congregation at the 6.30pm service was usually quick to respond. Some of the most memorable times of ministry there came from a very cold start.

Everything rises and falls on the commitment of God's people to prayer and worship. Worship is our priority – our first obligation and delight. All the way through the Bible the prosperity of the people of God follows the trajectory of their worship: when the leaders and the people devote themselves to worship, life tends to go well but when they fail to do so, it quickly falls apart. It's still true today. In the Old Testament there are many kings who follow God and who do good and great works, but the Bible records only one complaint of God against many of them: they failed to complete his instructions when it comes to worship. We're not called to pursue any other calling until we have given ourselves to God in worship first. And it's not a one-off deal; it has to be a lifestyle, a permanent attitude and approach. The book of Revelation makes it clear that worship is one of the central activities of heaven (along with fun, feasting and sight-seeing). Matt Redman often describes worship as he ad libs in 'Here for You': 'the people of God in the presence of God pouring out the praises of God.'

However, if the truth be told, in church we all put almost everything else above worship. When we turn to God in the midst of our mess, worship is the place to start rebuilding our lives but, compounding our first error, we often start to rebuild elsewhere. We think that we can shortcut worship and get straight on to more tangible things. But worship is where everything begins, and can begin again, and again, and again. Following its failure to worship, leading to just about every other evil imaginable, in 586 BC Jerusalem fell to the Babylonians and Solomon's temple was destroyed. The Israelite nation was defeated, its humiliation complete with mass deportations to Babylon. There, Daniel refused to worship foreign gods or the king, continuing courageously to worship the one true God he knew. His faithfulness began to reverse the nation's fortunes, ushering in the new start for them that God had desired. Years later, the returning exiles rebuilt Jerusalem, starting with the temple. They began at the place of worship; the city walls weren't rebuilt until Nehemiah returned years after that. Their first priority was the temple, restoring the sacred heart of worship at the centre of the nation. Ezra 3:1-2 describes how 'The people assembled as one man [and] began to build the altar of the God of Israel . . . despite their fear of the peoples around them, they built the altar on its foundation and sacrificed burnt offerings on it to the Lord.' They understood that worship was their first duty, their first opportunity, their priority, the *sine qua non*, the first thing to put right and rebuild. It's no different for the church in the UK today. This is where we must start. That's why I'm a huge fan of initiatives like Worship Central and 24-7 Prayer. We can go to all the church-planting conferences and leadership conventions we like, but until we're praying and worshipping almost as if that's all that matters, then every other effort will be in vain.

At St Swithun's we worship together constantly, at all levels of church and in all types of meeting, not just on a Sunday. We worship as a staff team, on Alpha, in connect groups, even the mothers and toddlers group on Thursday mornings has worship. Running nights of prayer and worship has unlocked so much depth for us as we've taken time to interact with God in worship as a whole church.

Without doubt, the most important meeting in our weekly church calendar is one of the smallest, not the largest. Every Tuesday morning at 7.00a.m. a group of about thirty intercessors meet to pray. It's one of the very few things in the church that I've not delegated. I probably should ask someone else to lead it but, selfishly, I've kept hold of it. The focus of our prayer has always been the wider church in Bournemouth, though naturally we pray for what God is doing at St Swithun's and St Clement's too. This group keep me constantly returning home to our heavenly Father's house, to converse with him each week. Occasionally these meetings have been charged with the heights of power and depths of profundity but are usually more mundane: we gulp a coffee, then worship, study Scripture and pray. That's it – no frills and nothing fancy, just what Christians have been doing since Pentecost. We always take time to listen to God, primarily in Scripture, tentatively sharing visions, prophecy and words of knowledge that we sense the Holy Spirit might be trying to communicate to us. As I reflect on the four years of meetings so far, it seems extraordinary how God has spoken and what prayers he has first inspired and then answered.

One significant danger for people like myself, who love worship and occasionally get caught up in intense spiritual experiences, is pride. It appears from Ezekiel 28 that Lucifer was a beautiful angelic being, perhaps a kind of heavenly worship leader before pride began to grip his heart. He got fed up with God getting the glory and began to desire some of it for himself. Way too often I flirt with this same, deadly evil and I'm not the only church leader who has to confess an ongoing battle with inner voices telling us to seek a share of the glory that should all be bestowed upon God. So I'll tell you a secret: sometimes when lovely, godly people compliment me in order to encourage me, I find I have to whisper to myself,

'Get behind me, Satan!' Spiritual pride is treacherous and we must deal with it ruthlessly.

If we allow our worship of God to cool and give pride a foothold in our hearts, we become foolish and sooner or later it will be our undoing. When it came to our first church plant at St Clement's we prayed a lot in advance and took time to test the call and wait until we had the leader and finance in place. But still, as I look back now, I see that I was far too keen to get going. I certainly had a godly ambition to see St Clement's come back to life, but I also wanted to be able to say that we'd planted out. I was too keen and allowed myself to be egged on to rush ahead, wanting to seize the slender chance we had to relaunch the site for mission. With more patience our plans would have been better, the team would have been stronger, and we'd have had an adequate financial package in place. Blinded by my pride, I allowed St Swithun's to pay the stipend of the plant leader and even agreed to rent the vicarage from the diocese rather than pressing to be given it. As a result, we came perilously close to pushing St Swithun's finances beyond the danger zone during the first half of 2017. Had I been humble and more patient we'd have all been better off for it.

I wasn't the only one who needed to deal with spiritual pride. At St Swithun's we'd planted from scratch into a blank venue with no existing congregation, structures or expectations. But at St Clement's a small congregation was already in place and we faced the very different challenge of revitalising a church community already in existence. It took a great deal of courage for the congregation of St Swithun's to take on a project like that; it also took a lot of humility from the receiving congregation at St Clement's to admit it needed help. The deep spiritual issue that both congregations have had to address is pride. None of us likes admitting that we're not doing very well and need help and few of us are willing to sacrifice and risk our hard-won, carefully managed reputations on high-risk new ventures. So we had endless discussions over finding the right language to use as a metaphor for what we were doing. 'Church planting' was rejected because it made it sound as if there was no church there already. I then, rather insensitively, described St Clement's as being 'on life support' with St Swithun's acting as an organ donor – not surprisingly, that upset a lot of people, sounding as it did as though St Clement's would be dead without St Swithun's; although some felt that was factually accurate, who would want to be described like that? It's absurd to offer to help someone, only to rub their nose in it as we do so. Such an approach would only reveal a lack of true love in the motive. Finally, some of the St Swithun's people got offended that the St Clement's people were offended. It got messy and all revealed pride – on both sides.

Spiritual pride mixed with impatience is a toxic mix and deadly for Christian leaders. 1 Samuel 13 tells the woeful tale of the mistakes that King Saul made while under the influence of these sins. He wouldn't wait for Samuel beyond the absolute minimum period. Regarding himself as invincible and self-validating the righteousness of his cause and decisions, he rushed ahead. In the Lord's eyes, Saul's kingship was over from that point onwards (cf. 1 Sam. 13:13–14). I imagine that if leaders like me in the church today were exposed to the same level of real-time judgement few of us would survive long.

Eventually, with handfuls of hair torn out of my own head after many long meetings, we worked out how to stop the rot: humility was required, mixed with a renewed focus on Christ. I apologised for any offence I'd caused and worked instead to focus us on what the Holy Spirit was doing. We gathered around the name of neither St Clement's nor St Swithun's – those names began to become meaningless to us – only the name of Jesus and his church. Affairs quickly improved and we found the language of 'relaunching the church in partnership' very useful; it conveyed the sense that each church was in partnership with the other, and that we were also in partnership with our two church schools, the local community and the diocese. Mostly, however, it conveyed that we were in partnership with Jesus. We recovered our worship as we focused on building the Kingdom of God and letting go of trying to gain glory for any other name than the name of Jesus.

It's peculiarly shocking that strong views on worship are often what causes divisions in a church, or else what turns it inwards upon itself until it's little more than a private members' club for those who appreciate a certain style. This is the complete opposite of true worship, which reminds us that it is not *my* church but God's alone. If 'our' churches are actually fully under God's ownership and control then he's perfectly entitled to do with them whatever he wants. He can give a church to someone else to run without needing to explain anything to us. To worship God is to deny ourselves and all we own or control and surrender it all to God. Worship reminds me that the world doesn't revolve around us and our views; it revolves around Jesus and his views. Worship puts Jesus back at the heart of every individual, every family, every church, every town and therefore every nation. As I worship I sometimes imagine myself switching positions with Jesus in my life, picturing, in my mind's eye, driving along in a car with Jesus at the wheel instead of me. Worship is about me letting God be the driver and accepting his invitation to be his passenger. Worship reflects God's character; thereby keeping

God's core values central. It keeps love, mercy and justice as the central aims and attributes of our lives and the life of our churches.

To resist spiritual pride when I worship, I frequently raise my hands in a posture of surrender; when in prayer, I'll occasionally fall to my knees in total submission. Curiously, I have found myself growing in confidence as I focus more on Christ and less on myself. In Exodus 17 Moses worships in the face of dire circumstances. He overlooked the field of battle as the people of God fought for their very lives. Moses' contribution wasn't military strategy, though; it was worship. He stood with hands held high in praise. Such was the dependency of that battle on the quality of Moses' worship that when his arms got heavy and his hands fell, the battle started to turn against them and others rushed in to help him keep worshipping. Surely our success is ultimately not conditional on anything we do, but on the grace of God only. However, propped up by Aaron and Hur, Moses worshipped as the battle raged and his praise continued until the battle was won – or perhaps it's more accurate to say that the battle continued until Moses' worship session was complete.

At one national conference during our second year, I sat next to a bishop who started pumping me with increasingly aggressive questions about St Swithun's. After a while he brutally turned away, muttering, 'Humph! It all sounds like a bit of a heroic leader model.' I was mortified. I honestly didn't think that's how I'd talked about it. I knew too that he was right about that model being a danger. Although I know better, I'm sometimes tempted to put celebrity church leaders on a pedestal so they can be my heroes too. But that particular day I felt the accusation was unfair. I had been invited to speak at the conference about what I had seen God do, and had tried to be both humble and confident. However mistaken it was on that occasion, the admonishing I received was a useful reminder to me that I must genuinely work against any pride within, rather than learn a well-practised rhetoric of humility. A deep life of prayer and worship always seems to accompany those people I've met in whom the quality of humility seems so rich. He might wear a fetching purple shirt, a large cross and a bishop's ring but one bishop I know has trousers that always appear worn at the knees. I know why: nearly every time I pray with him he falls to his knees and simply says, 'Come, Holy Spirit.' He also kneels to say the Lord's Prayer whenever he boils a kettle to make a hot drink.

Pride leads to spiritual complacency and that presents the devil with the opportunity to bring about great evil in and through our lives. When King David was at his peak he made a fatal and wicked error: instead of going out with his army to war, he relaxed in his palace. There he saw a beautiful woman bathing, and, blinded by his own power, he took advantage of her and had her husband killed. Their love child died. Even so, their next child, Solomon, became a great king in the ancestry of Jesus (Matthew 1:6). God has an endless ability to redeem any situation, no matter how bad and messed-up it gets. The story also teaches us something about worship: that progress in our spiritual battles is tied to quality in our worship. King David showed us how *not* to do it by turning away from his calling to battle and lusting after a woman rather than loving after God. He committed adultery and murder rather than remain faithful to his calling. In David's errors we see how we can succeed: we are to pursue our calling to battle, full of passionate love for God. When, as a result of worship, we're full of God's love for us, and of our love for God, it's impossible not to love the world around us. It is then impossible not to advance in power. Great worship starts and fuels that virtuous cycle, and poor worship is the reason it falters.

One Thursday night early in 2015, Debi and I had the huge privilege of being invited to Abbey Road studios in London to sing along at a live recording of Matt Redman's worship album *Unbroken Praise*. We don't usually mix in circles anywhere near that cool, so it was a real treat for us and we were a little bit star-struck. Just as we were about to go in, from which point you have to turn off all phones, I got a call saying there had been a fire back at St Swithun's, with the police and firefighters in attendance suspecting arson. The various reports were bewildering and Debi and I didn't know what to do. We were at least three hours away and the truth was that we couldn't have done very much anyway – the team back in Bournemouth was doing everything that could be done. Still, it was pretty dramatic, possibly dangerous, and we weren't there. We felt helpless. There was nothing we could do, was there? Then the penny dropped with us. There *was* something we could do: we could worship. We realised that God had so arranged things that while the church we led was under attack, we would be led in worship by one of the world's finest worship leaders. That night we really gave ourselves in worship and as I lifted my hands I understood a tiny bit more of what it means to lead.

I get to meet a lot of leaders now who want to plant churches. They want to talk all about the place, the church, the project – just as I used to. I've learned to do for them what people far wiser than I did for me. I begin by asking them about their personal prayer and worship lives because at the core of every church is the senior leader's daily time of prayer. When we turn to discuss their plans for a church plant, I start by asking them about their plans for prayer and worship. Out of all the things that we can prepare and plan for, nothing is more important than that. Every church needs a worship leader. Every church needs lead worshippers. Every church needs leaders who worship.

During the planning phase of St Swithun's while we were still living in London, I had the enormous pleasure of meeting several times with Sandy Millar. Sandy was previously the Vicar of HTB and is now a retired bishop, still very much on fire for Jesus. I'd chatted to him a few times about the project from its infancy. When I was worried and anxious he taught me to trust in God's sovereignty. Once we met in a café near Putney Bridge. I'd been working on plans and budgets galore, drawing up documents for all the various decision-makers I was trying to convince to back the project at that time. I had files of documentation and had become so bogged-down in the detail that I'd lost the thread of what I was really doing – and I'd forgotten why I was doing it. Sandy visibly recoiled as I pushed the files across the table at him asking for his help to make sense of it all and to advise on what to do next. Then he looked at me quite sternly and said, 'Dear Tim, do try not to plan too much! All you want to do is to go down there and run up a flag, open the doors, and do what we do. But pray like mad that during those first weeks, months and years, someone gets healed. If God is there, word will get round.' Then he sat back, as though that was the sum total of his wisdom.

I didn't think much of Sandy's advice at the time: planning was all anyone else wanted from me. But I've reflected on it frequently ever since, asking God to etch on my heart: 'If God is there, word will get round.' Now it's like a mantra for us at St Swithun's that we ask of God and repeat to each other constantly. That's what we have seen: God has given us his presence. People have started to cry as they've walked through the doors on occasion – God is there and word has got round! I remember asking one newcomer why they'd come and recall the mystified look on their face as they replied, 'God's here. Why wouldn't I come?'

God's presence in our midst is what we pray for all the time; it's our number one prayer request. Our approach places great emphasis on encounter. Hospitality to us is much more than just being nice; it's our chance to display the character of God. I often tell our hospitality teams that they are the most important ministers there because they get to give people their first impression of who God might really be. They get the chance either to confirm or to break the negative preconceptions that newcomers will hold about the character of God and what church is like.

In Exodus 33 Moses asks God for his presence to be the defining difference between the community of God's people and any other community on earth. He says: 'If your presence doesn't take the lead here, call this trip off right now. How else will it be known that you're with me in this, with me and your people? Are you traveling with us or not? How else will we know that we're special, I and your people, among all other people on this planet Earth?' (Exod. 33:16, *The Message*). One translation has Moses asking, 'What else will distinguish me and your people from all the other people on the face of the earth?' (Exod. 33:16, NIV).

That God is with us is all that matters. One of Jesus' titles is 'Emmanuel', meaning 'God with us'. In life it's who we are and who we are *with* that determines our wellbeing. Our closest relationships cause us happiness or sadness. Everyone wants good relationships and intimacy, and we all fear isolation and loneliness. Unfortunately, our society has little sense of having God among us and many live with a sense of dislocation and loneliness. There are more single adults in our society now than ever before. The result is widespread loneliness. In the summer of 2014, just before we started St Swithun's, the *Guardian* described loneliness as 'a silent plague that is hurting young people most'. That same summer the *Telegraph* reported that there are five million people in Britain who feel they have no real friends, commenting on a study that found students are four times more likely than pensioners to feel lonely 'most of the time.'

Mother Teresa cautioned:

> The greatest disease in the West today is not Tuberculosis or leprosy; it is being unwanted, unloved, and uncared for. We can cure physical diseases with medicine, but the only cure for loneliness, despair, and hopelessness is love. There are many in the world who are dying for a piece of bread but there are many more dying for a little love . . . it is not only a poverty of loneliness but also of spirituality. There's a hunger for love, as there is a hunger for God.[1]

The presence of God satisfies our universal need for intimacy, that sense of being truly known and loved unconditionally.

Advertising executives are only too well aware that we have this need and try to propose their products as the answer to it. To do this they often use sex to sell. It's a tempting idea that we can find the intimacy we're craving by increasing our sexual attractiveness and so we're urged to equate success in life with the degree to which we achieve our sexual ambitions. The problem is it's a big fat lie: it doesn't work. Using sex to try and gain unconditional love in order to meet our need for intimacy is like using any other drug to self-medicate an unmet deep inner need: it only leaves us feeling more needy than ever. Sexual longings aren't wrong – they're good;

we are made for intimacy and we're not wrong to desire it. It's just that so many of us look to meet those needs in the wrong ways with the wrong people. But God helps us to find the right way. He made us, and he dreamed up sex in the first place.

I often hear Christian people describing their frustration at trying to communicate the gospel to friends who they love and are trying to witness to. They'll say things like, 'They're just so perfect, they're good looking, they're in love, they have plenty of money, they have a beautiful home and they're happy. They have no need of Jesus whatsoever.' We must refuse to believe that is true, because it never is. Everyone needs Jesus. And anyway, accepting that the claims of Jesus are actually true and placing our trust in him is a decision that we must all make irrespective of success, health or ability. As it happens, as I write this we have at least two tragic and very serious pastoral situations going on with people who, if you'd met them only a few weeks ago, you'd have been tempted to think that they had perfect lives. It is heartbreaking to see the catastrophe unfolding as sin is discovered. I've only been in ordained ministry ten years but I've learned already that sooner or later things will surely happen in life that shatter such manicured facades. We need to be there when they do, demonstrating love, grace and practical help, not standing back moralising and saying, 'I told you so!' No one is beyond God's grace, forgiveness and healing. Anyone who turns to God will discover that he is willing and able to meet our core need for intimate, unconditional love and transform and restore any life. That's why Jesus came to earth.

On the Sunday following the death of Billy Graham we cancelled our preaching plans and instead screened the last film he'd recorded for the UK at all of our services. It had a huge impact and over twenty people came forwards that day to commit their lives to

Christ. One of them was a beautiful young woman who'd had a debilitating problem with self-harming for years that had led her to the brink of suicide many times. As she watched the film she was filled with the Holy Spirit and set free there and then: she fully understood that Jesus' blood had been spilled for her, taking all her pain away and replacing it with the love of God. Afterwards, she wrote to me telling her story, ending by saying:

I have only recently started coming to St Swithun's and I really feel the presence of God during the services and the overwhelming feeling that I have found the home I was looking for and where God wants me to be. I am hoping that in time I can be baptised there. My thirtieth birthday was spent in a cardiac intensive care unit, hopeless and broken and extremely afraid but with the vague idea that God in his mercy had given me a second chance. Next Sunday I will turn thirty-one, which in itself is a miracle, and I am full of excitement for the future and peace is growing within me. My fear is turning to faith and I know that God will take care of me if I let him. My life, and the world, make so much more sense to me with Jesus in it and I am so grateful.

Chapter 12

Battleship, not cruise ship

> For we are God's handiwork, created in Christ Jesus to do
> good works, which God prepared in advance for us to do.
> Ephesians 2:10

There are many upsides to being linked to the HTB family of churches. However, HTB has become a bit of a brand among those who are highly churched, who often imagine it's about a great gathered experience – worship, preaching and a range of helpful courses – which is simply a caricature of a church whose real nature is much deeper and wider. As with most large churches, its growth owes much more to its zeal in real-world evangelism, its effectiveness in community-based discipleship, and its enabling of believers to put their God-given gifts to work for the coming of God's Kingdom. All that happens outside of what you'll see on a Sunday if you visit.

I knew there was a danger that some churched people might visit St Swithun's and perceive it to be a show they could enjoy but not really input into. The church doesn't have a membership list; instead, we say that while all are welcome to come and receive, our vision is that everyone who counts themselves a member will pray

175

and worship regularly, everyone will serve in some way, and everyone will give. Aware of a number of visitors from other churches in Bournemouth in the months immediately after we opened, I announced that we were here for unchurched younger generations: existing Christians were welcome to join in if they felt called by God and were commissioned by their existing church to do so; otherwise, while we thanked them for visiting, we asked them to return to their church. I didn't want unchurched visitors feeling crowded out and suspected that if masses of churched people came it would all feel very 'churchy'. I warned existing Christians that if they wanted to join it would be hard work and found myself using an image that may be attributable to John Wimber or Sandy Millar: as a church we are more like a battleship than a cruise ship; we don't take passengers. I still warn the congregation now that if you're on board then you're in the crew and my advice is to find a job that you want to do before you're asked to do one that you don't. As I mentioned earlier, we certainly will also serve as a hospital ship and seek the healing and wholeness of everyone we encounter. But out of respect and love for everyone who comes we seek to speak life into one another in the name of Jesus and stand against the enemy's deception that anyone is without worth, hope or ability. We believe that every person is made by God, known by God, loved by God and has a God-given identity and gifts. Jesus gave his life for every person to demonstrate how much God loves them. The Holy Spirit is ready to live within anyone who will ask and pour God's love into them and every person is therefore of inestimable worth to God. This earth-shattering mindset is paradigmatic for every Christian and has inspired the church throughout history to break injustice and oppression.

Of course, it's easy to talk like this. But helping deeply damaged people rediscover their God-given sense of hope, worth and ability takes time and a lot of love from many compassionate people. To a greater or lesser extent, we've all been damaged by past sin and we all need the help of others to recover from it; we'll also all need that help again at some point in the future because no one is perfect and the ageing process will make us dependent on others anyway. So we love and serve one another here knowing that, sooner or later, we'll be the ones requiring help. I guess a proof of all this actually happening within any church would be in the strength of its volunteer teams. You might think that's just a function of the size of a church but I'd disagree. In my experience so far, welcoming newcomers and properly connecting them into groups, ministries and teams gets harder as the church gets bigger. As I write this, we're actually on the cusp of reinventing our entire approach because having reached an average Sunday attendance of six to seven hundred our historic system, which seemed to work well when we were below five hundred, simply isn't effective anymore and that's causing problems, letting people down and hindering further growth.

I believe it's crucial not just to support key volunteers but to thank them consistently and celebrate what's being achieved. During our first summer we threw a big party for all the volunteers in the church. It has become an annual fixture and we love it. We strung up festoons down the church drive, booked a hog roast and some of the guys put together a covers band. Late that night I sat back overjoyed. Less than a year after we'd started, I could see two hundred people laughing, eating, drinking and dancing the night away under the stars. It was such a celebration and you can't beat that. God is deeply into teams.

A few months later I was putting together a mortgage application to buy the building we had been renting. The bank advised me that, along with strategy documents, factual reports and financial forecasts, what they really wanted to know about was our team. The bank manager told me:

> It's all too easy to write a strategy and populate a spreadsheet. But the bank will be entrusting the money to a team of people – they're the most decisive factor in your success or failure. So we want to know about who we're lending to just as much as we want to know about what their plans are. At the end of the day it's about trust – not in the strengths of a pretty project plan but in the strengths of your team.

As I began to gather brief biographies of our leadership team for the bank, I saw what a phenomenal team God had drawn together.

One volunteer on the marriage course typifies the character of so many. Phil started helping out on the course even though he was single because he believed that marriage was a good thing and wanted to help. So he offered to help the catering team as well as the production team. One night he parked outside and in doing so disturbed a homeless guy who can be very charming and very unpleasant in equal measure – he's unpredictable and volatile. He was sleeping in the fire escape and Phil advised him to move because they'd be opening the venue up soon and would be checking the doorways. I'm not great when I'm woken up either, but this man was really threatening towards Phil and muttered, 'I'll give you fire exits. I'll get you – and your car.' Phil apologised again for disturbing his sleep but politely reiterated the need to move on in order to keep the fire exits clear. Shortly after Phil had gone inside, one of the other volunteers arrived and rushed in saying, 'Phil, your car's on fire!' And so it was. Many suspected that the homeless guy had lit a fire underneath Phil's car in revenge.

The fire service was called and they promptly extinguished the fire but the car was a write-off. The police came too and together they began to investigate, knowing it was highly unlikely that a parked car in good working order would suddenly burst into flames after half an hour. However, Phil did everything he could to dissuade them from suspecting a malicious cause and, in the end, convinced them to stop their investigation. If he was bothered about his car, it didn't show. Phil said 'it's only metal, no one was hurt,' and persuaded everyone that it was probably caused by an electrical fault. Do you know why? He didn't want any homeless people blamed. He was sure that news of a revenge arson attack by a homeless person would make it harder to get other volunteers and churches involved in homeless ministries. That's just so inspiring to me; it's such a Christ-like attitude.

I don't particularly like the word 'volunteer' because to me it lacks a sense of value and ownership over the roles that people take up. At church we very rarely draw up lists of our 'volunteer needs', but we do regularly sit back and consider individuals trying to figure out who they really are and where they'd be best placed in service. That way people will flourish and roles will be performed to a high standard: the church wins twice over. Sometimes people come into the church with such low self-esteem that they feel they have nothing to give. As gently as I can, I respectfully disagree with them and try to empower a belief that God has enriched them with unique gifts and experiences that the church will always be short of until they put them into play. One such guy was my friend Andy.

As a young kid, Andy had attended his family's traditional church, even joining in as a bellringer. But, as his teens approached, football took over and he was scouted from club to club working towards a professional career until, aged seventeen, he snapped his cruciate ligament. He dropped out and fell in with a bad crowd, quickly becoming involved in a local gang. Discovering the mind-bending effects of drugs and alcohol, he took part in drugs-crazed escapades that became increasingly dangerous and illegal. Vandalism and joyriding gave way to theft and eventually smash-and-grab raids on shops. He was soon caught by the police red-handed and received a twelve-month prison sentence, serving six months. This short, sharp shock did little to dent his enthusiasm for crime, most of which he hid from his girlfriend, with whom he had a baby daughter. He was a terrible father. When opportunities came to get in on the eye-watering profits that could be made from dealing drugs, Andy grasped them with both hands. Three years later he was arrested for possession and intent to supply, with three 10lb bags of heroin and £840 cash stuffed in his pockets. By this time Andy had himself become addicted to heroin. He was sentenced to three years in prison and handed an order to pay £54,000.

When Andy got out of jail he was clean from drugs and stayed clean, eventually moving to Bournemouth with a new girlfriend. He felt life was offering him a fresh chance. By 23 December 2008 he'd been clean and had no contact with drugs for five years. That morning, Andy stepped out of the door of the flat his girlfriend had found near an area called Boscombe, and knew he was in trouble: the place was awash with drugs and dealers. He wasn't in work and had plenty of cash on hand from a house he'd sold. Sadly, he started using again and in no time at all had burned through £10,000 of savings. His girlfriend tried her best to stay with him and help him but by 2012 admitted defeat and left. Andy found himself addicted, penniless and, being unable to afford the rent, with no secure income and a serious drug habit, homeless. He started shoplifting and spent several short spells in prison as a result. In 2014 Andy's body began to shut down owing to the drugs and he began to suffer seizures that became increasingly severe and regular. That winter, he had a seizure during which he ruptured his spleen and fractured his ribs. Thankful to be in hospital, a single thought swirled around his broken mind: he believed he was dying and would never again see his daughter, who had already been missing from his life for ten years.

Out of hospital and once more living on the streets, Andy somehow stayed clean and turned up at the crisis homeless shelter that St Swithun's hosted in partnership with several other local churches. There he met a volunteer called Paul Noble, who befriended him and helped him move into local secure accommodation. Andy began to come to all that he could at St Swithun's, attending the end of that term's Recovery Course to face up to his addictions and then on to Alpha. On Alpha, Andy discovered the God he never knew; he received deep forgiveness and began to live again. Out of the collapsed shell of a broken man, a new Andy began to emerge. We talked long into the evenings and prayed often, as did his whole Alpha group and many others at church. As Andy prayed, God helped him rebuild his life and he stayed clean. He began to serve in many ways at church, joining the Alpha team for the next course and helping at the homeless shelter the next winter. One desire became stronger and stronger as he repeated it over and over in prayer, 'God, I'd love to see my daughter.' Sadly, there was no hope of that happening. Andy had burned the bridges with his own mother long ago, the only remaining link to his daughter.

One Sunday, early in the summer of 2017, I remember seeing Andy at the afternoon service. He was beaming. His brother had texted him, having somehow been contacted by his daughter's social worker, to ask if Andy would be willing to see his daughter, just once, as she felt she needed some answers to move on in life. We calmed him down and told him not to expect anything from her. He went to Birmingham for the meeting and we all prayed like mad. When he saw her, Andy told her the whole truth, including his conversion, and apologised to her, stopping short of asking her for forgiveness as he didn't even want to put that on to her, feeling he had no right to ask anything of her. The tears flowed on both sides. On the way out of the meeting Andy saw his mum sitting in a car but walked on, not wanting to put a foot wrong with anyone. One month later the social worker called him again, asking if he'd return for another meeting, this time with his mother attending too. Once again, Andy told the whole truth, retelling the story of his conversion as a Christian, and assured them that he loved them even though he could not expect their love in return. Andy now speaks two to three times a week with his mum and is in regular contact with his daughter who, to Andy's huge pride and with wonderful irony, is now at university studying for a law degree in Criminology.

Chapter 13

Finding freedom

It is for freedom that Christ has set us free.
Stand firm, then, and do not let yourself be burdened
again by a yoke of slavery.
Galatians 5:1

Where the Spirit of the Lord is there is freedom.
2 Corinthians 3:17

We've seen how Bournemouth has a massive problem with drug addiction and homelessness. When we were planning St Swithun's we knew it would be a driving factor in our approach. Official government statistics released in 2015 revealed that Bournemouth has the UK's highest proportion of benefit claimants unable to work because of alcohol and drug addiction.[1] Council officials point to the high number of unregulated rehab venues as a root cause.[2] Some of those are close to the site of St Swithun's, with many others in the parish of our first church plant at St Clement's in Boscombe. Bournemouth also has one of the highest rates of homelessness anywhere on the South Coast.

Having first opened our doors for Sunday services on 14

September 2014, we were quickly confronted by addiction and homelessness. Before we reopened it the closed site had become something of a magnet for both conditions. That winter the town's crisis shelter couldn't find a home anywhere and they asked if we could help. At that point we had not yet moved into the church hall on our site, choosing instead to focus on getting the main building up and running. Our leadership group didn't talk about it for too long. We didn't feel at all ready or equipped for it, but nevertheless we felt compelled – so we just did it. None of us was comfortable with the notion of walking past homeless people that winter knowing that we had the keys to a warm, dry, empty venue in a perfect location, that we'd been simply too scared to open for them. So on 1 December 2014 we opened a homeless shelter and kept it open every night throughout that first winter. The scheme is now shared with other churches, which is a great model because although it was a great privilege to host the shelter here all winter, it did place quite a burden on the church.

At about the same time, two incredible women began to worship with us: Emma, whose story I mentioned earlier, and Susie. They were both former alcoholics who had come to faith in Jesus and seen their lives completely transformed as a result. They felt called to start up a ministry to reach addicts in the town and support them through a recovery process. A friend of mine, Nigel Skelsey, came down to speak one Sunday in our second term in the New Year. He is a deliciously maverick, huge, straight-speaking character with a total contempt for false religion but an utmost regard for the person and mission of Jesus. Formerly a successful journalist, photographer and high-functioning addict, Nigel has devoted his life more recently to helping addicts experience the freedom uniquely available for them in Jesus. He lit a fire in these two women as well as in me, and from that point we planned to start an addiction recovery ministry. Emma and Susie were both busily employed in regular jobs but so full of enthusiasm to start things up that I had to battle to hold them back. I was desperate not to begin a project without a really strong team in place, because I knew that without it we'd be quickly overrun and chaos could ensue. So Emma and Susie gathered a team and they trained and prayed together until March 2015, when we launched our first Recovery Course.

We all want to be free. No one wants to be tied down or restricted: my three young children certainly don't; they find sitting on their chair at meal times nearly impossible; school ties and top buttons are branded as 'strangling'; straps on bike helmets are hated and car seatbelts have to be constantly reinforced. But give them the freedom of a football pitch, beach or large garden and they're away, free at last. Anyone who's had to teach their toddler to make the transition from a cot with bars to a bed at night will know what I'm talking about. Children have an innate desire to break free.

Often we are less free than we like to imagine. I have several bad habits that I'd like to break but find myself incapable of doing so. These sins of mine are never quite as private as I'd hope and always reduce not just my own freedom but the freedom of others around me. Even if we seem free on the outside, there's a kind of inner freedom we can lose: when we hold on to the hurt, anger and vengeance of wrong that has been done to us, we lose our freedom and get bound up on the inside. When we hold on to the shame, guilt and resentment we feel for having done wrong things, or for having wrong things done to us, we lose our freedom. A loss of freedom isn't just the price we pay for our own sin; we reduce other people's freedom too and their sins affect us. Tragically, this lost freedom can often be all-encompassing – think of the long-term emotional damage caused by abuse for instance.

The nagging sense of lost freedom, what the Bible calls 'condemnation', is extremely powerful. It refuses to be drowned out by alcohol or drugs. No amount of self-inflicted pain can silence it and no amount of sexual encounters can restore our lost sense of worth and value. Although these choices may provide fleeting relief by obliterating all other thoughts and emotions in that moment, they hasten our decline into a deeper pit. Our sins enslave us and they enslave others. Addictions to drugs, alcohol, gambling or pornography are obvious examples of lost freedom. If we can't choose *not* to do an activity, we've lost our freedom. Jesus labelled such things thieves and liars, saying that they, 'come to steal, kill and destroy' (John 10:10). How right he was! I'm opposed to hard drugs not only on moral grounds, but also because they promise an ecstatic fantasy and in the end deliver the exact opposite: utter misery. They lie. In that sense they are truly demonic.

From the outset, we've tried very hard at St Swithun's to resist the world's 'them and us' approach when it comes to people who are addicted or homeless, any more than when it comes to bankers and doctors. Actually, at St Swithun's there is no 'them and us' on any issue. Just 'us' – we're in it together. No one in a church should live life on their own because a church is a community, a family. You don't have to be addicted to crack cocaine to know what it feels like to be unable to choose to stop doing something destructive or self-comforting. We're all addicted to a life of sin, the very thing that Jesus is trying to bust us out of. So at St Swithun's we never look down on those who are in the process of breaking free from addictions. By contrast, the world heaps shame on them. I've spoken to many addicts whose self-perpetuating sense of guilt and shame is the biggest barrier to their coming forward to receive the help that's available. But that's not how they're received nor viewed by God nor anyone at St Swithun's. We just think, 'Yup, you're one of us.'

One of the most distressing features to see in those who have been in addiction is the deeply destructive effect on their mental and emotional health. Jesus once met an infamously violent man who was so deeply under the influence of demonic forces that he simply called himself 'Legion' (Mark 5:1–20; Matt. 8:28–34; Luke 8:26–37). A Legion was a Roman regiment of six thousand troops. This guy was completely overwhelmed by everything that had gone wrong in his life; we don't know the details but we do know the results. He was mentally and emotionally derailed, isolated and estranged from his family and friends, and in deep confusion and distress. He was clearly known as a very violent person because the local population treated him like a wild animal and chained him up, although he frequently escaped. He self-harmed by cutting and thought of himself as dead inside, so much so that the Bible says he 'lived among the tombs'. He was abused by others and tormented inside. His life was in total disarray and he felt his whole person was occupied by other evil personalities. He'd lost his freedom in nearly every respect imaginable.

I've noticed sometimes how people who have been through unspeakable horrors in life frequently have a keen spiritual insight, but, cruelly, their experiences have left them with an incorrect and very negative view of God's nature. They've come to see that evil really does exist on the one hand, but don't know who God really is on the other. They're sometimes hard to help because they see themselves as a lost cause, beyond redemption and without hope.

But we never do. They see God as judging and unknowable and think of themselves as cursed. The Bible says this is what the world looked like to Legion who, 'When he saw Jesus from a distance . . . ran and fell on his knees in front of him. He shouted at the top of his voice, "What do you want with me, Jesus, Son of the Most High God? In God's name don't torture me!"' (Mark 5:7).

Legion had spiritual insight but an entirely false view of God. Jesus does *not* want to torture the oppressed but do the exact opposite: he wants to set them free. Jesus said this about himself at the outset of his public ministry: 'The Spirit of the Lord is on me, because he has anointed me . . . to proclaim freedom for the prisoners . . . to set the oppressed free' (Luke 4:18). That day, Jesus set Legion free from every evil that had enslaved him.

When we encounter Jesus we can experience freedom too, just like Legion. But how can we experience Jesus now? He's not physically here on earth but here by his Spirit. Jesus said that was even better for us (John 16:7) – not least because he could then be everywhere rather than in one physical place, even taking up residence within us. The Apostle Paul writes, 'Now the Lord is the Spirit, and where the Spirit of the Lord is, there is freedom' (2 Cor. 3:17). To encounter Jesus is to encounter the Holy Spirit, and to receive the Holy Spirit is to gain the keys to freedom. When we pursue Jesus we find freedom.

Many of us fear that submitting to Jesus will actually *reduce* our freedom, but nothing could be further from the truth. The exact opposite occurs: in Jesus we find our freedom; it starts on the inside so at first it's often in spite of our circumstances. But Jesus is very much interested in changing our outer circumstances too. As a deranged demoniac, Legion could break chains but he was very much *not* free. However, once in his right mind as a free man, he chooses to sit in submission at the feet of Jesus. The man experienced recovery of that rare dramatic sort which is full and instantaneous deliverance. I sometimes wonder why we don't see more of that happening today. I'm sure the fact that the church as a whole tends not to attempt it is a factor; it may be, however, that most of us couldn't handle being given that degree of freedom so quickly. I've seen it go wrong several times when a recovering addict receives with great euphoria their first taste of freedom but, realising they're an addict no more, then expresses this freedom by going on a bender, returning to the very thing that enslaved them in the first place. Although the man Jesus delivered got full, total freedom immediately, he didn't freak out. Perhaps God in his mercy and wisdom allows most of us to grow into our freedom over time, step by step. This is exactly what the Recovery Course helps people to do over a number of weeks.

Whenever I speak to these walking miracles of deliverance in our community, I'm reminded not only of Jesus' victory over the demons that ruled Legion, but of his victory over all sin and the devil himself. The writer of Revelation promises us that at the end of time we're going to look down on the devil and be surprised at how small and weak he is. We're going to shake our heads and say, 'That's the devil? That's the one who caused so much damage?' (Isaiah 14:16–17). And Jesus is going to destroy him not through any actions – it doesn't need that – nor even words. The Bible states that just his arrival and a single breath will be enough (2 Thess. 2:8). If the devil really isn't that powerful, after all, then how do we end up in so many problems; how do we lose our freedom so easily?

The Bible shows us that the devil's main way of attacking us is to impact our thinking, causing us to doubt God's good character and tempting us to pursue our own desires. The devil asks us to imagine a world free from the control of a restrictive God who does not want us to flourish. Satan wants to trick us into accepting the false premises inherent in everything he suggests. Every statement the devil ever suggests to us will be based on the false premise that God is not good and is not sovereign. We accept these lies partly because we want to be in control of our own lives and partly because the existence of human suffering seems to support them. But God is good and God is sovereign. Deep down I believe we all want leaders under whom we can flourish and realise our greatest potential. That's the truth about who God is; he is the ultimate good leader for our lives. How can we defend our thinking to retain the freedom that Christ has won for us?

The Apostle Paul, picturing the protective equipment that every Christian needs in battle, told the churches in Ephesus and Thessalonica that to protect themselves from the enemy they'd need to put on a 'helmet of salvation' (Eph. 6:17, 1 Thess. 5:8). We all have to protect our minds by constantly recalling Jesus, who he is to us and what he has done for us. Paul has in mind a serious piece of protective headgear: it's not like a baseball cap; it's like a motorcycle helmet! I used to ride motorbikes and I can vouch that a helmet has a very weird effect. With it on you feel completely invincible and ready to take on the world. That's the impact Jesus has on us.

The battle is in our minds. I once went to a black Pentecostal church which I absolutely loved. There the preacher and congregation worked together to craft the sermon through a call-and-response partnership. In the middle of his exposition of one Scripture the preacher kept calling out the phrase, 'God is good!' to which the congregation kept replying, 'All the time!' God is good all the time. That's truth. Life may not always feel like it's true, but it's especially important in those moments that we remind one another that it is indeed true!

Jesus said: 'If you hold to my teaching, you are really my disciples. Then you will know the truth, and the truth will set you free . . . If the Son sets you free, you will be free indeed' (John 8:32, 36). Jesus' teaching shows us not just how to get free but how to stay free. He warns us that after we've experienced freedom we need to change the way we live, otherwise we can end up in a worse state than before. What do we change? First, we're not to use our freedom to indulge ourselves in the very things that enslaved us in the first place. That would be crazy – a kind of warped logic. Paul tells the Galatian church, 'Do not use your freedom to indulge the flesh; rather serve one another humbly in love' (Gal. 5:13).

Second, we've got to get a grip on our minds. Paul tells the Corinthian church 'We demolish arguments and every pretension that sets itself up against the knowledge of God, and we take captive every thought to make it obedient to Christ' (2 Corinthians 10:5). We do that by turning our thoughts to Christ, asking him to remake us into the people he made us to be. A restored relationship with our creator restores our true identity, and true freedom is becoming more and more ourselves. This is a fundamental aim of the Spirit's work in our lives, resisting the world's suffocating, conforming pressure and helping us to restore our God-given identity, one could say our birthright. As the influential psychologist Clare W. Graves put it, 'Damn it all, a person has a right to be who he is.'

Third, spiritual change is always resisted. Look at the response of the villagers in the story about Legion: Jesus had transformed that community, but even though he had freed and healed the one who had terrorised them, tragically they pleaded with Jesus to leave them alone. They were so fearful of change. Those in the St

Swithun's family who have experienced freedom can all tell stories about how not everyone in their lives was pleased for them. Some try and talk them out of it; others sneer. Recovering addicts know full well that their freedom will be tested. Old contacts and friends will want them to rejoin them in substance abuse, encouraging them to readopt the slavery of former addictions. It sounds senseless but it's very tempting. That's the life they knew. One of the things that has made me most angry is seeing drug dealers loitering outside our church site on Thursday evenings ready to try and sell to recovering addicts who have been attending the course inside. The local police help us stop that but we have to remain very vigilant.

Fourth, freedom means forgiveness – receiving forgiveness from God and extending it to others, and having done so to resist returning to resentful, angry thoughts. Paul tells the Ephesian church, 'In your anger do not sin: do not let the sun go down while you are still angry, and do not give the devil a foothold' (Eph. 4:26–7). Anger resulting from unforgiveness in our lives, gives the devil a foothold. Anger is a natural and important human emotion and can help drive us to resist oppression and right injustice; however, long-term, unexpressed and unresolved anger damages us and others, taking away freedom. We can so easily become consumed by hate that pollutes and diminishes any human heart over time. The antidote is to receive God's love and forgiveness, and to learn how to extend it. We'll often need the help of a friend, a prayer minister, a pastor or a counsellor to learn how to do that.

I certainly did. I found the help of prayer ministry, mentors and counselling so helpful in my own life. Having freed the man formerly known as Legion from the demons that enslaved him, Jesus does a very surprising thing. He didn't let the guy leave with him on the boat, but commissioned him to 'Go home to your own people and tell them how much the Lord has done for you, and how he has had mercy on you' (Mark 5:19). The man did exactly that. And an amazing thing happens: flick from Mark chapter 5 to chapter 7 and you'll see the impact he had: in Mark chapter 5 the people of the region beg Jesus to leave. He obliges them, but in his mercy leaves them just one witness – the man they'd previously been terrified of when he was enslaved by demons. What a powerful message of transformation that man must have taken back to his people, just as Jesus had told him to. By Mark chapter 7, when Jesus returns, they beg him to stay. They then bring all their sick and enslaved people to him. Mark 7:37 tells us that 'People were overwhelmed with amazement. "He has done everything well," they said.' That's the impact we all can have to transform the places where God has put us, to bring the freedom that Jesus has given us to others.

In his life, death and resurrection, Jesus secured victory over the devil. On the cross we see an amazing exchange: Jesus dies in our place taking on our sin, and we take on his life. Jesus took on to himself all the power of every evil in our lives that takes away our freedom, and in return he gives us his wonderful, freeing life and power. The Bible says that power is our inheritance and Paul describes it as

His incomparably great power for us who believe. That power is the same as the mighty strength he exerted when he raised Christ from the dead and seated him at his right hand in the heavenly realms, far above all rule and authority, power and dominion, and every name that is invoked, not only in the present age but also in the one to come (Eph. 1:19–21).

This power, this victory of Jesus, is available for us today, even though we live in the midst of an evil that is still retreating.

The theologian Oscar Cullmann saw the 'now and not yet' experience of life for a follower of Jesus as being analogous to someone who lived during the period of time in the Second World War between D-Day (when allied troops landed on mainland Europe and began to push the enemy back) and V-E Day (when the final victory was claimed). The decisive battle occurred for us on the cross and is realised by us at the point of our conversion. But the battle continues for us all as we defeat the retreating enemy, until a future moment of final victory. This analogy means a lot to me because, as I've recounted, my grandfather on my mother's side was in that war and was part of the army that saw total victory and the liberation of Europe from the evil grip of the Nazis. He got his finger shot off and saw many terrible things, but he survived to tell the tale.

I used to love hearing him tell war stories as a child. One story was of arriving at a French village, driving his truck in a convoy to resupply the frontlines. They were told that the village had most probably been mined by the retreating German army and had not yet been cleared. There was no viable alternative route and the frontlines had to be resupplied immediately so the convoy had been ordered to take its chances and drive through the village.

The Commanding Officer approached my grandad in the cab of his truck and said, 'Albert, you're a Christian, aren't you?' My grandad replied that he was. So the CO said, 'Well since you know where you're going when you die, you can drive an empty front truck, and the rest of the convoy will follow your tyre tracks. If you get through the mines, so will we. If you get blown up, we'll know to take a different route!' Grandad said a prayer, set off, and drove straight through the village without incident.

Likewise, having rescued us, given us our freedom and secured the final victory, Jesus sends us back into the world to join him in bringing freedom to others, even at great cost and sacrifice to ourselves. My grandad's story is certainly heroic; but it also reminds me that followers of Christ are already dead to the world and have nothing to lose – but everything to gain – by giving their lives in order to save others around them. My grandad's faith was transformative not just for his own life, but for the lives of many others. This is what Jesus has done for each of us, and what we are commanded to do for others.

I love hearing testimonies in our services from those who have had their lives transformed by Jesus, often by attending Alpha, the Recovery Course, or through other ministries and courses. I'm frequently struck that the change in their heart can also be seen so visibly in their faces. At the beginning of the Recovery Course I have met lovely people whose faces are nevertheless drawn, their heads drooped in defeat and their eyes cast downwards in shame. But as the inner state of their lives is transformed, so their bodies and whole demeanour change. They blossom like flowers.

It just happens that there are a number of professional and amateur photographers who worship at St Swithun's, and in May 2016 they decided to club together and put on a photographic exhibition called 'Transformed Lives', displaying the portraits of those whose lives had been changed in some way by church. Alongside each photo was a short testimony written by each subject, telling their story. It was a fantastic and deeply moving exhibition. I watched visitor after visitor first glance at a portrait photo, then read the story, and return to the portrait again to gaze at a life transformed by Christ, some weeping as they did so.

Chapter 14

How to lose £0.5m in thirty seconds

Set a guard over my mouth, Lord;
keep watch over the door of my lips.
Psalm 141:3

Soon after we started our morning service I mentioned to the small congregation that we'd like to buy some Bibles if anyone felt called to give us some money to do so. After that service a seventy-year-old woman came up to me and asked, 'Why do you want to buy Bibles?' I stumbled out, 'Well, err, we're a church whose faith is rooted in Scripture, so we want people to be able to read the Bible.' 'So do I, you dummy,' said the lady. 'It's all here on my phone but what I needed this morning was a good Wi-Fi connection. Why don't you get that instead?' With that she whipped out her phone, which I noted was the very latest iPhone, and waved it in my face. I'd just like to record in print that this beautiful woman didn't look seventy and knew me well enough to talk to me straight: she was my mother.

St Swithun's was, is and always will be an experiment. That first day when Ric Thorpe and I visited Bournemouth, the archdeacon showed us around various churches that were in need of something new happening. We concluded that there was indeed great potential at every location he showed us. In more and more places there are opportunities for church planting, because existing leaders and congregations are welcoming new schemes with open arms. Contrary to popular myth, I've often found that many older people in churches are some of the most forward-looking and ready for change.

As the archdeacon slowed to park at the last site he wanted to show us, he said apologetically, 'I hesitate even to show you this site. It's highly unlikely that it would ever become available and even more unlikely that we'd ever be able to afford it. And there's almost no way we'd be allowed to set up here.' He paused briefly and then continued more firmly, 'But I think we should be considering everything at this stage and I didn't want to keep it from you. I'll tell you one thing right now, though: if it ever happened here we could be sure it was God, because on human terms this is the most impossible site in Bournemouth.' We walked around the outside and noted that it was directly across the street from the Bournemouth University Students Union building and very close to several offices housing entrepreneurial digital companies where creative young professionals were doing exciting things. Then we walked inside and found a massive, empty box, almost entirely cleared of all the usual ancient visual cues of traditional churches. There were several side rooms and a hall which was in need of a new lick of paint, but basically in sound order. I looked at Ric and he looked at me: we both knew what the other was thinking. This was it. It was St Swithun's.

I discovered that St Swithun's was itself originally a church plant built in 1882. In those days they didn't look for existing sites, but built whole new facilities. Oh my, how the level of ambition in the Church of England has fallen! The guy who built it was Bournemouth's first vicar, the Revd Alexander Morden Bennett.

He was a gifted evangelist and a leader with seemingly limitless energy and vision. In his day he crossed both parish and diocesan boundaries to found schools for the poor and hold open-air meetings to evangelise Dorset's pottery workers. He was a maverick church planter motivated to enable everyone in society to encounter Jesus as he really is and his church as Jesus meant it to be. As a Tractarian and a mover and shaker within the so-called Oxford Movement that led to Anglo-Catholicism, Bennett's tradition was very different from my own. But I like to think we'd have got on.

It doesn't surprise me one bit that Revd Bennett decided to name the church plant after Saint Swithun. Dear old Swithun was cut from the same Jesus-revolutionary cloth as Bennett. Swithun was an Anglo-Saxon Bishop of Winchester from around 852 to 865. He was an outdoors man, deeply committed to planting churches in order to reach the unchurched and the poor. He loved those outside the church and liked nothing better than seeing them welcomed in. William of Malmesbury reports that at Swithun's own controversial request, he was buried outside the Old Minster in Winchester rather than inside it, so that his grave, 'might be subject to the feet of passers-by and to the raindrops pouring from on high'. However, in 971 he was adopted as the patron saint of the restored church and his body was transferred to a shrine inside it since it was thought inappropriate to leave a bishop's grave outside the building. Legend has it that there were many miraculous healings on that occasion but it also poured with rain and continued to do so for the following forty days. This was taken as a sign of Bishop Swithun's displeasure at being moved away from a position where he could monitor how many outsiders were being welcomed in.'[1]

Swithun had a reputation as an evangelist who performed sometimes bizarre miracles to authenticate the power of the gospel he so relentlessly proclaimed. He was an incessant planter and restorer, hence the many dedications to Swithun at churches across Southern England, especially in Hampshire, as well as in Western Norway. Oxford's Magdalen College also has a quadrangle dedicated to his honour. *The Golden Legend*, a medieval book of saints' stories, records: 'If any church fell down, or was in decay, St. Swithin would anon amend it at his own cost. Or if any church were not hallowed, he would go thither afoot and hallow it. For he loved no pride, ne to ride on gay horses, ne to be praised ne flattered of the people.'[2]

Moreover, William of Malmesbury observes that:

Though this good bishop was a rich treasure of all virtues, those in which he took most delight were humility and charity to the poor; and in the discharge of his episcopal functions he omitted nothing belonging to a true pastor. He built diverse churches, and repaired others; and made his journeys on foot, accompanied with his clerks, and often by night to avoid ostentation. Being to dedicate any church, he with all humility used to go barefoot to the place. His feasting was not with the rich, but with the needy and the poor. His mouth was always open to invite sinners to repentance, and to admonish those who stood to beware of falling. He was most severe to himself, and abstemious in his diet, never eating to satisfy his appetite, but barely to sustain nature; and as to sleep, he admitted no more than what after long watching and much labour was absolutely necessary. He was always delighted with psalms and spiritual canticles, and in conversation would bear no discourse but what tended to edification.'[3]

Swithun was uncompromising in his commitment to evangelism, social action and personal holiness. On top of all that, he was a church planter who had a refuse-to-die positive attitude. I'm proud to use his name on our site and I can well imagine how Revd Bennett got excited about all this too. Under Bennett's guiding vision the second half of the nineteenth century in Bournemouth saw a rush of church building as the local population grew. From St Peters in the town centre, Bennett planted three new parishes in fifteen years at Holy Trinity in 1867, St Michael in 1874 and St Stephen in 1882. He also built St Swithun's and All Saints' Branksome as chapels of ease. Further parishes were also carved out of Christchurch and Holdenhurst: St James Pokesdown in 1859, St Clement's in 1871, St John the Baptist Moordown in 1874 and St Catherine's Southbourne in 1885. Bournemouth's parishes continued to subdivide: St John the Evangelist from St Clements and St Paul from St Michael, both in 1890, and St Augustin from St Stephen in 1900. You can't help but admire the pace of ambition and action in church planting in those days.

However illustrious its history, by the 1990s St Swithun's was disused and deteriorating. Most fittings were removed by 1999, at which point it was purchased for £18,000 by Bournemouth Family Church (later Citygate), a Newfrontiers church. Citygate carried out extensive renovations including the roof and flooring, fitting new heating and electrical systems, building kitchen and toilets and an extension suite along the north side. The remaining fittings were moved to the sanctuary and the orientation reversed. Citygate also purchased the Tudor Hall that shares the site with the main building. In September 2013 Citygate relocated to a purpose-built new venue near the station leaving the site available for hire or purchase. And so it was that an opportunity presented itself for the Church of England to plant once again into the site.

When I first met the leaders of Citygate church here, Guy Miller and Andrew Lawrence, I was impressed by their godliness and their attitude. It seemed to me that they had what might be described as a Kingdom mindset that was focused on Christ, generous and able to see past denominational differences. If every church leader here had the attitude they'd had over the last twenty years, Bournemouth's society today would look very different. They've really been flying the flag for the gospel here for years now. And since getting to know them it doesn't surprise me one bit that Citygate continues to thrive as a large resource church for the whole Commission sphere within the great family of Newfrontiers.

The next eighteen months was a wild, unpredictable, rollercoaster. Like one of those scary rides built to feel as if it's literally falling apart underneath you. I've mentioned how at one point or another, everyone said 'no' to St Swithun's as at the time most people seemed to think that Bournemouth already had too many church buildings. Personally, I don't think there's anywhere near enough. In the end, the lease contract we signed on St Swithun's that contained a two-year purchase option as well meant that everyone would win: if only we could afford it, we would have a secure base for mission and Citygate would have the capital back to reinvest elsewhere.

We waited for 100 days, to see if the St Swithun's experiment looked as if it was working, and concluded that it was. By then we had about two-hundred-and-fifty regulars coming along. So I picked up the phone and began making calls, trying to find a way by which we could buy the premises. The restrictive covenants on our site, which made it much more difficult to secure commercial lending against it, presented awkward complications, but over time, as we explained things, met key decision-makers, wrote more planning documents, drafted cashflow budgets – and prayed like crazy – we eventually found a bank willing to lend some money. We also sourced some lending from within the Church of England's own structures too. It was miraculous: after just one year, we were on the brink of purchasing our own site. Four days before we were due to complete the deal, Debi and I dropped in on our solicitor to sign some final documents. After we had done so, our solicitor shook my hand and said, 'Congratulations! We're there!'

To this day I'm not sure what came over me but I replied, 'Thanks. To be honest, I didn't think it could happen. I'm still not sure how we convinced the bank to believe they could sell the property if we ever defaulted on our payments. I mean those restrictive covenants on the site really do affect its market value.' 'How do you mean?' asked the solicitor. And in the most mindless way, I outlined to him all the worst-case scenarios I could think of, missing out of course all the reasoning as to why they wouldn't occur. Blinded by my own pride at having stitched it all together I made the most stupid of blunders.

I left that meeting on cloud nine, happy that we'd signed on the dotted line and idiotically pretty smug about my success. The Bible promises us that as a principle of life 'pride precedes destruction; an arrogant spirit appears before a fall' (Pro. 16:18, ISV). That's definitely true. Because while I was walking out of that meeting feeling great, the solicitor felt worried. He emailed the bank checking with them that they really had looked closely at the restrictive covenants. The bank started to look again and while they did, asked the independent firm who had done the valuation to do the same thing. All those investigations came back negative. The bank could no longer lend us money. The deal was off.

Two days after I'd met the solicitor, our bank called me. I'll never forget that call. I was exhausted as I'd been working early and late and had fallen ill and our young children had been up in the nights too. I'd crept off to bed for a mid-afternoon power nap before heading out again that evening to more meetings. The bank manager was slightly embarrassed about the eleventh-hour rethink, but he delivered the bad news. I asked for time to think, ended the call and sank back into the pillow in a daze, as if having been given a knock-out punch. I realised what had happened – it had all gone wrong as a result of a single unguarded moment when I'd shot my mouth off. I felt ashamed and distraught and could barely pray anything other than, 'Help God!' I was embarrassed and I was angry. My mind began clicking through some aggressive options: how could I cause enough trouble to get them to change their minds? Could I call Citygate and tell them that the bank thought their site was worthless? Could I get the bank to cut their business with the valuation company if they didn't retract their revised view, because they were no longer reliable and trustworthy? Could I call the local newspaper and begin a campaign against the bank? But a single Scripture came to mind from Exodus 14:14: 'The Lord will fight for you; you need only be still.'

Sometimes it's harder to do nothing than it is to do something. But I resisted rushing around shaking all the trees I could think of; I simply shared the mistake I'd made with a few people and asked them to pray. I shared my mistake with my leadership team and the staff and asked them to pray too. I also tried hard not to be too harsh on myself, though I felt awful about it for the first few days. Then I stopped beating myself up. That wasn't going to help. I'd made a mistake; I'd admitted it and apologised; I'd learned from it and now I was focused on fixing it. I re-engaged all the parties and re-explained the basis for security. It helped that I used to be a chartered accountant so I could call on all of that experience. The funny thing is this, though: that's not what swung it. Someone senior at the bank got wind of the whole thing and intervened on the basis of supporting all the great charitable works we were carrying out for the community. To my knowledge, they weren't even a believer. They visited, liked what they saw and signed off on it. God had rescued me once again.

Chapter 15

Unblock the flow

And now what are you waiting for?
Get up, be baptised and wash your sins away,
calling on his name.
Acts 22:16

I love Easter. The annual focus on the cross and resurrection of Jesus always floors me in some new way. There are many Jewish people living in the immediate area around St Swithun's and just down the road is an Orthodox college linked to the very conservative local synagogue. I have a deep and enduring respect for all our local residents who put up with a lot of coming and going at all hours on our site. And I'm also mindful that Easter is a very significant time for both Jewish and Christian communities, with plenty of potential not only for friendship but also tension between them. A Christian friend with Jewish roots gave me an intriguing book by Brandt Pitre entitled *Jesus and the Jewish Roots of the Eucharist: Unlocking the Secrets of the Last Supper.*[1] So for our second Easter we held a Passover Meal together on Maundy Thursday. This celebrates the occasion of the Passover feast, the Last Supper that Jesus shared with his disciples, laying down the pattern for every

Communion, Mass or Eucharist that has followed. We wanted to get closer to the action, so about a hundred of us sat down to go through this meal together. We didn't put out any chairs and kept our coats on in the Passover style, ready to move.

It's amazing how much unleavened bread, dips, wine and lamb a hundred or so people can consume. For the whole day before the meal our house was filled with the smell of roasting lamb, with the herbs and spices that go into the various components of a seder or Passover meal. It was marvellous: I'd never led a seder meal before, and finding out about the order and significance of the components of the meal was fascinating. I found out that midway through the seder meal, the leader of the Jewish household would traditionally have taken the first sop, or morsel, of food and offered it to the most honoured guest at the table. Who did Jesus hand it to at the Last Supper? Judas. The one who was going to betray him later that same night, as Jesus knew full well. In the midst of the great themes and scenes of the Easter story, that one small act still blows me away.

In our second year on Easter Sunday over five hundred people turned up to celebrate. We had an amazing day, with dramas and performances and basically a huge knees-up celebrating the defeat of death and victory of new life in Christ. It was wonderful to worship Jesus anew in all those ways and I felt as though the church was beginning to mature. We'd been going eighteen months or so and we'd travelled beyond the initial phase of getting everything going. Equally, the adrenaline had begun to wear off; I felt myself becoming more tired and knew that this was affecting my leadership. My early morning quiet times had become much harder as I wrestled to wake my mind up and focus on Scripture and prayer. The minor discouragements and criticisms were landing a bit more personally with me than they used to. I knew it was time for a break, and fortunately we had a holiday booked after Easter. It was time to unplug, unwind and be recreated by doing something recreational.

We travelled up to Debi's parents' house in the North and spent simple, happy days playing football with our boys and teaching Rebekah to ride a bike. Debi and her parents then took the children over to York, to visit their great grandpa, and the excellent National Railway Museum to boot. That left me with the chance to go up to the Lake District with three friends to walk, climb, cycle and get generally cold, wet and muddy. Just the tonic I needed.

On the second afternoon of our outdoor adventure mini-break the guys wanted to climb up through a stream, which flows down the steep side of one of those glorious Lake District fells. They told me all about how they'd done it a few summers ago under a warm sun. Despite some sheer sections they assured me the route was fun, easy and involved minimal risk. But the Lake District had been in the news during the preceding months because of the continued heavy rainfall. When we arrived at the foot of the climb it was cold and raining; steel-grey skies gave the whole thing a menacing look. One glance at the stream that flowed past where we'd parked the car told us that conditions were quite different from the last time they'd been here. What had been a trickle before had now become a fast-flowing river. We watched the wide, churning torrent in silence for a moment, probably all thinking the same thing: is this a wise route to climb today? But still, the egos of four guys out on a climb and up for a challenge is virtually impossible to knock, and so we began our ascent.

The sheer power of the rushing water was mesmerizing. We quickly became soaked from the spray and all slipped on the early, supposedly easy sections. Inside, I was getting nervous, but the guys were experienced and tough, and inwardly I leant on their strength to push on. We reached one section which was a climb up the side of a series of waterfalls. The roar of the water was immense. In front of me, Andy, an able climber, seemed to run up the climb with ease and I began to follow. About halfway up I realised I was way out of my league and, glancing over my shoulder saw that going down would be as treacherous as continuing up. That glance was enough to shock me that falling here would be serious and, in these conditions, easy enough to do. By this stage, the water once contained in the middle stream was flowing over the rocks I was climbing. I had a moment of panic, pinned to the rock, gripping with all my might to the slippery, sketchy handholds I'd found. I knew the only way on was up. Making sure of every hold before moving, I slowly climbed on. The guys who had made it encouraged me, but unbeknown to me, they'd been signalling to each other about how much danger I was in and what to do about it. When I made it to the top, I felt exhilarated, but my jelly-legs reminded me how foolish I'd been. I stood looking at the river running past me, over me, through me, mesmerized by its power, considering anew the huge rocks it had moved and carved its way past.

Later that night after a hot bath and a relaxing evening with friends, I thought about King David's words as he grappled to describe God's overwhelming, yet intimate, power over his life: 'Deep calls to deep in the roar of your waterfalls; all your waves and breakers have swept over me' (Ps. 42:7). I began to pray for a renewed belief and experience of God's power in my life. I realised I didn't want to splash around in a trickle and yearned to know anew God's raw, fundamental, unstoppable power.

I returned to St Swithun's knowing I had to make some changes if I was to seek after the power of the Holy Spirit. I began to meditate on Jesus' words, 'Let anyone who is thirsty come to me and drink. Whoever believes in me, as Scripture has said, rivers of living water will flow from within them' (John 7:38). The Gospel writer John immediately notes, 'By this he meant the Spirit, whom those who believed in him were later to receive' (John 7:39). I considered my own life and asked two questions: How desperately am I thirsting for Jesus? And is what flows through my life a trickle or a river? I was disappointed by my honest answers: I don't ardently thirst after Jesus or drink deeply from him and so much of the time my life has all the flow of a dripping tap. The two are linked. But Lord, I prayed, take me to the river.

You don't have to be a top theologian to work out what Jesus meant when he said that our experience of the Spirit should be akin to rivers of living water. The start of the book of Genesis describes the idyllic Garden of Eden, whose central feature was a mighty river that led to four further life-giving rivers. The Nile, the Jordan and the Euphrates all feature throughout the Old Testament as rivers of living water, vital to the life of the people of God who are delivered from oppression when the Nile is cursed and led into the Promised Land when the Jordan is blessed. King David sang, 'How priceless is your unfailing love, O God! People take refuge in the shadow of your wings. They feast on the abundance of your house; you give them drink from your river of delights' (Ps. 36:7–8). Although there isn't a river in the real-world city of Jerusalem, David also sang, 'There is a river whose streams make glad the city of God, the holy place where the Most High dwells' (Ps. 46:4). He was talking metaphorically in the same way as Jesus. Famously, the prophet Ezekiel records the extraordinary visions he saw when wandering along the banks of the Kebar river. An angel shows him a river flowing out from a temple and leads him deeper into it until

'He measured off another thousand, but now it was a river that I could not cross, because the water had risen and was deep enough to swim in – a river that no one could cross' (Ezekiel 47:5). Wherever the waters of this river flows, it brings life and along its banks grow trees bearing fruit every month, with 'leaves for healing' (Ezekiel 47:12). All this is what Jesus had in mind for what could flow through the lives of anyone who welcomed his presence into their lives by drinking in the Holy Spirit. It is striking that the last chapter of the Bible chooses the image of a life-giving river to capture what a life lived for and with Jesus looks like. The NIV version of the Bible beautifully entitles the passage 'Eden Restored'. The water of life in this river is 'as clear as crystal' (Rev. 22:1). Purity matters. There's no room for our muddy morality and mixed motives. The river runs, 'down the middle of the great street of the city [of God]' (Rev. 22:2). This is an image of prominence and power, like Ezekiel's river that no one could cross. How badly we underestimate the power of a life transformed by Jesus, lived in partnership with the Holy Spirit. In Revelation, as in Ezekiel, the trees growing on the banks yield 'fruit every month. And the leaves of the tree are for the healing of the nations' (Rev. 22:2). Our lives are supposed to be fruitful. We're supposed to feed others. Others are supposed to experience healing because of how we live.

As I thought about all this, I realised that a gap had emerged between what we said we were about at St Swithun's and what in reality we actually revealed. One Sunday I watched as people came in for our main morning service. We'd put a huge effort into the welcome team when we began, but now I watched our door team hurry people in and vaguely point them in the direction of the café where they could shuffle forward in a long queue for a coffee, in the hope that the limited number and range of pastries hadn't already been swiped by all the kids and pre-service set-up team. The following week I received a barrage of complaints from our key volunteers about staff members' attitudes towards them. At the same time, those staff members were in tears with me, feeling overwhelmed by the scale of the task they faced and desperate over why their teams were no longer as motivated as they were at first.

Jesus' vision of the river of life that was supposed to be flowing through us was of a divine love that is pure, powerful and productive. But as I considered my leadership of St Swithun's, with the approach that I'd inevitably passed on to my leadership team, I felt God pulling me up short and I acknowledged that my inner, spiritual growth needed to be matched by some outward changes.

A friend who's a senior management coach helped me see what was going on, introducing me to Larry Greiner's seminal *Harvard Business Review* article entitled, 'Evolution and Revolution as Organisations Grow'.[2] He argued that organisations get set in their ways by the force of history and rarely change until the structures, people and processes reach a point of crisis because the way they're working is no longer appropriate for the level of growth they've reached. At that point a revolution can unleash the next phase of growth and avoid the alternative, which is to plateau for a while at best, before sooner or later moving into decline. As I read the article I realised, with some satisfaction, that we'd made it through phase one as a start-up; but I also realised we were at a point of crisis that, if I'd allow it, would precipitate a very healthy, if a little painful, revolution.

We took Greiner's advice and did three things. First, we empowered our strongest administrative staff member to lead more. We were very fortunate in that she had fantastic leadership potential and had always been much more than my assistant. That gave the staff a key figurehead and she was much better than I was at bringing clarity and authority to our office without losing any of our values, which she embodied so readily. Second, we restructured into four key leadership teams, with a clear mandate and vision: overall strategy, operations, ministry and discipleship (who also led on pastoral care). Third, I launched a project called 'St Swithun's 2.0' that aimed to bring professional management to areas where our initial creative and informal approach had lapsed into serious inefficiency, if not outright chaos. Nowhere was that more true than in the whole area of our communications, where we had to recruit a new staff member to get a grip on things. It helped that he was a very gifted worship leader into the bargain, so he strengthened us there too.

I was still leading as though we were in the initial phases of a new start-up. The rest of the organisation and its people had moved on and I had to do the same. I'd been a factor driving growth forward at the beginning but was now actually preventing growth because I hadn't changed the way I was leading. I'd thought, read, prayed and consulted; now it was time to take a deep breath and take action. Rightly or wrongly, I did two things. I sent out a strongly worded email to the whole team pulling us all up short, saying we'd violated our core value and stopped loving people wholeheartedly. I gave anyone who wanted to the option to leave now if they didn't want to stay and devote themselves to that principle. Then I sat down with my leadership team and told them I'd worked out what our number one problem was: me. That might sound harsh, but its real purpose was to put us on notice that I would be changing and because we were all together in this thing, so would they. If they weren't up for it, I gave everyone the option to exit with honour now rather than resist the changes that would be coming.

Another fascinating article was published in the *Harvard Business Review* in 2000 by Daniel Goleman called 'Leadership That Gets Results'.[3] In it he writes about the relative benefits of six leadership styles found among a worldwide study of emotionally intelligent executives. I was devastated as I reread the article. I realised that my early pacesetting leadership style had got quick results from our group of highly motivated people, but there's a serious downside for leaders who fail to transition as what they're leading grows: it can destroy any chance of building a climate of trust. The team had begun to feel harassed by my continued demand for excellent performance and their morale had dropped. I'd started to get frustrated and hadn't taken the time to articulate any goals clearly. In my blind arrogance I expected people to read my mind, and if they couldn't I thought that meant they were the wrong people for the job. I'd stopped giving effective feedback and motivating people, which meant the team had to second-guess me all the time and quite understandably didn't feel at all trusted, so they'd stopped taking initiative as the risks of getting it wrong were too high. Just as Goleman predicts, flexibility had evaporated and we'd all stopped taking responsibility. Not good. No wonder God's flow through us had diminished.

The remedy seemed relatively simple: recast our vision and change my leadership approach to put more trust into my team. But I've found that much more difficult to do than it sounds. To use a footballing metaphor, I began to learn how to operate less as a talismanic mid-field captain on the pitch and more like a coach, or manager, on the sidelines. I'm still learning: it's not easy and I don't think many church leaders know how to do it well. It is counter-intuitive to step away from directive leadership and divert time and energy away from operational decisions. More money and larger staff teams do not by themselves solve the issue – they just increase the burden of operational leadership. There are very few UK churches who have appointed senior operational leaders alongside their senior pastoral leaders – what might be loosely known as the 'Executive Pastor' role in the US. And having made such an appointment, there are even fewer UK church leaders who can change their approach and style to fit that new model. I'm convinced this is one reason why we're not seeing a greater number of larger churches in the UK.

If leaders are not there to supply all the answers and tell everyone what to do, then a reasonable question to ask is: What, then, do leaders actually do? I've found Brendon Burchard's book *The Student Leadership Guide*[4] a useful summary and I've used it as a checklist on occasion to review my own leadership. Burchard argues that leaders do six things: envision; enlist; embody; empower; evaluate; and encourage. If you're a leader, stop reading for a moment and think about whether you're active in each of those ways in your network, organisation or family. A wise man I know urged me that to get the best out of the team of people God had given me, I needed to change my approach. He advised me to stop saying 'Here's what I want you to do' and start asking 'What would you like to do and how can I help you?' It's extraordinary to me how that has unlocked so much potential. Now, having listened to a team member describe a challenging situation they're battling, I usually ask that question and listen to their answer. Nine times out of ten I agree with their suggestions, although I often tweak them a bit in the light of other factors, resources or solutions they might not have seen.

Occasionally, I'm really surprised at what they come up with. I remember hearing one team member describe a multitude of challenges she was facing as she planned to take a large group of our young people to a summer festival. 'What do you need from me to help?' I asked. 'Actually, I think we've got most of this in hand, I just wanted you to know about it so I didn't feel quite so alone in it,' she said. 'But do you know anyone with a caravan? We'll be up all hours and, to be honest, I don't sleep well in tents.' She didn't need detailed direction from me – all she wanted was a comfortable bed. That was an easy fix.

None of this would have been possible without my personal assistant stepping up into a leadership role. Lucie-Blue Paterson is one of the most objective and honest people I know, which proved invaluable when she became my assistant. Blue had a good upbringing in a middle-class home, her only Christian contact being the matriarch of the family, her beloved Oma (Dutch for grandmother), a Russian Orthodox who would pray with her granddaughters at bedtime. While her family had a passing acquaintance with the Russian Orthodox church at significant religious festivals, Jesus formed no part of their vocabulary or thought. Blue was a bright child, though, and went on to study Art History at Goldsmith's. She moved in with her boyfriend and got her first City job. The relationship was a disaster and soon ended; the job was much better, until she started dating a colleague and that got ugly. She started afresh working in Notting Hill for a time, before returning to the City while she lived in Hackney, enjoying all that London offers young professionals.

For eight years a series of relationships came and went as Blue worked hard and partied hard. She travelled internationally, had prestige, a good income and a rich social life, but somewhere deep inside a void was growing. Every time Oma saw Blue she would hand her a miniature icon which Blue would promptly drop into her latest designer handbag. Oma wouldn't be put off so easily, however, and always reassured Blue that God loved her and had a plan for her. Blue thought it was nothing but sweet, well-intentioned but naive words. In odd moments, Blue recalled that her grandmother had been held in a Japanese Prisoner of War camp in Java (Dutch East-India) and that her own mother had escaped Russia during the Revolution. Oma always claimed that only their faith in Jesus had got her and her mother through such ordeals. On the surface at least, Blue maintained her disinterested air. But she found herself wanting to carry Oma's icons with her at all times and, even though she didn't particularly know who it was aimed at, she began to pray. Every morning she'd step out of the lift from her block of flats, light a cigarette and pray as she walked to the bus stop, repeating under her breath, 'Guide me. Protect me. Give me strength.'

By Christmas 2011, Blue found herself breaking up with another boyfriend, having had a terrible row over, of all things, God. Her boyfriend was an ardent atheist but Blue resisted, clinging on to some kind of belief that God existed, even though she could answer none of her boyfriend's questions. Blue's younger sister suggested that she should try going to church and told her how much she and her husband had enjoyed attending Alpha at their local church. She recommended HTB in South Kensington. And so it was that in January 2012 Blue came to HTB for the start of that term's Alpha course. She could not believe her eyes at the numbers of perfectly normal people her age flooding into the church. Being the intelligent, conscientious person she is, Blue went every week and relished the group discussion where she was able to speak honestly and ask questions without fear. She enjoyed journeying with like-minded people who, as the weeks passed by, soon became friends. She eventually signed up for the weekend away although she was very nervous about going. On the Saturday evening, as someone prayed for her after the inspiring talk, Blue experienced something she'd not felt since her Oma had prayed with her as a child all those years ago: God's peace. The following morning, a helper in her group prayed for her again and this time she felt overwhelmed. She wept profusely and as everything came out the confusion left her. Drenched with a sense of God's love and joy, all Blue could say was, 'Gosh, I'm so sweaty!' She went outside and called her sister. In between the tears she said, 'Millie, thank you. It's true; I know God loves me.'

Two-and-a-half years later, I met Blue just as we were preparing to leave London to get ready for the launch of St Swithun's. She told me her sister, Millie, lived near Bournemouth in Poole and that she was also considering moving down to live nearby. She eventually did exactly that, although for a whole year she commuted the two hours to London every working day before she agreed to come and work for St Swithun's. By that stage, everyone was begging me to find a good assistant who could also take on the task of shaping our growing team and fledgling office into a professional organisation. She agreed on one condition: that she could take on leading Alpha too. We readily consented and never looked back. For two years Blue served us so faithfully, managed my office and built the organisation that enabled us not only to sustain our growth patterns but also to give us a platform to begin planting out churches. On top of all that, in the two years that she led Alpha while on staff, she ran twelve courses, seeing hundreds of people commit their lives to Christ. Blue's life *flows* with the grace of God, and because of that, so now do the lives of many others.

Chapter 16

Get risky, stay risky

'Lord, if it's you,' Peter replied,
'Tell me to come to you on the water'
Matthew 14:28

If you want the ultimate thrill,
you've got to be willing to pay the ultimate price.
Mark Foo, a big wave surfer who died at Mavericks in 1994

We'd just got back from a joy-filled, sun-kissed summer holiday at the end of our second year, camping as a family in France. Our four-year-old daughter was upstairs having an afternoon nap and I was beginning a meeting with my curate, Matt, in my study at the front of our house; Debi was there too, with our son Josiah, aged eight, who gate-crashed the meeting, bubbling over with excitement as he told Matt all about the fun we'd had on holiday. Bliss.

Suddenly, there was the unmistakable crash of breaking glass owing to repeated, sickening blows of something breaking the rear windows of the house with a great force of violence. Josiah ran to the dining room to see what was going on and froze in the doorway. At the window was a large, strange man, breaking through the glass and trying to climb into our house in a frenzied attack. Debi grabbed Josiah and rushed him upstairs. Matt immediately pulled out his phone and dialled 999. I ran over to the window to confront the stranger.

It was immediately clear to me that this guy was in the grip of a terrifying psychotic episode. He screamed at me to let him in. His eyes were full of pure panic as he lunged in blind frenzy at the windows and he hurled abuse, shouting about being chased by four men who were trying to kill him. He was totally out of control, frightened and desperate; I guessed he was therefore highly dangerous. With the backs of his hand and elbows he was smashing the outer layer of glass windows along the back of our house, but seemed utterly confused as to why he could not then get in. Thank God for the aged secondary glazing, which previous occupants had fitted to the house to try and cut down on the drafts that rattled through the house in winter.

I was scared stiff. As I watched the man handling huge dagger-shards of broken glass, blood beginning to stream down his arms, I knew that in order to protect my family I had to prevent him getting into the house at all costs. Instinctively, I realised that my best chances were to try and calm him down and play for time until the police arrived. I tried every trick I could think of. I asked him his name and repeatedly said, 'I'm here to help you.' I asked him to explain, reassured him that he was safe and that the strangers he believed were chasing him were not here. I asked him about who was chasing him and why. I tried to coax him round to the front of the property, assuming that he'd broken into the garden through our side gate. He hadn't – he'd actually come over the fence from the other surrounding properties. Thanks to Matt's work on the phone, within only a few minutes the police arrived. Out of their car unfolded the local sergeant – incidentally, one of the tallest men I've ever met. The man who had been so deluded and violent only seconds before became instantly mute and submissive. He was so wrapped in fear of the imaginary demons chasing him that he seemed quite relieved that the police had arrived. He felt safer with them there. I know for sure that I did.

A few days later, I was due to go away overnight on an off-site staff retreat. Although the attack was during daytime and there was no reason to think it would recur, I felt nervous about going away. I found myself fretting over the impact of Josiah having seen the man, as well as Debi's safety in the property when I wasn't there. My nerves were further frayed when a car shunted into ours while Debi was collecting our kids from their swimming lessons. No damage was done, but it served me renewed notice that we were vulnerable to faceless threats I could not control. I shared my feelings with Debi, saying that I was worried for them and asking whether she'd like me to come back so that they wouldn't be without me at night. Inside, I knew that I was projecting my own worry on to her; I just wasn't ready to admit that my nerves were shredded.

My wife is much tougher than I am. She looked me in the eye and said, 'Tim, we really are fine you know. Are you sure it's not you who has been most affected by this?' I denied it instantly. But I knew she was right. I had become fearful. I was jumping at unexpected sounds. I was catching my own reflection in a mirror or window and quickly looking back, thinking for a split-second that I'd seen someone there. I'd nearly wept in the police station as they'd taken a witness statement from me with great care and professionalism. I was becoming irrational.

Two weeks after the incident I was asked to prepare a statement for the court. I thought it was an opportunity to support the police and to ensure that through the justice system the guy might get the help that he needed. However, one week later I received a letter from the Crown Prosecution Service telling me that they were not going to pursue charges against the offence involving me, because the same guy had now been arrested on a murder charge. It turned out that I was right to have thought he was dangerous. I wept for a bit, then realised I had to face up to the effect that fear was having on me.

Since then I've reflected a lot on fear. That episode was the first time in a while that I have felt physically, primitively afraid. I guess, like many average men, I don't think I'm particularly cowardly nor especially brave. But I've thought about the extreme fear I saw in that man and my own fear that came about as a result. Even though I know many people who have gone through far more frightening things, I've ruminated about the effect of fear on my family, and about my own fears for my family. Fear is like a rapidly spreading weed: it multiplies damage and is very difficult to contain once it's taken root. None of us will get rid of fear completely. I've received love and support, counselling and prayer ministry and I'm fine; so is my family. But it was a painful lesson to learn: if we're to move forward in life, sooner or later we have to learn to face our fears.

Fear can paralyse us, or panic us into wildly inappropriate action, or send us beating a hasty retreat into our places of safety. So it's critical to understand and master it. Fear is not irrational because there always are risks and things can indeed go wrong. But fear amplifies the negative and diminishes the positive; it makes the worst-case scenario seem most probable and success highly unlikely. The adrenaline that fear releases causes our brains to shortcut longer neural pathways that consider various perspectives of wisdom. Instead, our thinking is routed along lightning-fast pathways leading

224

to freeze, fight or flight reactions. Of course, that's a God-given response and under fire it is essential; but most of us in that state are not really making considered choices. This is how some people live most of the time: their fears determine their lives. Courage is not the absence of fear, but the mastery of it.

The adventurer, Bear Grylls, advises fathers to teach their sons about courage. He has taught his own sons: 'Don't be held back, either by fear or by lack of confidence. Go for it, despite these very normal emotions that we all feel occasionally.'[1] There's nothing wrong with feeling fear; it would actually be dysfunctional if we didn't feel it. The question is, will we learn to acknowledge its influence and, having considered other wisdom, enable ourselves to move forwards in spite of it? Will we rule it or will it rule us? I've had to revisit this question regularly in my adult life and certainly in my vocation as a church leader.

In Matthew 14:22–36 we read the famous episode after the feeding of the 5,000 when Jesus sends his disciples out on a fishing boat that gets caught in a storm. In the middle of the night, they're still battling the storm out on the lake. Jesus walks on the water to them and, thinking he's a ghost, they are undone with fear. Jesus makes four statements to them, serving as the antidote to their fear and ours: 'Take courage! It is I. Don't be afraid . . . Come.' (vv.27–9).

'Take courage!' is spoken by Jesus as a very strong command. He's not saying, 'Pull yourselves together!' He's saying he has the courage we do not have and that we need to take it from him. The root of the word 'courage' is the Latin for heart, 'cor'. Courage means inner strength. I find it most comforting to hear that Jesus is commanding me to allow myself to be inwardly strengthened by him. He knows that without this inner encouragement of his Spirit

I will remain weak and fearful. In my fearfulness I must reconnect to God my creator, the source of life itself. Disconnected from him, we become consumed with fear; reconnected to him, we flourish and grow towards eternal life. Sadly, it seems to me that many Christians resist God's desire to provide the encouragement that we do not possess. God does not ask us to free ourselves from fear. He commands us to be willing to receive that process as a free gift from him.

'It is I' really does speak to the crux of the matter: we can take strength from Christ only once we recall who he is. We must constantly remind ourselves exactly who we're dealing with, and this is yet another reason why a rich, varied and continual worship life is so vital. Jesus said, 'Courage, it's me' (Matt. 14:27, *The Message*). The disciples, we are told, thought that the figure walking on water was a ghost, their old watermen superstitions getting the better of them. They were scared to death. The corrective was seeing Jesus with a renewed perspective, doing something 'impossible' for anyone to do. Within a short time they'd have to get their heads around Jesus doing much more than that. If we can't get our heads around Jesus walking on water, how are we ever going to accept he's risen from the dead?

The Gospel writer Matthew knew all this full well. As elsewhere in his literary masterpiece, he's reminding his readers in this passage that Jesus is the fulfilment of what was promised in the Old Testament. There, God revealed himself to Moses who asked God to reveal himself to those he was sending him to, with messages of wrath unless they released God's people whom they were oppressing. God self-authenticates – there's nothing else you can appeal to validate who he is. So he told Moses to tell Pharaoh that if he wants to know who is speaking to him, it is 'I AM'. Through Moses, God parted the waters so that his people could escape to safety. It was a partial victory at a particular time. Now Matthew takes it to the next level: God, through Jesus, enables his church, personified in Peter, to walk on water. It demonstrates total victory for all time. The Amplified Version of the Bible actually translates Jesus' words as 'I AM' to highlight all this.

It's only after considering this that one can really grasp the full impact of Jesus' sharp command: 'Don't be afraid'. Without hearing the first two statements before it, this one will seem like a platitude. And that's what many people make of it. But once we take from the all-powerful Jesus the courage that he knows we need, we can hear this statement again with new ears. The reason to fear has been removed: all that remains is the pattern of our thoughts – our learned responses formed at a time when we did not know who Jesus was and had not received anything from him. About such outmoded ways of thinking the Bible tells us to 'demolish arguments and every pretension that sets itself up against the knowledge of God, and we take captive every thought to make it obedient to Christ' (2 Cor. 10:5).

Taken together, then, Jesus commanded the disciples to receive courage from him on the basis of a new level of belief in who he was. Jesus' first three statements provide a Trinitarian explanation of what's happening to the disciples and what they need to do about it: Jesus is creator and provider; Jesus is deliverer and redeemer; Jesus is spirit and life. This matches what Paul prayed for the church in Ephesus: 'I pray that out of his glorious riches he may strengthen you with power through his spirit in your inner being, so that Christ may dwell in your hearts through faith' (Eph. 3:16–17).

How do we respond to all this? Peter's reaction is instructive. How amazing that he should say, 'Lord, if it's you, tell me to come to you on the water.' Peter intuitively sensed that Jesus was inviting him out even though there's no indication in the passage up to this point that this was the case. Yet Peter saw that if Jesus really was calling him to be the rock on which his church would be built, that was a task way beyond his power, impossible but for Jesus enabling him to do that which he could not do on his own. So why not this also?

As I argued earlier, we must get it into our heads that the church is not called to do what is, humanly speaking, possible; we are called to do what is, humanly speaking, impossible. You don't need God for possible things – you just need to learn how to put on a good show, how to get organised, how to raise money, and how to make people feel good. As a church leader, I'm shocked at how easy it is to spend most of my time on such things. If we're called to do the impossible, however, a very different list of priorities emerges: worship, prayer, truth-speaking, culture-challenging. We must re-see Jesus and get out of the boat.

Which is why Jesus' last statement should shake us: 'Come.' Peter had to leave behind the familiar battles of a fisherman pitched against the elements in a world that he knew and instead pursue the miraculous. And so he goes for it. Thank God that Matthew resists turning the story into a kind of idealistic, unreal, spiritual trip at that point. No, this isn't a one-off decision that Peter makes, a kind of eureka moment that means he never has a spiritual struggle again; no, this is a miracle that involves ongoing risk and the need to keep believing. Having realised who Jesus is and having chosen to accept the courage he's offered, Peter has to keep giving his total attention to Jesus. When he reconsiders things and looks anew at the wind and waves, he becomes bound once again by what is only humanly possible. Jesus must remain our total focus.

I'm convinced that, in many corners of the UK, the Church of England has become far too risk-averse. At St Swithun's we've done our best to foster a permissive, supportive culture that encourages people to broaden their experience and simply to try new things. One young guy who had started to come along during our first year is an entrepreneur in his twenties who runs several stores and an online business that sells skateboards, scooters and all manner of cool stuff that appeals to kids and to big kids like me too. When I talked to him about some of the ideas I had to set up a café and bar to serve drinks after our evening service, I found myself reeling off the list of reasons why we probably shouldn't attempt it – how much it would cost, what we'd need to put in place first, and so on, talking myself out of it with every problem and objection I could think of. I remember him looking at me and saying:

> Why don't you just start small? You could easily do a pop-up bar after one evening service to see if people like it rather than create something physical that's fixed. Watch to see if it builds community. See if the unchurched young guys gravitate to it. If they do then you can grow it; if not then no problem – you've just learned a valuable lesson very cheaply and you can tell everyone it was just an experiment. You don't need to set up massive endeavours without testing them first.

He was spot on and we acted on his advice. Taking measured risks in leadership is essential. On the other hand, failing to investigate potential dangers of any course of action that we're considering can be deadly.

In his dashing RAF uniform, flying officer 153043 Aubrey Glyndwr Matthews must have looked impressive. He was the pilot of a Vickers Wellington Bomber, attached to the 19th Operational Training Unit in RAF Kinloss, Scotland. Just four months and fourteen days after the happy birth of his new son by his beautiful bride back in London, on 20 April 1945, Aubrey took off from RAF Kinloss at 11.52a.m. Nearly an hour into the flight at 12.40p.m. the plane broke up in mid-air and crashed to the ground just outside Edinburgh near Bank Head Farm, Humbie, East Lothian. All six members of the crew died. Aged twenty-six, Aubrey was the oldest member of the crew by three years. My dad has only a single photo of himself as a baby being held by his father. Just ten days later, the Reichstag would be captured by the Allied Forces signalling the defeat of the Nazi military and within days, the war would be over. My grandfather so very nearly survived it. That must have made my grandmother's tears all the more bitter. It was a grief from which she never recovered, and she never remarried.

Eyewitness reports say they noticed the Wellington flying at about five hundred feet when the overcast sky was lit up by a flash, followed by an explosion, whereupon they saw a section of the wing falling off and the aircraft tumbling out of the sky. Crash investigators concluded that the starboard wing had sheared away but the official report says that 'The pilot probably lost control in turbulent cloud due to not being strapped in.' There's a discrepancy between the eyewitness accounts and official report. For starters, if the bomber was in turbulent cloud then people on the ground couldn't have seen it. But it's not an unreasonable report, in that many pilots did not strap in because seat straps were tight and necessarily restrictive and would make exiting the plane much harder. None the less, flying without them was a big no-no as the pilot needed them to maintain control of the aircraft in turbulence and during evasive manoeuvres under fire. Throughout the war, life expectancy in bomber command was perilously short, so one can understand why so many pilots took the risk. We owe that brave generation so much.

I will never know whether my grandfather flew in a way that was unsafe, costing his own life and the lives of others. Did he unstrap himself before the mid-air explosion or after it? It's impossible to say. But it's an interesting story against which I sometimes review my own spiritual life and leadership of the church. Am I still strapped in or have I, for the sake of short-term expediency, removed the safety devices in my life that are crucial for my long-term health and the health of those I lead? My private integrity would be so easy to compromise. My personal spiritual habits often feel boring and ill-fitting. My close relationships with those I am accountable to are sometimes tempting to pull back from. It's more tempting to hide my sins and frustrations than it is to remain honest and vulnerable with my prayer partners. But all these things are essential safety devices in my Christian life and leadership. Tragically, many people fly along without them in place, apparently without any consequence until they enter turbulent times.

At St Swithun's we follow nearly every message with a time of worship during which people can come forwards to receive prayer. I've frequently seen how the Holy Spirit uses such occasions to give his seal of approval as to how the gospel message is being communicated by addressing a specific issue in someone's life where they have an unrealised dream or a positive, unmet desire – or else are suffering or caught in sin, difficulty or failure of some kind. Following Paul's words to Timothy, we have a team of trained people who will respectfully lay hands on those who come forward requesting prayer and ask Jesus to fill them with his Spirit. And he does. Physical and emotional reactions vary greatly according to the personality, circumstances and mood of those being prayed for, but

God is always present. I love watching people receive this kind of ministry because it authenticates the spoken gospel. As Paul wrote to the Corinthians, 'My message and my preaching were not with wise and persuasive words, but with a demonstration of the Spirit's power, so that your faith might not rest on human wisdom, but on God's power' (1 Cor. 2:4–5).

When I introduce these periods of ministry at our Sunday services I'll often admit that it might feel very risky to come forward for prayer. But I'll do all that I can to encourage people. Personally, I suspect we all probably need to come forwards for prayer at least once a month. Sometimes I'll say, 'Come and join me, I'm going to ask others to pray for me too' and I'll go and stand at the front to receive prayer. It is wonderful and I've often felt free and full of joy afterwards, or felt that I have heard from God on a matter that previously I was confused about. God is always ready to give but we can be surprisingly unwilling to receive.

One of the risky things I did soon after starting St Swithun's was to decide to preach about real-life issues rather than abstract religious concepts. A General Election beckoned, so I preached a message that looked at key parts of each party's manifesto and compared them to New Testament teaching. Of any message I'd preached up to that point in my life, that was the one I was most nervous about. I was sick with worry about it beforehand and felt I did a terrible job. When I had finished I walked straight off the stage and went and hid in the toilet, I was so embarrassed! I felt the same way after I preached ahead of both the EU Referendum and the next General Election.

It felt risky to preach on such matters, but we'd taken a decision as a team not to duck tough subjects. Although I felt I hadn't executed any of those messages very well, in each of the weeks that followed many people wrote thank-you notes telling me how I had helped them. One man thanked me particularly for my courage in choosing to preach about politics and current affairs. He added that he'd listened to my talks while lying in his bath in the Lake District! I didn't know quite how to reply to this, but he encouraged me onwards and for that I'm grateful.

Chapter 17

Transition times

The Lord our God said to us at Horeb, 'You have stayed long
enough at this mountain. Break camp and advance . . .'
Deuteronomy 1:6–8

Although I'll always love the latest version of St Swithun's, the
time I enjoyed most of all was when it had just been born, when
there were just thirty or forty of us. We didn't have any structure
or infrastructure, no staff or teams, not even a bank account.
Everyone knew everyone else and our meetings just felt like an
excuse to meet up with new friends. The level of excitement about
what God was doing, and the level of expectation about what he
was going to do, was sky-high. If there was a need, someone offered
to lend, source or buy it; if there was a pastoral crisis we rallied
around so that the load was spread out, even though the level of
care was very high. That all lasted about a month.

As we grew, life got more complex. We had to start thinking
about meeting agendas, governance structures, processes and data-
bases, legal issues, communication channels, finances, information
technology, budgets and human resource policies. These are all good
things and in today's world you can't run even a small church

without them. However, although my accountancy background helped a little, my theological college training in no way prepared me to deal with them. On reflection, two years at a sleepy, ivory-tower Bible college plus a long curacy had actually deskilled me from so many abilities and the knowledge base that I have needed. I've swiftly had to relearn them, this time under fire.

As I mentioned, the uncomfortable truth was that, as our numbers grew past 250, I quickly became the bottleneck and felt drained by the never-ending demand for operational decisions, as well as pastoral attention and message preparation. It didn't take a rocket-scientist to work out that the model had to change quickly, otherwise either we would fail or I would die. Neither of those seemed like a good idea, so we hired a few new people, set up a proper office and got in some leadership coaching to help us develop. We clarified our structure and introduced a somewhat grandiosely named 'Executive Leadership Team' to oversee the church and provide strategic direction; then we developed teams of leaders who ran the ministries and midweek connect groups. The launching of a third service late on Sunday afternoon relieved the pressure on our packed evening service. All these measures helped considerably.

While at HTB I'd seen the wisdom of managing change as 'evolution not revolution', such that whenever possible it's wise to adapt and tweak things as you go rather than changing nothing for a long time, before lurching out of slumber into radical, rash change out of sheer desperation. In hindsight, there have certainly been occasions when I've delayed change for too long and watched my options narrow to a point where only major surgery has saved me. That kind of strategy is very risky: it causes enormous upheaval and is likely to be much more expensive, less well informed and poorly planned. It is therefore much more likely to fail. Sometimes you've got no choice, but avoiding this scenario wherever possible, by taking the time to think change through and plan for it, nearly always pays off. That said, in the name of 'proper planning' I've sometimes deferred change for way too long. It's a balance, I guess: plan, but then get on with it. Anyway, that's what we had tried to do and I felt pleased that we'd spotted the need to transition at an early stage and had made the necessary changes. I was looking forward to the next five years with the structures, people and processes we had in place.

But just one year later we hit the buffers again. It was as though all the changes we'd made had simply papered over the cracks. As I thought about the health of the church, it seemed to me that those cracks were now showing through and some of them were huge. The state of our facilities epitomised the stage we'd reached: the event carpeting we'd first laid in the main church, expecting it to last ten weeks, had served us eighteen months but had become stretched and torn and was fast becoming a major trip hazard. It was the same story with our staff office: the team were still using a collection of old chairs and wobbly trestle tables that we'd collected as we'd grown and were experiencing neck and back problems as a result. To value our team (never mind our responsibilities as an employer) we should surely provide proper chairs and tables, with ergonomic keyboards and stuff like that. The Bible states, 'Don't muzzle the ox while it's treading the grain' and Richard Branson points out that 'The customer isn't king, your people are. Take care of your staff and they'll take care of your customers.' I realised that we weren't taking proper care of our key people and it was beginning to show. In pumping them full of vision, but then not giving them the tools they needed to carry it out, I was simply frustrating them. The office printer could no longer cope with what was being asked of it because it wasn't designed for that level of use; neither was the internet router, and so on. We'd survived the start-up phase and now we faced the challenge of investing for the long term.

Far harder to fix than office equipment was the team itself. Some of the people who had given the most in that initial period had reached their limit. In fact, we'd all reached the limit of our competency, including me. It's good to live with a sense of challenge where we're stretched and supported, but spend too long in the danger zone beyond that point, where we're over-stretched and under-supported, and stress will win. I had the deep pain of seeing some of our core team burn out, knowing that the way I'd led them had been a major contributing factor. I felt it too. I'd tried to change but each morning the person staring back at me in the mirror looked increasingly overwhelmed, alone and afraid. Was it all about to come crashing down? Or could we make the leap to something sustainable and healthy? As if all that wasn't bad enough, ridiculously, we had accepted that God was calling us to stretch ourselves further and plant out. I seriously considered whether we had gone raving mad.

As a teenager I once heard a great preacher from the deep south of the USA speak from Deuteronomy 1:6, urging us all to change and pursue the new things that God is doing. I can hear him now, in a delicious Southern drawl, repeatedly using the riff, 'You've stayed looooong enough at this mountain.' Those words came back to me one morning as I was praying through the future for St Swithun's. Moses told the Hebrews wandering around the wilderness, 'The Lord our God said to us at Horeb, "You have stayed long enough at this mountain. Break camp and advance"' (Deut. 1:6-7a). I heard those words in an entirely new way, instantly recognising that we were in a wilderness between two states also and I didn't want to return to where we'd been – 'Egypt', as it were. But I couldn't see how we could enter the next stage, our 'promised land' either. We were stuck at our 'Horeb'. Horeb had been the place of foundational miracles; it was where God first appeared to Moses in the burning bush (Exod. 3:1) and where God first provided the fledgling nation with its most basic of all human needs from the very rock they were standing on: water (Exod. 17:6).

It's hardly a surprise that the Hebrews settled down a bit at Horeb. I know this temptation all too well myself and I've seen it at work in St Swithun's. A kind of spiritual inertia sets in at those times and places when we've got just enough to survive on: we're not yet experiencing the full freedom we aspire towards but we're no longer caught in captivity and restriction. So we think, 'That will do for now' and stop growing. Although not a deeply satisfying place, nevertheless, with a resigned, tired attitude, we make our mediocrity semi-permanent and if anyone asks us how we are we shrug and say, 'Yeah, okay, I suppose.' Perhaps we become familiar with a fear of failure. Perhaps we start telling ourselves stories of great things that occurred an increasingly long time ago. Perhaps we drop our expectations. Perhaps a type of low-level continual grumbling sets in. Perhaps everything begins to feel a bit flat as joy departs. Then God's word comes to shake us from our settled-down, lack-lustre spirituality, telling us to leave Horeb and 'advance'. To do that, though, involves us 'breaking camp'.

Last summer when we went camping in France, we were considering visiting a couple of different campsites during our two weeks but ended up staying at the one we liked, in part because we couldn't face the hassle and upheaval of resetting everything. To move sites we'd lose a precious day of our holiday sorting everything out, taking down the tent, packing it all into the car – only to have to set it all up again after a few hours' drive down the coast. It simply didn't seem worth the hassle. It's the same so often in life: the pain of considering what has to be broken in order to move forwards is a tremendous disincentive to change. None the less, there really is no option if we're to obey God's call when he urges us to 'move on'. We must accept that change is always messy, confusing and difficult. As a leader, I know how powerful the temptation is to deny or try to evade my responsibility to 'grasp nettles' and address problems but sticking one's head in the sand is not a successful long-term strategy. So, on my own church-planting journey, the one question loomed large: should we consider 'moving on' by setting up a second site at this stage? There would be so much change involved in taking one on – could God really be asking us to do it?

Until that point the vision of St Swithun's had been the re-evangelisation of Bournemouth and the transformation of its society. Now the time seemed right to introduce a third element: the revitalisation of the church. Previously I'd kept that part a bit hidden if I'm honest. I feared that, as a very young church, we wouldn't be taken seriously or, with a kind of youthful pride, might get ahead of ourselves. I believed that until we'd built something sustainable at St Swithun's we didn't really have anything to give away to anyone else; we had to show what could be done here first to have any credibility in resourcing others elsewhere.

I'm a bit nervous of all the fanfare around the strategic funding now available for church plants that are launched as 'City Centre Resource Churches'. The grand, admittedly worthy, aim is that they'll grow quickly and soon be able to reinvigorate other churches right across the city. Using this designation for new plants before they've run a single service, however, heaps huge pressure on the small leadership teams and can squash creativity. The most helpful part of the designation would be to make it clear that in order to be or become a resource to others, these churches might need continual resourcing for many years, or at least relief from contributing colossal amounts back to the diocese. If initial funding for such churches is to be truly strategic, perhaps we also need to put in place further stages of coaching support, intervention and even new funding at each level of growth. As growth takes place, the church planter will either need to change their leadership approach radically and build an effective team or move on. Some leaders are brilliant at starting new initiatives but aren't so good at consolidating once the earlier years are done. I'm not at all sure that I'll prove very good at it, although I'm giving it a go. If a church planter is able to build to the stage where further church plants become possible, then the resource church is likely to need some kind of executive or associate pastor appointment to release the planter to do that effectively.

The hope for St Swithun's has always been that we might not just be a church plant, but to build and plant other churches. We acknowledged that to go from one site to two would be a huge transition but we felt called to keep pressing forwards in that direction. At the end of our second year we got our first opportunity. The bishops of Winchester and Southampton, the archdeacon of Bournemouth and the wardens and PCC of St Clement's Boscombe invited us to plant into that parish and relaunch it for local mission. St Clement's is a mile down the road from the St Swithun's site, in the heart of an area that had been described as possibly the most deprived neighbourhood in the South West.

The gospel has to be the starting point for church planting, rather than any desire to preserve historic buildings or make deprived neighbourhoods nicer places to live. Even after we'd been there for a while, from the outside St Swithun's looked sad, closed and forgotten and was not a good advert for our message. I received a letter from a member of our congregation, who had sent me a cheque to pay for new notice boards on the church site since our old ones were such an embarrassment. About the old notice board, she wrote: 'I only hope it is enough, as I see that one side needs new glass and the other side's woodwork needs attention. I'm sending this because when I mention to my neighbours that I attend St Swithun's they always exclaim that they thought it was derelict!'

There are myriad factors in the success of a church plant, but location is certainly one of the most important. We believed that God was giving us a very specific vision for the local community of Boscombe. Even though it's only one mile away from St Swithun's, within easy walking distance, culturally it feels much further. We sensed many in the community of Boscombe would be attracted to a relaunched St Clement's who might not normally consider coming to St Swithun's. St Clement's is an iconic building in the heart of Boscombe. However, we soon discovered that the building is Grade I listed, so would be fantastically expensive to maintain and difficult to develop – this in a deprived neighbourhood where incomes are low. The reputation of the church in the community was not healthy: the gardens had become a market-place for drug dealers and prostitutes. But just as we'd seen at St Swithun's, we believed that demonstrated it was something of a natural meeting-point for the very people whom Jesus loves so much and are in such need of him. St Clement's had been in decline and difficulty for many years, but thanks to the faithful endurance of a small group of believers who had battled to keep it going, an opportunity for mission was retained.

The bishop and archdeacon invited me to meet with the PCC at St Clement's. I was so inspired by them, because I knew that stylistically we were chalk and cheese. They favoured traditional Anglo-Catholic liturgical and eucharistic worship style while I preferred informality, loud guitars and drums. However, as we talked and prayed we were united in our vision for those in Boscombe who did not yet know Jesus and who were in such need of the kind of ministries that a vibrant church could bring. Through tears, the PCC shared their heart with me that all they really longed to see was the Kingdom of God in Boscombe and they were prepared to risk everything they had worked so hard to sustain in order to see it occur. All they asked for was some understanding and help to make the transition. What could I do but respond to their faith? That small group was so courageous in inviting St Swithun's to partner with them to relaunch St Clement's as a base for mission to Boscombe. We agreed that St Clement's could only be relaunched if St Swithun's brought to it the full backing of established office, finance, ministry support and leadership. That meant appointing me as priest-in-charge and running the two sites as one church. We'd be joined at the hip and in it for the long haul.

At several points in the story so far I have mentioned how difficult it can be to find the right language to describe church planting. Some have settled on the idea, attributable to Jonny Gumbel at St Peter's Brighton, of relaunched churches being like a child of two parents. In our case, St Swithun's and St Clement's were the parents and the relaunched church would be the child. Like any child, St Clement's would reflect certain attributes of each parent and for a while, maybe even years, remain dependent upon them; but the new church would nevertheless have an autonomous identity and, like a child, would need to discover who God has made it to be as it grows. Perhaps resource churches should talk more about church parenting than church planting?

A large piece of the jigsaw for the St Clement's project fell into place when I met Simon Nicholls. Si was on staff at Soul Survivor Watford, where for many years he'd served at the heart of that great church, with its summer youth festivals and social justice ministries too. I'd been introduced to him by one of our trustees in London and when we met I instinctively knew he'd make a great point-person for the St Clement's project. I took the idea to the St Swithun's executive team back in Bournemouth – most of whom had never even met him – and was surprised by the strength of their agreement. I outlined the financial commitment we'd have to make to bring Si, his wife Chloe and young son down to Bournemouth and the upheaval they'd have to make – all with no guarantee at that stage that the St Clement's project was actually going to happen. In the end, it was our cautious-but-faith-filled treasurer who clinched it: 'You're asking us to take this decision on the basis of faith, not factual certainty,' he began 'but would we want it any other way? If it's a God thing it will always involve faith so we should be very cautious about making major investments that don't require faith. He sounds ideal! If they're willing to risk everything to move down here, then let's add our faith to theirs.'

God had also been moving in Si's heart, speaking to him and Chloe about it. When we first met, Si was in the final year of his theological training for ordained ministry in the Church of England. Shortly beforehand, Si's father had died. The guy I met was weak, not strong; he was grieving but still choosing to say to God, 'I'm full of pain and loss but I'm not going to stop trusting you and following you. You give and take away. Blessed be the name of the Lord' (Job 1:21). Like everyone else here, Si is a wounded healer, a leader with a limp. He has learned that God's power is made perfect in his weakness. When I met him and heard his story, I knew he was our man.

Chapter 18

Second site

'The glory of this present house will be greater than the glory of the former house,' says the Lord Almighty.

Haggai 2:9

Like most church planters, I've memorised Haggai's prophetic encouragement to the returning exiles. And this is exactly what is now occurring in many locations around the UK as tired buildings are being given a new lease of life through church planting. This promise was given to me as a specific prophecy over St Swithun's before we began and we're certainly seeing that fulfilled. I've researched the history at the site and seen that soon after the building was completed the congregation became embroiled in dispute and discord. But in recent years, first under the careful Kingdom-building work of a Newfrontiers congregation, then by our current team, something of God's glory has been made manifest.

When things at St Swithun's got tough, coinciding with the call to plant out to St Clement's, I began to restudy my way through the exile and return of God's people in the Old Testament. It's a very complex and rich piece of biblical history. Matching the events of the history books with the voice of the prophets and the narrative of books like Daniel, Ezra and Nehemiah is something I find endlessly fascinating. I spent a long time studying, praying and thinking through a book that, to be perfectly honest, I hadn't really appreciated before: the gem that is Zechariah. After a while, anyone involved in planting or rebuilding a church is going to need a very large amount of encouragement and guidance – and that was Zechariah's primary role to the returning exiles. They were given the incredibly demanding task of rebuilding a bombed-out temple and a war-shattered city. As if the project itself wasn't hard enough, the people frequently became discouraged and distracted, and their work was constantly under derision, diversion and danger from their surrounding enemies.

Into that cocktail of discouragement, Zechariah preaches: 'For who has despised the time of insignificant things? They will rejoice to see the plumb line in the hand of Zerubbabel' (Zech. 4:10, ISV). The returning exiles were few, weak, vulnerable and faced an overwhelming task – God often seems to choose such groups to do great things. Under Zerubbabel's wise and bold leadership they exercised faith and gave themselves to the project. Can you imagine yourself as one of them, despairing, looking up to see Zerubbabel, the master builder and leader, clambering up the scaffolding to encourage you, measure progress and assign the next tasks? What a pleasure it is to serve under leaders like that! Clearly, Zerubbabel prefigured Jesus himself, who invites us to join him as he promises, 'I will build my church' (Matt. 16:18).

The great biblical commentator, Matthew Henry writes:

It is a comfort to us that the same all-wise, almighty Providence, which governs the earth, is in particular conversant about the church. All that have the plummet in their hands, must look

248

up to the eyes of the Lord, have constant regard to Divine Providence, act in dependence on its guidance and submission to its disposals. Let us fix our faith on Christ, and view Him carrying on his work according to his own glorious plan, and daily bringing his spiritual building nearer to completion.[1]

Many old church buildings in the UK have become millstones around the necks of the dwindling, ageing congregations who have responsibility for them. Personally, I believe we should hold our civic responsibilities as custodians of historic buildings more lightly and be much bolder in using and adapting them to facilitate contemporary worship, prayer and mission. Many church ministers I know spend a large part of their time dealing with historic buildings usually ineffectively and/or unsuccessfully. We simply don't have the right training, skill set or resources. Although it's a well-worn cliché to say that 'church is the people not a building', we nevertheless desperately need to hear that truth again and again. It's not the Anglican Church's primary concern to safeguard 'national treasures' of stone and cement, however pleasingly arranged they are. Yet many Church of England sites are still somewhat iconic in localities right across the country; if reimagined and remodelled, they could make marvellous facilities for the church's gospel mission.

Long before actually doing anything, we knew we had to build friendships and pray. Some of us from St Swithun's started to join the ten or so people who attended the traditional Eucharist service at St Clement's every Thursday at 10.00a.m., then we moved our usual Tuesday 7.00a.m. prayer meeting there for more than half a year. I loved those meetings, despite their being freezing cold because at that time there was no heating in the room where we met: as late summer turned to autumn, then winter, the temperatures fell and the night stretched out. We'd arrive at 6.50a.m., croak out a few worship songs and then stomp around the building praying. The usual comforts of nice coffee, comfy chairs and professional sound and visual set-ups were all stripped away and it was brilliant! The presence of Jesus seemed so near and joyful. As word got round that the Lord was moving in power, numbers started to increase until we'd completely outgrown the small back room and had to move into the chancel where we sat in the old choir stalls. That was even colder. We praised, thanked, wept, wailed, prophesied and stomped up and down the aisles declaring the promises of God. We hoped, lamented, rejoiced, waited, listened and trusted. One morning I handed out packets of salt and bottles of oil and we went all over the building inside and out, cleansing and anointing the site. I tell you, I love intercessors – they're up for anything!

Of course, we were standing on the shoulders of some local prayer giants. Twenty years ago, a small group of people in Boscombe began to pray at St Clement's, moved by the decline of the church and the poverty of Boscombe. They fasted and wept as they continued to meet and pray. Their prayer was one of the prophecies God gave to Israel to give them hope while they were in exile mourning their defeat and loss: 'Your people will rebuild the ancient ruins and will raise up the age-old foundations; you will be called Repairer of Broken Walls, Restorer of Streets with Dwellings . . . they will rebuild the ancient ruins and restore the places long devastated; they will renew the ruined cities that have been devastated for generations' (Isa. 58:12; 61:4). They were sure that this was what the Lord was calling them to pray for. One of the women who had been in that original prayer group was contacted by a member of the Tuesday morning prayer group. The woman was overjoyed, believing that what she had heard was now happening at

St Clement's was the fulfilment of what her group had prayed for twenty years ago.

It was very humbling to know that so much prayer had gone before us. Yet, as I got to grips with the project and realised the immensity of what we were taking on, I found myself beginning to doubt whether we'd done the right thing. I also couldn't get it out of my mind that St Swithun's was a mere two years old. Were we really ready to plant a church? Wasn't there still so much to do back at the St Swithun's site? Surely we should be planting from a place of strength not weakness? Even on the surface, St Clement's didn't look great: much of it was dirty, ripped, peeling, rotting and crumbling; rooms and cupboards were full of clutter, junk and cobwebs. Beneath the surface lurked the far greater challenges of insufficient heating and electrical supplies, towers with falling stonework, rising damp, blocked guttering and leaking roofs. There was no carpet, no production system and no real kitchen to speak of. At the very same time, we were struggling to find enough people for the children, youth and Alpha teams at St Swithun's, so who was going to do those same things at St Clement's? I had many moments where my mind filled with a hundred such questions without answer and I'd mutter ridiculous prayers like, 'God, are you mad? Do you realise what you're getting us into?' Of course he did, and I knew that full well. But it helped me to say it none the less.

The fact was that, as a leadership team, we had become convinced that the Lord was calling us to 'break camp and advance' and was promising to provide the teams and money that the project would need. Our confidence grew by recalling that God promises us that he'll provide so we can do what he calls us to do. Paul told the Philippians that, 'my God will meet all your needs according to the riches of his glory in Christ Jesus' (Phil. 4:19). We remembered that God had provided for us so many times in the past; in fact, he'd never let us down. Moreover, the congregation at St Swithun's had responded with great faith and generosity on our previous gift days and we felt sure they'd respond to the vision when we were ready to launch.

The Bible describes repeatedly the processes of renewal, reform and rebuilding in the history of God's people; indeed a significant part of the Old Testament is devoted to this theme. In the sixth century BC, Israel deserted God and, as a direct result, the nation was conquered by the Babylonians, Jerusalem was sacked and the people were deported to Babylon. There, through the prophet Jeremiah, God commanded the Israelites to mourn, to lament what had happened, in the hope that they would turn back to God (cf. 2 Kings 24–5; Jer. 52). In the tenth month they fasted and lamented the beginning of Nebuchadnezzar's siege of Jerusalem. The fourth month fast lamented the breaching of the walls two-and-a-half years later in 586 BC. The fifth month fast lamented the burning of the temple and the breaking down of the walls. The seventh month fast lamented the assassination of Gedaliah – the last man of peace. With his death the final flicker of hope was extinguished. Defeated, humiliated and ashamed, the exiles mourned and fasted in exile. But God wasn't done: he had promised that new hope would emerge. And it did. While they were exiled in Babylon, Babylon itself was conquered. Subsequently, there was a change of policy and a small group of exiles was commissioned to return to Jerusalem and begin to rebuild the temple there.

The returning exiles faced an enormous task. God gave them not only money, materials and skilled people, but also prophets to teach, guide, correct, encourage and motivate them. One such prophet was our friend Zechariah. Those six months thinking and praying through the book of Zechariah as the St Clement's project was unfolding began to guide my thoughts as to how we might go about our own rebuilding task. Zechariah – what a man he must have been – encouraged the returning exiles, proclaiming: 'The Lord Almighty says, "The fasts of the fourth, fifth, seventh and tenth months will become joyful and glad occasions and happy festivals for Judah. Therefore love truth and peace"' (Zech. 8:18–19).

A week after moving down here, Si Nicholls travelled on the slow train from Southampton to Bournemouth. A lady and her young son sat around the same table opposite him. The mum and son were talking about each of the places they went through. As they pulled through Boscombe, the mum said, with deep sarcasm, 'Ah, your favourite place! Boscombe.' To which the son replied, 'I'm glad we're not getting off here. I hate Boscombe. It's rubbish! It's where all the crime happens.' Mum asked, 'Is it really?' And the boy replied, 'Well, no, I guess not. That's actually America isn't it!' Si got chatting to them and they told him story after story about the drugs and violence of Boscombe. That's the reputation of the place. Si told me all this the next day and added, 'We've got to work out how to change the story.'

That's exactly what Zechariah was talking about. The four fasts he referenced were laments, the exiles recalling the story of destruction, remembering with tears how everything had gone wrong. Now God tells them to continue to recall those events but to 'become joyful and happy'! Why? It's not a case of 'mind over matter' – they're still confronting the reality of what had happened. But Zechariah encouraged them to celebrate the fasts for a different reason, no longer simply to lament and look backwards, but henceforth to strengthen their new hope and look forwards. At St

Clement's we decided that we wouldn't deny the things that had gone wrong, the difficulties of the past, nor the scale of the challenge we faced. When we met to discuss those issues, however, we committed to a positive attitude, being thankful for the lessons learned and happy about the new life emerging.

Of course, this principle permeates the New Testament too. Jesus angered the religious authorities no end in saying that the temple the exiles rebuilt was a picture for us of himself: it represented his death and resurrection (this may be exposited from many passages, but for a particularly clear example, see John 2:19–22). Jesus died and was buried, but on the third day he rose again. Jesus did die, but you won't find him in the grave. Good Friday is called thus because, although we remember Jesus' pain, his separation from the Father and his death on that day each year, we know that his suffering made an atonement for our sins and he paid the price our sins deserved. Though he was without sin, he took our place, dying so that we don't have to. And, as his followers were to see, only three days later, death couldn't hold him. Jesus came back from the dead: he's alive! So instead of death, we have received, through Jesus, new life and joy and hope. St Paul writes, 'Just as Christ was raised from the dead through the glory of the Father, we too may live a new life' (Rom. 6:4).

Paul describes the church as being Jesus' body, the new temple on earth (1 Cor. 3:16) that God is building and living in (Eph. 2:22). All around the UK, old empty churches are being reopened, relaunched and seeing new life. I'm convinced that this is the beginning of a long-awaited new move of the Holy Spirit here. I feel so excited that God is inviting us to join in and get involved. Of course, to do that work of rebuilding means embracing change. Zechariah's advice was to 'love truth and peace' (Zech. 8:19).

Loving truth means facing the hard facts about the values and cultures of our congregations, the state of our buildings, scarcity of our resources, poor reputation of our churches and bluntness of mission initiatives. Loving peace means taking time to build friendship and trust with people who worship God and see things in different ways, and who have a different experience of life. It means remembering that what unites us is vastly more than what separates us. Whenever different people establish trust and mutual understanding, they can begin to journey together towards a different future.

When my dad was nearing his retirement, he and Mum decided to take on a very ambitious project: they decided to buy a 'do-er upper' and purchased a property that was the end result of several efforts at converting a nineteenth-century barn. It was functional but had become a bit of an incoherent and very much outdated bungalow. They partnered with a gifted architect and talented builder to set about the process of transformation. I vividly recall one winter's day in the middle of the process, walking around the squalid, bombed-out shell of a site with Mum. She was in tears – there was frozen mud everywhere, stacks of building materials, no ceilings in any rooms and the roof completely missing from others; walls had been knocked down and deep trenches ran everywhere. She was numb with the scale of the challenge. 'What have we done?' she asked, 'All this money, time and effort and all that remains looks like a war zone.' Had Mum and Dad genuinely believed that narrative, they would have lost their nerve, exited the project at great loss and missed out on all the joy that followed. But they had a vision distinct from what they saw with their eyes.

Mum wiped her tears away and began to change the story. She started to shine as she described what she saw in her mind, dancing across the mud pit that was to become her garden, imagining the flowers, fruits and produce that were to come and skipping along the scaffolding boards as she showed me where the kitchen cupboards would be. She chose to imagine and speak about what would be, not focus on what was. She drew me into her dream too. Mum and Dad believed the future would be different so they persevered through the present. Today, they own a beautiful country home that looks and works perfectly and are able to offer hospitality to so many needing a place of peace and retreat. If only we learned to do the same with our crumbling old, moribund churches.

Zechariah sets out the Lord's promises, enthusing: 'Many peoples and the inhabitants of many cities will yet come, and the inhabitants of one city will go to another and say, "Let us go at once to entreat the Lord and seek the Lord Almighty. I myself am going"' (Zech. 8:20–1). He was urging the exiles to imagine a great time of invitation. These are like the days we live in, even more so since the advent of social media, which vastly accelerates the grapevine effect. The good news about Jesus has always spread most effectively by word of mouth. We are to be Jesus' witnesses. When Jesus met his first disciples, they simply went and told their friends about him and said, 'Come and see' (John 1:39, 46). This is certainly the principal means by which St Swithun's has grown. I love the way Zechariah makes it so personal: he doesn't recommend others to go; he says 'Come with me'. That's ownership. I suspect many of us go to church more out of a sense of obligation than enthusiasm, but I've actually got to want to go to church myself if I'm to extend an authentic, warm invitation to others. If you don't enjoy your church gatherings yourself, why invite others to share your misery?

Like it or not, in our culture today the lighting, temperature, ambient music, smile on the face of the host, warmth of a friendly conversation, quality of the coffee – even the type of cup it's served up in – all communicate something to people who know so little about who God really is. And in our culture, the first impressions we give people are doubly important. I've learned from my marketing research that there are countless studies confirming that the way a salesperson interacts with you has a significant influence on whether or not you buy a product. An interesting addition to such studies is research showing that the influence of the salesperson is a relatively weak predictor of consumers deciding to buy the product, but a very strong predictor of consumers deciding *not* to buy it. In other words, salespeople have to work extremely hard to convince us to buy something but they can easily put us off doing so. Unfortunately, the same is true for those whom visitors first meet when they come to your church: a good welcome won't convert anyone but a bad one might put them off for years.

Our teams go out of their way to break visitors' negative preconceptions about who God might be. That's why, in the culture God has called us to reach, investing in our venues matters even though it's so expensive to do to. It's absolutely *not* about it feeling nice, cosy and religious to those who believe – we don't need all that stuff; we don't need a warm-up to worship. Its value lies in what it communicates about God to someone who *doesn't* yet believe. Zechariah promised God's people that if they invited others to worship in the way he advised, then: 'Many peoples and powerful nations will come to Jerusalem to seek the Lord Almighty and to entreat him' (Zech. 8:22).

I readily admit that as we seek to build beautiful worship venues, filled with large and capable staff and volunteer teams offering tailor-made ministry programmes, there is a risk that we'll forget about God. Trusting in our own ability, we may begin to engineer things too much. Fortunately for us, this was Zechariah's very next point to address when he prophesies: 'In those days ten people from all languages and nations will take firm hold of one Jew by the hem of his robe and say, "Let us go with you, because we have heard that God is with you."' (Zech. 8:23). That last sentence sometimes keeps me awake at night, consumed with the zeal to see it happen.

Unfortunately, I have no reference point in my own life for this. I've never yet seen it occur. I've glimpsed people queuing for church events and services a couple of times, but I've not experienced the kind of wide, public revival that Zechariah was talking about. I'm comforted by reminding myself that this isn't just a daydream, it's scriptural prophecy. Through Zechariah, the Lord Almighty is saying that there will be a time coming when people will *beg* us to take them to church with us. Why on earth would they do that? Because of God's presence there. They'll have heard that church is where they'll get the help they need and the answers they're desperately longing for.

I love reading revival stories and was recently reminded of the awakening at Wheaton College in the US.[2] In 1995 two students spoke at a regular Sunday evening chapel service and said they'd recently experienced the overwhelming love of God, having publicly confessed their sins. They set up two microphones on either side of the chapel and simply invited everyone to come forward and confess. Lyle W. Dorset, Professor of Educational Ministries and Evangelism at Wheaton, was there and collated several eye-witness accounts about what happened in his book *Accounts of a Campus Revival*. One by one, people began to confess their sins, from senior academics to fresher students. The meeting continued past midnight as students left the chapel to tell others that something extraordinary was happening, bringing these friends back with them to the chapel all through the night. The meeting was finally called to a halt at 6.00a.m. but because there were still scores of people queuing at both microphones they agreed to open the chapel again at 9.30p.m. that Monday evening. That night, more than a thousand students gathered and after worship and prayer, began to confess their sins in the same way as before. They continued until 2.00a.m., agreeing to reopen the chapel the following Tuesday evening too. That night they had 1,300 students and the same thing happened. On Wednesday night 1,500 students came to pray, worship and publicly repent of sin until 3.00a.m. The shattered but elated chaplain opened the doors again on Thursday night, when at least 1,800 staff and students filled every nook of the building. Latecomers stood in the hallways surrounding the chapel, so magnetic was the sense of God's presence. Dorsett collated many of the testimonies from students who became Christians during these meetings, commenting that, 'Hundreds of students admitted that they had been in rebellion against God . . . scores of others confessed they were in bondage to sexual sins, substance abuse, resentment, anger, hatred and pride. As they got right with God and others, they could scarcely contain their joy.'[3]

A young woman student who had been one of the courageous first to overcome shame and publicly repent of sexual sin at the first Sunday evening chapel service, came forward and gave a word of knowledge, based on Matthew 9:37–8 that God was challenging the students to respond to his love by committing their lives to work in the Lord's harvest fields as foreign missionaries. Many others came forward that night saying they'd sensed something similar. One student had done some research and traced the decline in numbers of foreign missionaries being sent out from Wheaton College from the illustrious class of 1950 where, after a similar multi-day revival, 127 men and women had dedicated themselves in this way. Another brave student leader stood up and asked for any who felt called to dedicate the rest of their lives to full-time Christian service, and who would like to receive prayer, to come forwards to the platform. Between two and three hundred students streamed forwards, completely blocking the aisles and pews. A party seemed to break out such that Dorsett writes, 'People who were there said they completely lost track of time and enjoyed an ecstasy unlike anything they had experienced before.'[4]

As I read about the revivals at Wheaton College, and others like it all around the world, I started dreaming about the role that church sites like St Swithun's and Clement's might have in Bournemouth. Most people in Bournemouth do not know how to call on God and many have a hugely negative view of churches. But from the way they're living and speaking, I'm convinced that they're desperate for him. I sense this too: all around those of us who believe, I'm sure people are silently screaming for what we have found – or rather, for the one who has found us. People haven't rejected Jesus: they've rejected what they perceive his church has become. But Jesus is forgiveness, love, truth, life, peace, freedom. Who doesn't want that? Everyone longs for those things; they just don't yet believe that's what can be found at church. Zechariah tells us that it's up to us to convince them that it's really true: God is indeed here, wanting and waiting to be found; he's even out there searching for them. At its best, Jesus' one global Church is an incredibly beautiful thing for which there is no substitute.

Think about those who are acutely lonely: where else in society can you now find real community other than in church? It's incredibly rare. Think about people who are homeless: who else in society is prepared to offer a bed unconditionally and free to utter strangers who are sometimes messy, chaotic and deeply scarred people? It's the church. Who's providing all the foodbanks? Who's providing free debt counselling? The church. Who's befriending elderly people and caring for ex-offenders? Who's helping addicts to be addicts no more? Who's educating hundreds of thousands of children in church schools? Who's mentoring young people and relieving their anxiety? Who's encouraging business people and helping them make ethical decisions and deal with stress? Who's coming alongside students to help unlock their God-given potential? Who's helping people to strengthen their marriages and families? Who's running international disaster relief agencies? Who's helping people restore their lives from separation and divorce? Who started most of our country's hospitals and hospices and visits thousands of sick people in hospital every day? Who's lobbying government to ensure justice and mercy for all in this nation and overseas? Who's weeping with those who have lost a loved one and gently helping them recover hope? Who's cooking meals for mothers with new babies? The church! People would be queuing around the block desperate to get into church if only they knew that all this was available.

Epilogue: Live again

I dreamed that I was holding a dead baby in my arms. All around me people were in deep grief. As I held the baby it came back to life. I gave it back to its mother and a bolt of pure, intense joy shot through me, so profound that it woke me up in an instant. I had a suspicion as to the meaning of my dream, confirmed when I shared it with one of our intercessors at that morning's prayer meeting. As she sat down after I'd told her about it, the Lord spoke to her in an instant and she jumped back up again, blurting out what I already knew: 'God just told me that your dream is about the church.'

I've hesitated to end this book by sharing my dream with you for fear that we'll fall into the same trap that Joseph and his brothers did. If I were you, I'd be tempted to think what an arrogant fool this dream makes me sound. That would be true if I thought the dream was about me or had anything to do with my own ability; but I can't reawaken a church any more than you can, or either one of us could resurrect a dying baby for that matter. Likewise, Joseph couldn't rule by his own might any more than he could make the sun, moon and stars bow down to him. It is God alone who makes these things occur and all any of us have to do is play our part in his plans. No one part in God's story is greater than any another. It's my name on the front cover of this book only because I've written the story down; the story itself is about the efforts and gifting of numerous people who have all had a vital part to play.

I've had the opportunity and permission to name only a small number of the big family of people at St Swithun's and St Clement's. I am deeply grateful to the few I have mentioned and the many I have not, that they would trust me enough to serve them as their leader and tell their story to try and inspire others. I hope the story I've told ignites faith in you. Despite our past failures, present weaknesses and future shortcomings, God is inviting us to partner with him in his mission to the earth. The church is his chosen vehicle for this magnificent project: living communities of worship, truth, hope, faith, mercy and justice in myriad colours and shapes. There are countless people who would do a better job than I am leading the church here and you can probably think of others who would do a better job than you at whatever God has you doing right now. But we all have to accept that God called *us* and be strong and courageous as we keep working at what he's entrusted to us. There are plenty of apparently good reasons why *not* to plant churches or any other new faith adventure. But none of that matters. When God says 'I choose you' or 'Do this' then it's the end of the matter: all we can do is trust God and get on with it, relying on his help every step of the way. The sooner we do so, the better our lives will become. Wholeheartedly pursuing God's purpose for our lives is the best decision any of us can ever make.

What does the future hold for St Swithun's and St Clement's? I hope we'll continue to play our part in the evangelisation of Bournemouth's unchurched younger generations, the revitalisation of other churches and the transformation of society. To help us do that we now express our unity not with the names of our sites, but with the verb that is our core value: love. We say we are

LOVECHURCH, a community of people who love God, love people and love life. 'Dear friends, let us love one another, for love comes from God' (1 John 4:7).

Notes

Introduction: 570,000 reasons to get out of bed
1 Rick Warren, *The Purpose Driven Church* (Zondervan, 1996).
2 Nigel Scotland, *Evangelical Anglicans in a Revolutionary Age, 1789–1901* (STL, 1969).
3 Graham Tomlin, *The Provocative Church* (SPCK, 2014).
4 Norman Grubb, C. T. Studd: *Famous Athlete and Pioneer* (Zondervan, 1933), p. 152.

1 Every day is a school day
1 Rick Warren, *The Purpose Driven Life* (Zondervan, 2002), 'What on earth am I here for?', Day 25, p. 193.
2 Richard Rohr, *Falling Upward* (SPCK, 2012).

3 Repurposed for hope
1 Diocese of London, *Buildings on Sure Foundations* (2018), available at https://www.london.anglican.org/articles/buildings-on-sure-foundations/
2 See Gwyneth Lewis, *Sunbathing in the Rain* (HarperCollins, 2003), a powerful book about living with depression.
3 Joyce Meyer, *Battlefield of the Mind: Winning the Battle of Your Mind* (FaithWords, 2002), p. 223.

4 Richard Rohr and Joelle Chase, *Essential Teachings on Love* (Orbis, 2018), p. 1.

4 The ones that got away

1 World Development Report 1994: Infrastructure for Development, (New York, N.Y.: Oxford University Press).

5 Your Macedonian moment

1 Bill Hybels, *Holy Discontent: Fueling the Fire that Ignites Personal Vision* (Zondervan, 2007).

6 My big but

1 Dietrich Bonhoeffer, 'Christ in the Psalms', lecture delivered on 31 July 1935.

2 Pete Greig, *God on Mute: Engaging the Silence of Unanswered Prayer* (Kingsway, 2007).

7 No turning back

1 Tom Wright, *John for Everyone: Part 2: Chapters 11—21* (SPCK, 2002), p. 161.

8 It's snowing money

1 Steven Furtick Jr, *Sun Stand Still: What Happens When You Dare to Ask God for the Impossible* (Multinomah UK, 2010), p. 7.

9 Budget for coffee

1 Anthony Uyl (ed.), *The Writings of Josephus*, trans. William Whitson (Kindle edn, 2016), Book 2, p. 177.

2 Brian Houston, *Live, Love, Lead* (Hodder & Stoughton, 2016), p. 150.

11 Worship like you mean it

1 Mother Teresa, *A Simple Path* (Rider, 1995), p. 83.

13 Finding freedom

1 Department for Work and Pensions 2015 statistics on IB, SDA and ESA claimants with a condition of obesity, alcohol misuse, drug misuse and severe stress (cf. DWP online statistical FOI releases, May 2010 to May 2014).

2 According to the *Bournemouth Echo*, 'More people are unable to work because of drugs and alcohol in Bournemouth than anywhere else – but no one is really surprised' (23 March 2015).

14 How to lose £0.5m in 30 seconds

1 Alban Butler, *Lives of the Saints*, Vol. VII (July 1866).

2 Jacobus de Voraigne, *The Golden Legend: Readings on the Saints*, trans. Williams G. Ryan (Princeton University Press, 2012).

3 William of Malmesbury, Gesta Regum Anglorum, ed. and trans. R.A.B. Mynors, R.M. Thomson, and M. Winterbottom, 2 vols (Oxford: Clarendon Press, 1998–9), I, p.xv.

15 Unblock the flow

1 Brandt Pitre, *Jesus and the Jewish Roots of the Eucharist: Unlocking the Secrets of the Last Supper* (Doubleday, 2016).

2 Larry Greiner, 'Evolution and Revolution as Organisations Grow', *Harvard Business Review*, May–June 1998.

3 Daniel Goleman, 'Leadership That Gets Results', *Harvard Business Review*, March–April 2000.

4 Brendan Burchard, *The Student Leadership Guide* (Morgan Ja, 2008).

16 Get risky, stay risky

1 Bear Grylls, *To My Sons: Lessons for the Wild Adventure Called Life* (Lion, 2012), p. 10.

18 Second site

1 *Matthew Henry's Concise Commentary on the Whole Bible* (Thomas Nelson, 2003), p. 00.[to follow]
2 Timothy K. Beougher and Lyle W. Dorsett (eds), *Accounts of a Campus Revival: Wheaton College 1995* (Wipf & Stock, 2002).
3 Ibid., p. 85.
4 Ibid., p. 83.

Acknowledgements

The danger of starting a list of people to thank is that I'll miss someone out. I'm paranoid that upon opening my first copy, I'll realise I've left someone off this list who means the world to me and I'll lose a valuable friend. However, several people put in significant time and skill to help me complete this project. So thank you to Andy Lyon and all the team at Hodder, Mark and Amanda Elsdon-Dew at Holy Trinity Brompton, as well as Bishop Jonathan Frost who has poured himself into this work since the beginning. Huge thanks to Blue Paterson, Tom and Lizzie Redman and Fifi Makhoana here in Bournemouth, who all gave me enormous assistance.

Rich and Tracey Elliott and the Pickwell Manor crew gave me a safe place to think and write, and, along with Kester Brewin, Si and Claire Sleight and Paul and Naomi Bulkeley, shouted me on. God answered some of my most desperate prayers through people like David Ingall, David and Rachel Cooke, Johannes and Tracey Radran, Marilyn Smith and Carol Williams. Mum, Dad and my sister Katie have not only made invaluable contributions but have all been tremendously gracious in allowing me to share my inevitably biased perspective on our family interactions.

Special thanks must also go to Blue, Emma, Andy, Mark and Mandy and many others in Bournemouth who courageously allowed me to share their personal stories with you. Thanks as well to our amazing staff team here who have worked so hard. Matt and Laura Clayton, with Jamie Matthews and later on Si and Chloe Nicholls, took the risk of their lives in joining Debi and me in our 'God or bust' adventure. We are so grateful to have had the privilege of starting the work here alongside friends like Tien and Charlene Tran, Pete and Gill Drysdale and Nikki Hunter.

All that has happened at St Swithun's and St Clement's is, of course, the work of the hundreds of people who have chosen to share their lives with one another in this place, and so this story is theirs as much as my own. I owe them a vast debt of thanks for their faith, willingness, generosity, sacrifice, enthusiasm and encouragement. Guys, I don't know where the story goes from here, but I know I want to go there with you – let's pursue Jesus with everything we've got and see what happens...

Thank you Debi, Josiah, Caleb and Rebekah for helping me to pursue this project, believing together that it was what God wanted us to do.

Love Tim

HODDER &
STOUGHTON

Hodder & Stoughton is the UK's
leading Christian publisher,
with a wide range of books from
the bestselling authors in the UK
and around the world ranging from
Christian lifestyle and theology to
apologetics, testimony and fiction.
We also publish the world's
most popular Bible translation
in modern English, the New
International Version, renowned
for its accuracy and readability.

Hodderfaith.com   Hodderbibles.co.uk
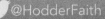 @HodderFaith    /HodderFaith